KT-452-243

The Complete Student Handbook

This book is dedicated to the memory of
Dr Eira Williams

The Complete Student Handbook

Edited by
Danny Saunders
University of Glamorgan

BLACKWELL
Oxford UK & Cambridge USA

Copyright © Staff and Educational Development Association 1994

First published 1994

Blackwell Publishers
108 Cowley Road
Oxford OX4 1JF

238 Main Street
Cambridge, Massachusetts 02142

All rights reserved. Except for the quotation of short passages for the purposes of criticism and review, no part of this publication may be reproduced, stored in a retrieval system, or transmitted, in any form or by any means, electronic, mechanical, photocopying, recording or otherwise, without the prior permission of the publisher.

Except in the United States of America, this book is sold subject to the condition that it shall not, by way of trade or otherwise, be lent, resold, hired out, or otherwise circulated without the publisher's prior consent in any form of binding or cover other than that in which it is published and without a similar condition including this condition being imposed on the subsequent purchaser.

British Library Cataloguing in Publication Data

A CIP catalogue record for this book is available from the British Library.

Library of Congress Cataloging-in-Publication Data

The Complete student's handbook / edited by Danny Saunders.
    p.   cm.
    Includes bibliographical references and index.
    ISBN 0–631–19373–1
    1. College student orientation—Handbooks, manuals, etc.
  2. Communication—Study and teaching—Handbooks, manuals, etc.
  3. College students—Employment—Handbooks, manuals, etc.
  I. Saunders, Danny.
  LB2343.3.C655   1994   93–39670
  378.1'98–dc20   CIP

Cartoons by Frances Tomlinson

Typeset in 11 on 13pt Palatino by Photoprint, Torquay, S. Devon.
Printed in Great Britain by T J Press Ltd, Padstow, Cornwall.

This book is printed on acid-free paper

Contents

Preface

When Alice was lost in Wonderland she asked which way she ought to go. The response she got was that it didn't matter as long as she went far enough because she would arrive somewhere sooner or later. Students have been similarly directionless in an academic world with confusing signposts and indistinct goals. Like Alice, the time has come for students, and people who work with students, to ask where they are going and how to recognize when they have arrived.

A student life becomes one of strategic travelling: in other words, a development towards achieving ends which are decided upon at the outset but which may be changed along the way. Who decides these ends and who evaluates when the ends have been achieved is the most critical part of the journey.

Students, and people working with students (like lecturers, employers, careers advisers and examiners), need to make these decisions together. To do this requires particular skills such as initiative, creativity and negotiation. In a wider context we often refer to a set of skills or competences that can be acquired or enhanced to improve the quality of life in education and the world of work which lies beyond it. Enterprising students are those who know where they are going, how to get there and what to identify as success at the end.

The Enterprise in Higher Education Programme did much to encourage the acquisition and extension of skills in students. Work is seen as an extension of classroom learning, as in the case of a sandwich work experience placement or a full time commitment to paid employment. Employers become part of the learning experience in this extension of learning to the world of work and so they become important signposts giving directions and distances to be travelled. They can also act as arbitrators in decisions about whether developmental goals have been met sufficiently well for students to leave education and move into other workplaces. Similarly with professional bodies (like those of engineering, building and accountancy), it becomes important for people 'working' to be involved in the process of education as much as with the product of it. As more people begin to have a say in such things, students need to be able to hold their own in discussion and negotiation of their own goals. This is called developing a self-centred axiom of learning. It becomes a case of students agreeing on a learning programme which can be called *learner centred* and in which students can identify a set of negotiated objectives, a personally preferred set of study habits and agreed attainment targets.

Traditionally, attainment has been considered to be something in which one student does better than another. A little story illustrates the folly of this assumption. It tells of two students walking along a road, when they are chased by a ferocious dog. They run until one of them stops to tie up her shoelace. 'What are you doing?' gasps the second student, 'Tying up your shoelaces won't help us outrun the dog'. 'No,' said the first student, 'but it will help me run faster than you, which is all I need to do'.

The successful student does not think of attainment and success in these crude competitive terms. Achievement is the *self* mastery of learning objectives agreed by the student who achieves them in a variety of ways and within a varied (although usually prescribed) time scale. It can also involve self or peer group assessment of assignments or projects without the lecturer in the traditional 'expert' role. A lecturer becomes a learning resource and as such will arbitrate and advise but not prescribe. The old story of lecturers who 'lecture to us in such a way as to show us how much they know and how little we do', becomes a redundant story. It marks a shift away from the old 'BBC model' of education in which lecturers were transmitters of knowledge and students were receptors of it, and when reception was judged faulty because of poor quality audiences.

The lecturer is, therefore, a facilitator of information and the student negotiates assessment and evaluation of learning as well as the procedures by which it is resourced. A new variety of assessment techniques becomes available in this context. Student portfolios can be personally written records of ongoing assessments, and profiles can be personally recorded 'can do's' of the term's work. These assessments become diagnostic with feedback potential, in a way that traditional techniques used at the end of a course cannot be.

In summary, students' skills are competences that can be acquired or extended, and which are critical for both academic life and the world of work. A planned journey is what Alice lacked in Wonderland and it is what students need, to avoid being lost. This book helps you to find the way.

Dr Eira Williams

Acknowledgements

Many thanks to all of the authors for their patience, effort and insight. I would especially like to thank Graeme Ewins, Phil Race, Chris Rust, Sally Brown and Maggy McNorton for all of their advice and support wherever it has been needed. Further acknowledgements are made to BP Chemicals (Baglan Bay), *Aiming for a College Education* – especially Winston Thomas and Ann Collins – for the overall management of materials and activities which help students of all ages to develop important skills. This book would not have seen the light of day had it not been for the support of the Standing Conference on Educational Development (now the Staff and Educational Development Association). Finally, I am most grateful to Maxine Hird for typing the final manuscript and to my wife Gail for putting up with all this editing.

The questionnaire on p. 251 is taken from the disk-format support material to *Enterprise Skills for Students* by Maureen Guirdham and Katherine Tyler, published by Butterworth-Heinemann, and is reproduced by kind permission.

Editor's Introduction

Being a student means more than just mastering a subject area or discipline, and then showing off what you know in an essay or an exam. There are many background skills which take you towards the final degree, diploma or certificate award. This book gives practical advice, hints and tips about many of those invisibles which many of your lecturers will take for granted but which greatly interest a later employer. So what are these skills?

> Over three years I must have been to four seminars a week – that's over 300 in total. None of it counted towards my final mark; most of that came from exams and essays. But when I went for my job interviews all they asked about was how good I was at discussing things in groups, talking to audiences, arguing and putting forward my views.

Employers, survey after survey tells us, value things like good communication, self-appraisal, organizational flair, efficiency, reliability and originality – to name but a handful of the transferable skills so often mentioned. What are equally important but less evident to people outside the academic world are the other qualities which contribute to a final qualification: taking notes, arguing and criticizing, revising, writing reports, working to deadlines, listening and making presentations.

There are also the crucial career decisions that students make during the course of their studies. This involves a lot of skill, too, such as criticizing yourself and weighing up the pros and cons of various types of employment. It means drawing up a curriculum vitae, applying for a job, preparing profiles and portfolios, and being interviewed.

The Complete Student Handbook helps you to develop and demonstrate all of these abilities. The book started with an idea from Chris Rust of the then Standing Conference on Educational Development (SCED). I sent him a paper on making presentations in the hope that SCED would circulate it more widely to student readers. He thought it a worthwhile venture and said that he had received some other papers with similar target audiences. The more we thought about it the more apparent it became that there was a lot of good material around, but it was mostly piecemeal and fragmented. What was needed was a book which brought it all together.

Since then, I have been asking colleagues from a number of colleges to write chapters that are useful, clearly written and student-centred. The response has been fantastic, not only in terms of content but also because of the immediate enthusiasm the proposal created.

Part of the reason for this is undoubtedly the changing pace of education. The idea of lecturers spending lots of time with a few students, or students reading lots of readily available books or journals, and of students then receiving individual tutorials or participating in small seminar groups is perhaps wonderful but with notable exceptions an impossibility. Student numbers have increased much faster than the number of lecturers. This means bigger classes, fewer seminars and tutorials and less detailed feedback about assessment by academic staff. Paradoxically, such happenings have suited the very different objectives of educational developers who for a long time have recognized the value of student-centred learning: where you own the curriculum and have a say in how you learn. Thus self and peer assessment, learning contracts, syndicate groups, peer tutoring, profiling, live projects and communication skills are all being introduced at various levels in further and higher education. Many lecturers are experimenting with initiatives as a reaction to educational expansion and student empowerment. This is, therefore, the time to give more support material for people on the receiving (or negotiating?) end.

We have identified three sections on 'getting yourself organized' (especially study skills), 'getting your message across' (especially communication skills) and 'getting out of college' (especially career skills). I am the first to say that there are huge overlaps and many chapters could be slotted into other sections. Take 'live projects' for example. These involve communicating with people outside college as well as with academic supervisors; they also require various study skills in terms of preparing, executing and presenting research activity. And there again, live projects prepare investigators for careers because the research is carried out in a workplace. All I can say is that after endlessly sorting and resorting material, these three categories seemed to be the simplest and easiest to understand.

I end this introduction on a sad note. One of the forces for encouraging student skills has been the Enterprise Initiative, which has affected over 70 institutions within the UK. For 18 months the head of the Enterprise Unit at the University of Glamorgan (then the Polytechnic of Wales) was Dr Eira Williams, a popular and respected teacher, and someone who always cared for students' well being. Eira wrote the preface for our book shortly before dying after a long illness. All of our authors have agreed that *The Complete Student Handbook* should be respectfully dedicated to her memory.

Danny Saunders
University of Glamorgan

How to Use This Book

This book is designed to last you throughout your degree or diploma, from starting at college (our use of this term includes universities, institutes and colleges of further or higher education) to sitting exams and being interviewed for jobs.

It is not a book for reading in one go, cover to cover. Instead, you are advised to turn to chapters as your needs arise. For example, your lecturers will ask you to write an essay – go to chapter 9. When exams start to loom, chapter 7 will be appropriate. If your seminars seem to be a waste of time, then chapter 14 will help. When planning what to do after finishing college you can turn to chapters 19 and 20.

Each contribution starts with a summary and at the end of each chapter we have added two further short sections. One provides an 'Action Plan': a series of practical steps for you to take when you have finished reading. This is an important, simple and easy way of making sense of material and ensuring that you remember the important points. The action plan is followed by a list of crosslinking chapters which build on what you have just read. In this way you are provided with chapter permutations based on your current needs and interests. When following up our suggested links, you will see that some chapters recur again and again – for example, the ones on personal transferable skills, profiling and creative problem solving. These are 'common denominators' which are relevant to everything and anything, so be warned!

The three sections of the book have already been introduced, and we recommend that you look at some of the first section ('Getting Yourself Organized') as soon as possible. All of our discussions with lecturers, students and past students have pointed to the importance of time management, problem solving and accurate self-assessment in learning skills at college which, in the long run, save a lot of time and energy. Our discussions with employers who eventually interview students also highlight the value of profiles and portfolios – in which case it is crucial that you establish a 'baseline' for your *present* skills: it is only by looking back at these baselines that you can monitor your progress and development. For this reason, we strongly recommend that you complete the questionnaire in chapter 15 as soon as possible.

Finally, our authors frequently suggest that lecturers, tutors and staff located in student and careers services can help you to assess and develop various skills. In an ideal world, this is obvious advice, but I have to admit that such help is not always forthcoming – even though in many ways you have the right to it. There are various reasons why academic and support staff are not always accessible, interested or expert in the development of student skills – a point I will return to in the Conclusion to this book. All that is emphasized here is the value of having one or more tutors who are prepared to spend some time with you – and it is you who should take the initiative in developing these special relationships.

Part I

Getting Yourself Organized

1
Time Management

Roger Coles

Further and higher education involves more private study and highlights the importance of organizing your time effectively. This opening chapter asks you to reflect about how you manage at the moment, and then sets out some diary-keeping exercises which introduce the advantages of being proactive through establishing routines and schedules for clusters of both academic and social activity.

Many of you will have moved into further or higher education from a strongly structured environment such as school or work. You will probably have discovered that you have a lot of control over your time, and in particular, you will be aware that some of this time is 'free' for you to do just what you like.

Freedom is a precious commodity, and can easily be frittered away. It is very pleasant to fill your time with socializing and trying new things, but it is all too easy to let the 'fun' things take over. This usually hits you when you realize that you have an uncomfortably short time to do an assignment or complete coursework.

You may find that the following ideas will help you to 'manage' your time more effectively – not to kill any enjoyment, but rather get a balance between your work time and your free time.

Why manage your time?

A bit of honest reflection

Have you ever:

- Left things to the last moment?

- Left things until it's too late, then not done them at all?
- Let someone down, either by not turning up or failing to do something you agreed?
- Got overloaded, and not done justice to your work?
- Simply forgotten things?
- Found resources (for example, library books, computer terminals) unavailable or heavily booked because you, like everyone else, left it to the last moment?

If the answer is 'no' to all these, then you need read no further. For the rest of us (and I include myself), it might be well worth reading on . . .

How about trying an example, simply to compare what you actually did with what you might have done. The table that follows has two columns: 'what I actually did' and 'what I would have preferred to do'. Try to remember what you did during each hour of yesterday and the day before, and put this in the first column next to the time at the start of that hour. Then think whether you would rather have done something else, and put this in the second column.

What I actually did	What I would have preferred to do
Yesterday	
0800	0800
0900	0900
1000	1000
1100	1100
1200	1200
1300	1300
1400	1400
1500	1500
1600	1600
1700	1700
1800	1800

1900	1900
2000	2000
2100	2100
2200	2200
2300	2300

The day before

0800	0800
0900	0900
1000	1000
1100	1100
1200	1200
1300	1300
1400	1400
1500	1500
1600	1600
1700	1700
1800	1800
1900	1900
2000	2000
2100	2100
2200	2200
2300	2300

When you have completed this table, ask yourself honestly whether you really could have done all the things in the second column. Even if you had only done some of them, would you have achieved a lot more than you actually did? For most of us, the answer is usually 'yes'. One of the main benefits of time management is achieving more: it makes you feel better and is marvellous at reducing stress.

Proactors and reactors

Even the most disorganized of us manage a little of our time. The essence of any time management system, however simple, is to make sure we do more of those things we want to do, and in good time (i.e. be proactive). This is clearly a better method than doing things because we have to (being reactive). A simple comparative example is as follows:

Two alternative scenarios – the reactor vs the proactor

Reactive version	Proactive version
Coursework to be typed on a word-processor for completion in four weeks' time on Thursday at 9.00 am. You put the brief on one side – it is in four weeks, after all!	Coursework to be typed on a word-processor for completion in four weeks' time on Thursday at 9.00 am. You guess it will take about three days. It needs a visit to the library, so you decide to go there straight away and make some notes before all copies of the books vanish. You put the notes you have made along with the brief in a named folder and put it on the shelf over your desk in your room.

You decide to start the remainder of the work the next week after watching the Wednesday college hockey match.

(One week later, after the hockey match). You do most of the rest of the coursework. However, you have a problem with your word-processor software. A friend solves the problem for you. |

(One week to go) The lecturer reminds you, but you cannot find the coursework brief – you go round to a friend to borrow his copy – and finish up in the Red Lion!

Hangover – forgot the coursework brief – you left it at the friend's. You go round there again (possibility of getting into a loop here!).

You get the coursework brief, go to the library – none of the books are there – you decide to ask around at tomorrow's lecture.

You try to load up the word-processor software – 'checksum error' – friend who usually solves your computing problems is out. You look for him – when you find him, he doesn't understand the problem from your description, so you take him back to your room – he sorts the problem, but you both miss the lecture.

(The day before the deadline) Would like to go on the caving trip, but nowhere yet with the

(Another week later) You finish the coursework.

(One week to go) The lecturer reminds you. You are tempted to hand the work in, but you hold back. You never know – you could improve it.

Go to Student's Union for lunch, meet one of last year's class. She gives you some new ideas – you look back over your answer – rework it, then print it off – fortunately the printer ribbon is new, so the work looks neat.

(The day before the deadline) Go on the caving trip. The minibus breaks down on the return journey coursework. Spend an hour trying to find the Caving Club Events Sec. but give up and go back to the library.

Later, and entirely unknown to you, most of the Caving Club are searching for you – they didn't think of looking in the library! Minibus delayed for half an hour.

(The day – Thursday at 9.00 am) Try to thread the completed coursework under the lecturer's door, but it won't go because there are too many others jammed underneath.

. . . And the lasting outcome

'42% – content sparse, and argued in an inconsistent and unstructured way. Get a new ribbon for the printer – the work was almost too faint to read'.

and you have to shelter in a lonely pub!

(The day – Thursday at 9.00 am) Sleeping soundly but get up in time for lecture at 9.00 am. Hand in assignment.

'71% – well set out and argued. You clearly drew on a greater range of material than I had suggested, and so came up with some novel ideas'.

You may find these scenarios a bit far-fetched, and perhaps the reactive version does not apply to you – but do you have a friend who is like that?

Investment in time

You will notice that the gaps in these two scenarios occur at different times: early in the reactive version and later in the proactive version. You may have heard the following argument, often used by reactors:

> I leave the work until later because the time pressure and adrenalin focus my mind and increase my motivation, so that I get a better result.

Maybe there is some truth in this, although we suspect perhaps that motivation aroused by time pressure is second rate compared with motivation inspired by interest. However, we cannot be expected to become interested in all aspects of our work all of the time. To acquire an interest takes time, and is probably better achieved if we are not under stress so that we can pick and choose when we work. As a friend once said:

> How easy life would be if we could learn everything in the same way as we learn a hobby.

Back to the scenarios – you have established that the proactor has done the work earlier rather than later. You can think of this early work as an 'investment' in time, which can then be spent later. This has several consequences for proactors:

- they have a well-founded feeling of achievement after finishing their work early;
- they are under less stress;
- they do not feel guilty about work, because more of it is completed;
- they have the opportunity to become more interested in their subject material, if they so choose.

Despite all of this, my experience is that proactors are not smug: rather they are happy and relaxed people, often very interesting to talk to simply because they have 'covered more ground' and, ultimately, they have more time to spend with you.

Becoming more proactive – preparing the way

So that you can take full advantage of the practical exercise in proactivity which follows, go back to the two lists you prepared earlier on your last two days' activities. Rethink, and amend where necessary, your right hand list until you are satisfied that it is really what you wanted to do.

Now try this:

1 Classify the items in the list under a few headings (no more than six) – for example 'Economics', 'Mathematics', 'Staying alive and keeping fit', 'Socializing', and so on.
2 For the two columns, (i.e. what you actually did, and what you would have liked to do), total up the amount of time under each of the headings, e.g. 'Mathematics = 2 hrs 15 mins'. Note when these activities occurred.
3 Also for each column, total up the unallocated times in hours and minutes, noting when these occurred.

Do you think these amounts of time spent on each heading were what you *really* wanted? Also, did you do the activities at the time of the day you would have preferred, or were you forced to do them in a hurry, when you had a spare moment? You will notice that (1) above is about *what* you did or planned to do, and (2) and (3) are about *when* you did things or planned to do them. Time management systems address both *what* and *when*, and so it is important to invest some time in thinking about them.

Becoming more proactive – a practical exercise

Invest an hour today (or tomorrow or on Sunday, but do it some time!) in making a *what* list. Don't forget to tell everyone that, for this hour, you are busy and not available.

Your list should not have too many major headings. Your main course subjects will probably be your first choices, but remember that the list has to cover the whole of your life (not simply the work bits), so include sporting activities, friends and family, and holiday plans, for instance.

When you are satisfied with your list, try to break down each heading to lower level subheadings. You may then find that you can break these subheadings down to a lower level again. At this stage, it really doesn't matter how many levels you go down to. Here is an example. You will notice that the individual headings and subheadings have a number: this can be used to create an index, to be discussed later.

Major headings   **Subheadings**

1 Computing

  1 Lectures

    1 Databases
    2 Software engineering
    3 Business applications

  2 Tutorials

  3 Team project

    1 Next deadline
    2 Own contribution
    3 Documentation

  4 Lab work

  5 Reading

    1 Current recommended book
    2 Manuals

  6 Coursework

    1 Lists and deadlines
    2 Marks so far

2 Sport

  1 Badminton

    1 Training night
    2 Fixture schedule

  2 Weight training

    1 Schedule and standards

  3 Aerobics

    1 Running
    2 Circuit training

  4 Sec. of Badminton Club

    1 Minutes of meetings
    2 Meeting plan
    3 Actionable items

3 Friends/family/social

  1 Birthdays

    1 Home
    2 College

  2 Parties/events

  3 Visits home

Once you have made your *what* list, put it in a handy place – the ideal is to bind it into a loose leaf folder and add to it when you think of new ideas. Don't restrict yourself to what you do now: include what you would like to do in future.

Lastly, make a provision to invest another hour in the *what* and *when* exercise which follows (the process of making provision ahead of time is a major part of time management, so getting into the practice is a good idea).

Using Daily Plans

Filling in the Daily Plan

This Daily Plan combines ideas from many time management systems. A quick look at it shows the use of shortened *what* headings or subheadings (some people use the numbers in their *what* list as an indexing system, so that they would enter '2.1.2' instead of 'Bad. Sched.' I can never remember what the numbers mean, but you might get it to work. It has the added advantage that it is more secure than words, and retains some secrecy from prying eyes). Also note the 'how long' arrows (in the narrow column), which give a time span to the *when* aspect of each activity.

You should have several of these dated pages, covering up to a month ahead, say, in your loose leaf folder or similar binding. Then, as you begin to think of activities or copy them forward from a diary, you write a suitable reminder in the 'Tasks to be done' column for the appropriate dated page. Also, fill in the 'Make time for' box – this is for tasks that you really want to complete, but are large and need to be broken down into manageable units and fitted in where possible.

Note also the completed items marked by ticks which you enter when you review the day. These are there to reinforce the proactor's well-founded feeling of achievement. They are the pay-back for the time invested on the previous day in drawing up the plan. Carried forward to tomorrow's plan will be the items marked with an 'X' which you have decided will still be relevant tomorrow. Once you have moved these forward, you can relax, safe in the knowledge that they have been taken into account. However, if you have let someone down by not doing one of the crossed items, set aside time for an apology in tomorrow's plan.

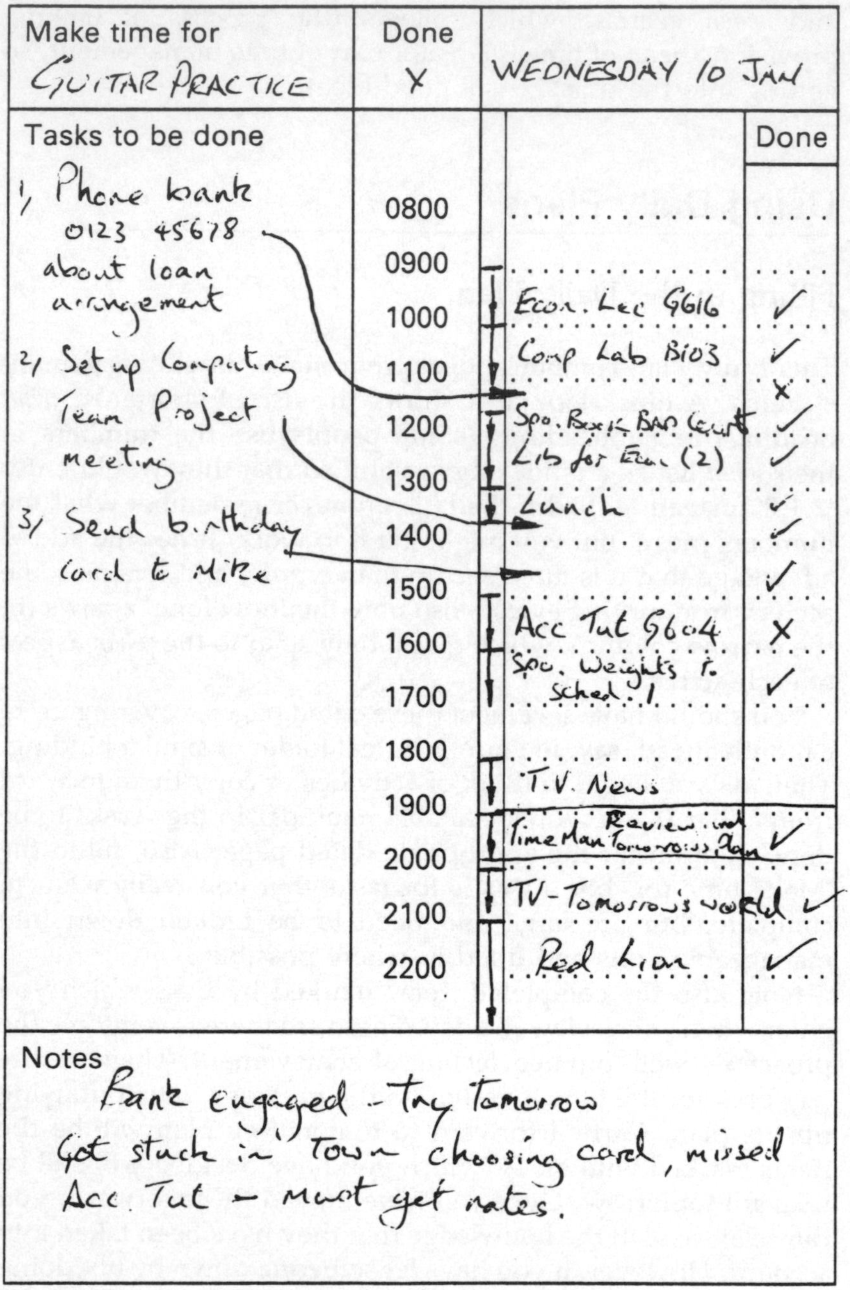

Make time for GUITAR PRACTICE	Done X	WEDNESDAY 10 JAN	
Tasks to be done			Done

1, Phone bank
   0123 45678
   about loan
   arrangement
 	
2, Set up Computing
   Team Project
   meeting
 	
3, Send birthday
   card to Mike
	0800
	0900
	1000
	1100
	1200
	1300
	1400
	1500
	1600
	1700
	1800
	1900
	2000
	2100
	2200
		Econ. Lec G616
		Comp Lab B103
		
		Spo. Bask BAD Court
		Lib for Econ (2)
		Lunch
		
		Acc Tut G604
		Spo. Weights to
		Sched. 1
		
		T.V. News
		Time Man Review and
		Tomorrow's 2am
		TV - Tomorrow's world
		Red Lion
			✓
			✓
			X
			✓
			✓
			✓
			✓
			✓
			X
			✓
			
			✓
			✓
			✓

Notes Bank engaged - try tomorrow Got stuck in Town choosing card, missed Acc. Tut - must get notes.			

Figure 1.1   An example of a daily plan – the heart of time management.

The bonuses gained from completing a Daily Plan

This daily planning investment therefore has a strong confidence-building effect and reduces stress and guilt. Notice also some bonuses from this format. There will be gaps between the arrows - denoting as yet unplanned time. You can use these for simple relaxation, or to give convincing answers to people who ask 'When will you be available today?'

Another advantage is that you can schedule 'do not disturb' blocks of time ahead, and publicize them to your friends. This is particularly valuable if you are doing research for a project or dissertation, where social or other unwanted interruptions can be very destructive.

Sorting out your priorities, and being nice to people

There will be times when the arrows try to overlap – the double-booking problem. If you identify these well ahead, they can usually be resolved by rearrangement. However, if you cannot rearrange them, then you must decide your priorities – if this means letting someone down, apologize as soon as possible (preferably before the event), and schedule your apology into your plan.

Of course, it may not be your priorities that determine events. 'See me straight after the lecture' or 'Phone home urgently' are events that must overtake a planned activity. Get on and attend to them; return to your plan as soon as possible – don't forget to schedule the necessary apologies.

Last, but not least, you can schedule 'pleasant' activities, or 'strokes' as they are sometimes known, into your plan. 'Send birthday card to grandmother' is an example. The choice is yours - try to fit in a 'stroke' whenever you can.

Now try a Daily Plan for yourself on the form on page 17. Use pencil – don't be afraid to make changes. Plan tomorrow, if that is a weekday, or the next weekday if not. (Of course there will not be any ticks or crosses marked on the plan yet – they will appear when you reach the review. Don't forget to plan a slot for the review activity – 15 minutes should be enough.)

Try to make sure that the items you fill in are headings from your *what* list. If not, add to your *what* list.

Keep the plan in a pocket or diary or wallet during the day, and try to follow it when the planned day arrives. When you reach the slot you have set aside for the daily review, fill in the ticks and crosses. Then make the plan for the following day. Continue for a few more days, until you are in a good position to reflect on the value of time management to you.

Rating your performance at time management

Based on the simple exercises you have done, do you consider time management:

1 *A great success* – you feel much better about your use of time, and would like to improve your management of it further.
2 *OK, but a bit bureaucratic* – what is wrong here? Do you dislike bureaucracy, or do you simply need a bit more 'oomph' to keep your time management up?
3 *A struggle* – you couldn't keep to it; you left the plan behind and forgot to do the following day's plan.
4 *A disaster* – forgot all about it until you found this book in a drawer some months later!

Let's have a look at each of these performance groups.

1 Great success

Try the weekly sheet on p. 17. If you can make these work (photocopy it as necessary), then it might be worth going on to a professional scheme: for example, a personal organizer or filofax. See the section 'Researching and implementing a time management and personal organization system', which follows.

Daily and Weekly Plan sheets

Make time for	Done		
Tasks to be done			Done
	0800	. . . .	. . . . .
	0900	. . . .	. . . . .
	1000	. . . .	. . . . .
	1100	. . . .	. . . . .
	1200	. . . .	. . . . .
	1300	. . . .	. . . . .
	1400	. . . .	. . . . .
	1500	. . . .	. . . . .
	1600	. . . .	. . . . .
	1700	. . . .	. . . . .
	1800	. . . .	. . . . .
	1900	. . . .	. . . . .
	2000	. . . .	. . . . .
	2100	. . . .	. . . . .
	2200	. . . .	. . . . .
Notes			

2   OK, but a bit bureaucratic

Keep trying. Motivation cannot be turned on at the flick of a switch. Maybe you should ask a friend, who has made time management work, to act as a supervisor and keep you on track. Or if you don't have any friends like that, seek out a member of your class who openly flouts his or her leather-bound personal organizer (they are certain to be able to find the time to see you!)

3   A struggle

You really are the person who could do with some time management, and a bit of personal organization, aren't you? You have to decide for yourself. Maybe you find being proactive hard work, and keep sliding back to being reactive. How about giving it another try? Follow the advice in (2) above. Using others to help you can often give that psychological shove to keep you going.

4   Disaster

Have you acquired a reputation for being unreliable? It is often said that you can work with people you love and people you hate, but unreliable people . . .

Researching and implementing a time management and personal organization system

These systems comprise a variety of features. Plan some time to research each, then choose one that suits you best. You might start your investigations in the college or union shop.

Diary systems or appointments books

These can give you a simplified version of time management. They can be cheap, but are not really effective unless the days have time scales. Their basic downfall is that they are weak on *what* aspects, and concentrate on the *when*. Maybe they are adequate if you fall into group 2 (see above). Also they are more compact than an organizer. Don't forget that diaries are available which are based on the academic year, rather than the January to December type.

You could use a combination of a diary and photocopies of the weekly sheet (p. 17) as a substitute for a more complete system, but you will need to design and incorporate your own *what* sheets – perhaps you should read on first.

Organizers

These have time management and personal data sections, usually in a loose leaf binder which has a durable cover (leather in the more expensive ones). The time management parts allow yearly, weekly and daily planning on pre-dated, replaceable pages. Also pages of fixtures such as birthdays and college timetables are available. These pages answer the *when* aspects very fully.

In addition, there are many pages which allow you to build up a personal database. This holds your *what* information, including your list of headings on which your time management system is built. Many more types of pages exist, for example, addresses and telephone numbers, useful books, who you lent books to, knot-in-handkerchief reminders, graph paper. These organizers are my own personal choice – they are low-tech, portable and do not lose their contents if the power fails or a battery runs out. However, you must keep them secure or in your sight, because the contents accumulate into a very valuable resource and life becomes very fraught without them.

Pocket electronic organizers

These fulfil many of the functions of ordinary organizers, and go some way towards the fully computerized systems. They are good if you like pressing lots of buttons and reading rather cramped liquid crystal displays. They must be physically chained to you at all times – a very 'liftable' commodity.

A computer (for example, a PC) based organizing system

These can be really smart, and can do things like automatically carrying forward uncompleted activities, or sounding the bleeper when a time-critical activity is five minutes ahead. If they form part of a networked system, you can (on a password) gain access to other people's schedules and so arrange meetings at mutually convenient times. They also have electronic mailing facilities, integrated word-processing and other features, often marketed under the generic name of 'electronic office'.

If you have fallen in love with your PC, and experience withdrawal symptoms when away from the keyboard for any length of time, these are definitely for you. Personally I find them very heavy to carry about (even the lap-top ones), and keyboards – yuk! A pencil is much simpler.

Action plan

- List activities and time allocations for the last two days, and state what you would have preferred to do.
- Identify areas where you could be more efficient with your time; are you a reactor or a proactor?
- Classify your overall academic and social activities, and total the amount of time that you would like or think you should spend on each category.
- Draw up a Daily Plan based on the *what* and *when* exercise.
- Rate your actual performance with what you said you would do – and revise plans for the next few days.
- Try to incorporate revised time management within a personal organizer system.

Crosslink chapters

5 Live Projects
7 Tackling Exams
9 Writing Essays
16 Employment Profiles

Useful addresses

- Time Manager International, who are probably the top in virtually all types of time management and personal organizers. TMI, 50 High Street, Henley-in-Arden, Solihull, West Midlands B95 5AN.
- Microfile, who manufacture reasonably-priced organizers, based on loose leaf refills. Available through various retail outlets – check with your college or local bookshop.
- Interactive Information Systems market an interactive video package, which comes as two video discs and associated texts. Maybe your Media Resources department has this package; if not it can be obtained from Interactive Systems Ltd, 24 Ray Street, London EC1R 3DJ.
- Most of the major book chains have various titles on time management, but be careful because many of these are for use in the world of work, rather than in education. I think you will find that the contents of this chapter will suffice to get you started – and save you money!

2

Making Notes in Lectures

Phil Race

One of the major teaching forums in university or college is 'the lecture'. You may be part of a huge audience seated in tiered rows in a vast room, and a lecturer then talks to you for about an hour. This chapter reminds you that it's not such a good idea simply to write down everything that is said. Instead, there are ways that you can make your notes more meaningful and – especially useful for later revision – more memorable.

When you've worked through this chapter, I hope that you will feel that you *make* notes, rather than just *take* notes. There's a lot of difference between the two. Making notes is something you do in lectures, but also you need to be good at making notes during discussions, from books and papers you read, from watching videos and television programmes, and simply 'out of head' when putting down first thoughts for reports. I'll be giving you some ideas about taking notes in lectures in particular, and I'll leave it to you to apply the ideas to any other circumstances where you need to make notes.

In any course of study, notes are important. There are various sorts of notes, including:

- notes you make as you study books and other learning materials;
- notes you make in lectures;
- notes you make for the purpose of intensive revision before an exam.

Everyone tends to have their own way of making notes. However, our instinctive way may not always be the best way – and it can be well worth learning new tricks regarding note-making. At school or sixth-form college, you may remember having had dictated notes, where you didn't have much choice regarding what you wrote down. Now, it should be quite different! The thing to remember is that you want your notes to be helpful regarding your task of learning their contents – some kinds of notes are much easier to learn from than others.

Why have lectures?

A good question! Is it because lecturers like to give them? Is it because that's what they see themselves as being paid to do? Is it because it's an accountable form of teaching, where there is some sort of measurement, associated with how many people are sitting there, and for how long? There are some genuine, useful purposes for having lectures, including:

- to give everyone in the group a shared learning experience;
- to give overviews of broad areas of a subject;
- to give you the chance to develop your attitudes to ideas and concepts;
- to give all members of a group a base of information;
- to give everyone inspiration.

In many courses, lecture notes cover all the main themes. Lectures deal with the central ideas. You're often expected to remember all the main things that were covered in lectures. If something was dealt with in lectures, it's fair game to set an exam question on it. In general, it is agreed that someone who thoroughly knows the lecture notes should be able to pass the average exam (with extra marks coming from all the other reading you're expected to do, and from work done in other learning situations).

A lecture has been defined as follows:

An event where the lecturer's notes are transferred to the students' notebooks, without the content passing through the minds of either the students – or the lecturer! (See figure 2.1.)

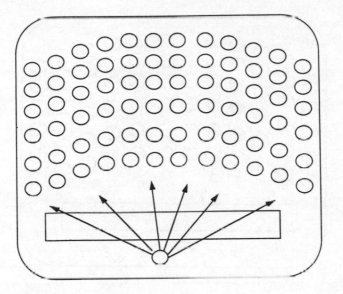

Figure 2.1 One-way information flow during a lecture.

Have you felt this at lectures? The situation doesn't really lend itself to active learning (unless you consciously decide to remain active, and use various ways of maintaining the activity of your mind).

The lecturer is often very busy talking, showing things on the screen, writing things on a board but for the most part you're simply sitting there, relatively motionless. Keeping very still is one of the best ways of preparing to go to sleep.

What do you do during lectures?

Suppose you're sitting there and not understanding it all. Do you ask a question? It can be very embarrassing if you do:

- the lecturer may resent being stopped;
- the lecturer may think it is a silly question;

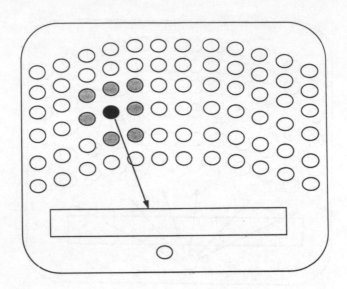

Figure 2.2   Sometimes it's difficult for you to ask a question.

- people around you may think you've asked a silly question;
- people around you may not like you stopping the proceedings.

More often than not, you don't ask – not surprisingly (see figure 2.2). Instead, you soon learn to sit there, looking alert, intelligent, awake and fascinated by the lecturer. Everyone around you looks like this too. So, naturally, the lecturer on seeing all these intelligent, alert faces, assumes that the lecture is going brilliantly, with each of you hanging on every word and idea – total attention.

Back on your side of the room, you quickly learn that if you continue to look alert and intelligent (and awake), no one is likely to put you on the spot by asking you any sudden questions. So the safest way to survive a lecture becomes sitting there *looking* attentive – but it's easy to look attentive while being practically asleep.

Choosing what you do

Here are some of the things students do in lectures.

1 Copying down what you see on the board or screen.
2 Writing down things that the lecturer says.
3 Writing down your own thoughts and ideas.
4 Asking the lecturer questions.
5 Asking *yourself* questions – jotting them down so you can research the answers later.
6 Answering the questions posed by the lecturer.
7 Doing calculations, solving problems and so on.
8 Yawning, shuffling, fidgeting, staring out of the window (if there is one), watching fellow students, chattering to them, muttering to yourself.
9 Thinking about what you will be doing later on.
10 Looking at the lecturer, the blackboard or the screen.
11 Discussing things with students near to you, when directed to do so by the lecturer.

To some extent, which of the above activities you engage in depends on the lecturer. However, you still have a lot of control over what you do. What you write, for example, is up to you. What you think is also up to you. What you decide is up to you.

It's worth looking at each of the activities you do in lectures, in terms of the *learning payoff* you get from them. This payoff is a measure of what you take out of the lecture room when you leave, that will be useful in your future studying. The learning payoff also includes the learning you can do *while actually in the lecture*.

Next, I'd like to look in turn at each of the activities we've mentioned, this time deciding whether it is 'active' or 'passive' (in other words whether it has a substantial learning payoff or not). In the table which follows, enter a tick to indicate whether you find each of the lecture activities 'active' or 'passive'.

How I find lectures: active or passive

		Active	Passive
1	Copying down what you see on the board or screen.		
2	Writing things down that the lecturer says.		
3	Writing down your own thoughts and ideas.		
4	Asking the lecturer questions.		
5	Asking *yourself* questions – jotting them down so you can research the answers later.		
6	Answering questions posed by the lecturer.		
7	Doing calculations, solving problems and so on.		
8	Yawning, shuffling, fidgeting, staring out of the window (if there is one), watching fellow students, chattering to them, muttering to yourself.		
9	Thinking about what you will be doing later on.		
10	Looking at the lecturer, the blackboard or the screen.		
11	Discussing things with students near to you, when directed to do so by the lecturer.		

Now, compare the items you've ticked with those on my list which follows.

Analysing lecture activities

		Active	Passive
1	Copying down what you see on the board or screen.		✓
2	Writing things down that the lecturer says.		✓
3	Writing down your own thoughts and ideas.	✓	
4	Asking the lecturer questions.	✓	
5	Asking *yourself* questions – jotting them down so you can research the answers later.	✓	

6   Answering questions posed by the lecturer. ✓
7   Doing calculations, solving problems and so on. ✓
8   Yawning, shuffling, fidgeting, staring out of the ✓
    window (if there is one), watching fellow
    students, chattering to them, muttering to
    yourself.
9   Thinking about what you will be doing later on. ✓
10 Looking at the lecturer, the blackboard or the ✓
    screen.
11 Discussing things with students near to you, ✓
    when directed to do so by the lecturer.

Next, let's go through each of the things in turn, and see if you agree with the reasons why I made my decisions about 'active' versus 'passive'.

1   Copying down what you see on the board or screen

You may have thought this would be 'active' – yet I chose 'passive'. Your pen may be active if you're busily copying things down, but it's all too easy for your mind to go into limbo while you do it! You can get into the mode of a human photocopier – or a shorthand typist. You may indeed be making faithful records of what's going on, but without much of it really going through your mind. If someone were to stop you, when in the 'copying' mode, and ask you 'Explain to me what you were writing about ten minutes ago' would you be able to do it? If it's not going through your mind, your notes will not have the benefit of any real attempt to structure them and make them as useful as possible. It will be much more difficult to make sense of these notes when it comes to exam revision.

2   Writing down things that the lecturer says

I put this as 'passive' too! Of course, there will be times when you need to write down things the lecturer says, word for word

– but only occasionally (for example, when a definition or a memorable quotation is given). My advice is to make notes *about* things the lecturer says – which is a different matter altogether from just writing it all down. Making notes is about making decisions. You can decide what is important enough to make notes of, and what just to listen to without writing anything. It takes a bit of practice (and courage) not to write everything down at first, but it will pay dividends.

3   Writing down your own thoughts and ideas

'When will I get time for this?' you may ask. It's worth making time for it. I ticked it as an 'active' process – and it can have a very high learning payoff in the long run. If you've got a lot of lectures, your own ideas and thoughts in today's lecture will soon fade and be swamped by other information – but not if you've written your thoughts down. Don't let your thoughts and ideas go to waste, but store them so you can exploit them later. Besides, writing down your own thoughts and ideas can help alleviate the boredom of some lectures!

4   Asking the lecturer questions

This is of course active, and useful. If you ask a question, you are automatically awake and thinking. However, as we've already seen, you may not feel like putting yourself under the spotlight. Some lecturers don't welcome interruptions. You may be afraid that you'll be ridiculed for asking the question (and therefore not knowing the answer). However, almost every time someone asks a question in a lecture there are several other students who also did not know the answer – and who are glad that someone asked the question. There are also several other students who did not realize that they should have been able to answer – in other words they didn't even think of the question until someone asked it.

However, if you still don't feel like asking questions (and who can blame you in some lectures!) there's always (5) below.

5 Asking *yourself* questions – jotting them down so you can research the answers later

This too is 'active' of course. If you don't write your questions down, two hours later you may not even be able to remember what the questions were, let alone research the answers. Writing down your questions doesn't take a lot of time – it takes less than a second to draw a large '?' next to something that you don't understand. It may be worth a few extra seconds to add a word or two to remind you of exactly what it is that you don't yet understand. If you know what the questions are, there's every chance you can find out the answers – for example:

- ask friends;
- look up books;
- approach a lecturer later;
- work it out for yourself.

6 Answering questions posed by the lecturer

Naturally, this is 'active' – at least for you when you're picked on to give an answer. However, when you are picked on (or when you volunteer to answer) there's every chance that everyone else in the room will mentally switch off for a few moments, while you get on with it. If you've got lecturers who ask a lot of questions, make sure that you benefit by trying to answer them (privately) by jotting down a word or two of the question, and a short answer.

7 Doing calculations, solving problems and so on

These are 'active' processes, and are useful practice for things you may be leading up to in exams. In a large group at least you have the chance to ask for help if you get stuck – you can't do that in exams!

8 Yawning, shuffling, fidgeting . . .

Obviously, you're not doing much learning if you're inextricably engaged in these processes! You may be achieving one useful outcome – letting the lecturer see that you're bored. However, it is usually better to engage in active learning strategies of your own (for example, making sense of last week's lecture – or even looking back at a completely different subject, if the present lecture is totally useless).

9 Thinking about what you will be doing later on

You're not alone! After all, you may have several lectures in a week, and each particular lecture can't be the highlight of your life. When you have problems outside college, it's quite natural that they will creep into your mind whenever there's not much else going on. If you're excited about the prospect of something you've been looking forward to, it's natural that your thoughts will stray (even during quite splendid lectures). The only real way to get your thoughts back to the subject of the lecture is to give yourself something quite definite to do – for example, concentrate on making particularly well-structured notes (maybe in a pattern, or a table of questions, or a diagram showing how one thing relates to others).

10 Looking at the lecturer, the blackboard or the screen

Almost everyone does these things during lectures – but the learning payoff can be small. It's possible to *look* at something or someone, without actually *thinking* much about what you see. So don't imagine because you're busy looking at things, that these things are automatically getting filed and sorted in your mind.

11 Discussing things with students near to
    you, when directed to do so by the lecturer

This can be a very useful way to get the most out of large-group
sessions. Sadly, some lecturers seem to feel that *they* should be
the ones doing the talking and discussing, and that 'other
discussions' are a challenge to their authority. Enlightened
lecturers realize that when everyone is involved in a vigorous
discussion (even if only for a minute or two at a time), everyone
is thinking.

Staying in the decision-making mode

That's the secret of good notemaking. If, during a lecture (or
equally, when making notes from books), you can maintain
your mental stance in the active way where you're constantly
deciding things, you can rest assured that the learning payoff
will be maximized. Also, your notes will be useful ones. Here
are some of the decision-making activities you can do while
notemaking.

Deciding what is most important – prioritizing

In any lecture, there's important stuff and there's 'padding'.
Obviously, you don't have to remember the padding. Yet the
padding is often interesting, and there's a tendency to
remember the anecdotes and forget the fundamental principles. Your best chance of deciding exactly what is important
is during the lecture, when you have tone of voice, emphasis,
facial expression and other clues to help you. If you simply
were to write everything down, can you imagine how much
harder it would be to read through it all some weeks later, and
to work out what was really important? Many fast writers
produce inefficient and difficult-to-remember notes. Therefore,
make decisions about importance during the lecture.

Making important things *look* important

What you need is for your notes to contain all the 'codes of importance', so that a glance at your notes reminds you of the key points from each lecture. There are many different ways of making things 'stand out' in your notes, including:

- highlighter pens;
- using different colours for different kinds of information: maybe red for important questions, green for key references;
- underlining things;
- drawing boxes round things;
- using big writing or printing for key points.

Deciding what you don't know yet

We've already mentioned the value of writing down your own questions as a natural part of making lecture notes. Look at it this way: the more you know about what you don't yet know, the more likely you are to be in a position to be able to find out. (Sorry – read that sentence twice!) The real enemy is 'not knowing what you don't know'. Therefore, make it a conscious strategy during any lecture to build up a list of things that you don't know yet. You can always cross things out later – for example, when you find out that you don't need to know them. Many good notemakers leave wide margins which allow them to record separate comments about what they are unsure of.

Making notes which are learning tools

For many of us, colour can be a useful way of making notes which are:

- more interesting to make in the first place;
- more stimulating to look at;

- more memorable;
- better at showing what is crucial and what isn't.

Suppose you wrote an important piece of information (for example, a definition, or an important quotation) in purple, surrounded by a green box. You'd probably remember the information because it looked different to anything else on the page.

Colour can be one of the most successful ways of coding the importance of different kinds of information during a lecture – it only takes seconds for you to change pens or pencils, or to draw coloured rings and boxes round key points.

If all the pages of your notes look alike, it should come as no surprise that your memory won't have much to go on when it comes to remembering them. Many of us learned to conserve paper at school. We were conditioned to fill each page, starting at the top left hand corner and finishing at the bottom right hand corner. If you make lecture notes like this, you could end up with hundreds of pages all looking very similar. The challenge comes with making *memorable* lecture notes, even in lectures which aren't particularly memorable.

Memorable layout

Most of us have highly visual minds. We remember things in different formats and appearances. The visual side of notes can give you something to hang your memories on. In the following examples, imagine you were at a lecture on vulcanology, the study of volcanoes. We'll look at some different ways of building up the lecture notes, and you can decide which technique may work best for you. Even better, you may wish to experiment with several techniques, to add variety to your notemaking activities in lectures.

Here are several kinds of notes you may choose to take:

- 'Complete notes': trying to write down everything you hear and see.

- 'Detailed linear notes': writing down all the main points in the order that you hear about them.
- 'Keyword' linear notes: writing down the main ideas, each followed by a word or two of detail.
- Keyword mental-map or 'pattern' notes.
- 'Question-bank' notes.

Let's look at some of these various forms of notes in more detail.

'Complete' notes

Lots of people try to write it all down – they usually fail! Trying to write down everything you see and hear in most lectures is impossible! The lecturer or presenter normally talks a lot faster than any of us can write. The danger is that you'll spend all your time writing, and not much time thinking about the subject matter: the result is usually notes which aren't very logical or organized. I'll not give an example of these kinds of notes as I expect you can lay hands on examples of your own. So let's look at the alternatives.

'Detailed linear notes'

In fact, these are only 'better' than complete notes in that they're a bit shorter and (with a little more time for you to think) a bit more coherent. Here's an example (imagine the extract below in your own handwriting):

Effects of Volcanoes

First is Plinian, extremely violent. Named after Pliny (Vesuvius 79 AD). Hot ash fired over the countryside.

Next, Mont Pelee – W. Indies: Peleean. This is the most destructive.

Here ash, lava and rock sent in eruption in 1902 and cinders killed everyone bar two.

Third type is Hawaiian, not explosive. Slow seepage of lava causes gentle sloping cone.

Fourth type is Strombolian eruption. Quite a lot of noise and spectacular. Does not cause many disasters.

These are better than trying to write it all down. However, when it comes to learning the subject for an exam, detailed linear notes are boring and hard to work from, and they don't do very much for your memory. On the other hand, if you're studying mathematics or some science/technology subject, there are parts where you do indeed need to take detailed linear notes – for example, proofs, derivations and worked examples.

But in general, notes such as these may not be easy to learn from and one of the key reasons for making good notes is so that you have something from which you can learn effectively and efficiently. So let's move on again.

'Keyword' linear notes

There's a major step forward here. Have a look at the example below.

Types of volcanic eruption

(1)	Plinian	V.violent. Pliny (Vesuvius 79 AD) Hot ash
(2)	Peleean	Most destructive. Ash/rock/lava 1902: killed all – 2
(3)	Hawaiian	Not explosive. Slow lava – gentle slope
(4)	Strombolian	Noisy. Not disastrous

Keyword linear notes are easier to learn from. With a bit of practice, they're quicker to write as you listen to lectures or programmes. The keywords help you to see at once what the main topics discussed are, and the notes give brief details rather than full sentences, keeping the writing task manageable. Advantages of keyword linear notes include:

- Shorter, to the point, leave you more time to think during lectures.
- Easier to learn from. Serve as an index.

Keyword mental-map or 'pattern' notes

Look at the example below. These notes contain all the important information in the previous examples, but look very different.

The main advantage is that pattern notes are visual. Imagine yourself in an exam room, about to answer a question on types of volcanoes. If you'd studied using pattern notes such as in the example below, you'd almost certainly remember that there were four kinds spread about the page of notes. With a little luck, the exact details of each of the four kinds would come back to your visual memory too.

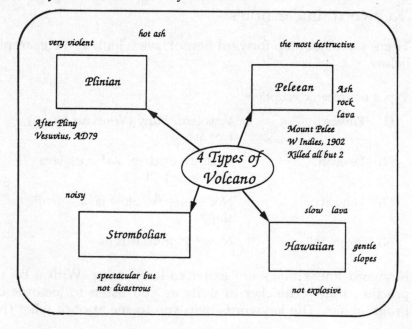

Keyword mental-map or pattern notes (see also chapter 4 on creative problem solving) come into their own when the subject matter is descriptive. However, pattern notes may not be suitable if you're studying mathematics or some science/ technology subjects, where the argument of the lecture may be much more linear.

'Question-bank' notes

You may not know what I mean by 'question-bank' notes, so we'll look at an example straightaway.

Types of volcano

(1)	Name four types of volcano	Plinian Peleean Hawaiian Strombolian
(2)	What is a Plinian volcano?	v. violent described by Pliny – (Vesuvius, 79 AD) Hot ash/cinders
(3)	Is Peleean more destructive?	Yes: all but 2 killed in St. Pierre 1902. Ash/Nuee Ardente quick/little warning
(4)	What's the difference between Hawaiian and Strombolian eruptions?	H: slow lava; not explosive S: noisy, little lava; quite explosive

Question-bank notes are ideal for learning from for exams. You can use them in any subject area. The main benefit is if you've got a test coming up, you can use your notes to test yourself again and again until you're quite certain to get each question right every time. After all, any test measures your ability to answer questions, so the more practice you have at answering questions the better you're bound to do in the test.

Follow up lectures

What are you doing with your lecture notes? Filing them for later? The more often you look at them the more memorable they become. One of the best things you can do with lecture notes is to make summaries of them – it's a way of reminding yourself once again about what the most important things were.

An excellent way to follow up lectures is to compare your notes with those of fellow students. You may well have written things they missed – and they will almost certainly have captured things you missed. If each of you improves your own set of notes, it serves everyone well.

Action plan

Notetaking or notemaking?

- Don't be a human photocopier. Just writing down what you see doesn't mean that you're on the way to learning it.
- Don't be a human tape recorder. Just writing down what you hear doesn't mean you're on the way to understanding it.
- Keep *active*:

  - make decisions;
  - make your notes *yours*;
  - show importance ratings;
  - write questions.

- Follow up your notes – soon:

  - process them;
  - compare with others;
  - fill gaps;
  - decide what you need to know;
  - make summaries.

Crosslink chapters

3 Active Reading
4 Creative Problem Solving
7 Tackling Exams
14 Making the Most of Seminars

Further reading

Race, P. (1992) *Five Hundred Tips for Students*. Oxford: Blackwell Publishers.
Race, P. and Bourner, T. (1990) *How to Win as a Part-Time Student*. London: Kogan-Page-Nichols.

3
Active Reading

Phil Race

When you've worked through this chapter, and tried out the ideas in it for yourself, you should be rewarded as follows:

1 You'll be able to read faster, when safe to do so.
2 You'll waste less time tracking down what you need to read.
3 You'll be quicker at finding the most relevant parts of the books and papers you read.
4 You'll get better value in terms of learning payoff from your reading.
5 You'll be able to make useful 'learning tools' while you read – often saving you having to re-read important materials time and time again.

Can you read?

For many people, reading is a difficult hurdle to overcome. You're already over this hurdle, or else you would not be reading this chapter. You've probably been reading for many years now, and you've probably succeeded in most things that depended upon you being able to read. So far, anyway. But reading is a skill in its own right – and as such it's something you can consciously decide to improve and develop.

How did you learn to read?

Most people learn to read at school, and often by reading one word at a time, and following along the line with a finger or pencil. More important, when most people start to read, there's quite a lot of emphasis on reading aloud. Although this is very useful in some ways (for example, so teachers can keep up with what's happening) it's actually very limiting. This is because many adults (you perhaps?) never really shake off the habit of 'mentally reciting' as they read. This limits the speed at which many people read, to the speed at which they can hear themselves reading out loud. In fact, we can quite easily learn to read a great deal faster, and this is particularly useful when 'scanning' a large amount of information aiming to track down that which is most useful.

Reading and memory

Try reading the following passage. Note that you'll have to read down the page, not across it. I'll explain why shortly. It may be interesting for you to time yourself – see how long it takes when you have to read 'vertically'.

How	bit	We'd	Reading
much	awkward	know	can
of	if	so	be
what	we	much	a
we	remembered	that	pleasurable
read	everything	when	activity.
do	we	it	It
we	saw	came	can
remember?	in	to	be
Not	newspapers,	answering	relaxing
a	on	any	as
lot,	television	question	well
I	screens,	we	as
think.	in	wouldn't	stimulating.
It	books,	know	Reading
would	and	where	something
be	so	to	you're
a	on.	start!	not

really	certain	to	we
interested	to	instinct,	don't
in,	need	most	usually
however,	to	of	expect
can	read	us	an
be	at	tend	imminent
boring	least	to	quiz
and	some	read	on
frustrating.	things	rather	what
And	you	passively.	we've
if	don't	This	just
you're	like	is	finished
studying,	much.	partly	reading.
you're	Left	because	

Now try reading it as follows (time yourself again if you like):

How much of what we read do we remember? Not a lot, I think.
It would be a bit awkward if we remembered everything we saw
in newspapers, on television screens, in books, and so on. We'd
know so much that when it came to answering any questions,
we wouldn't know where to start!

Reading can be a pleasurable activity. It can be relaxing as well
as stimulating. Reading something you're not really interested
in, however, can be boring and frustrating. And if you're
studying, you're certain to need to read at least some things you
don't like much. Left to instinct, most of us tend to read rather
passively. This is partly because we don't expect an imminent
quiz on what we've just finished reading.

The first time you read the passage, when it was in 'vertical
lists', you were forced to read one word at a time, and it was
much harder to make sense of the words as connected together
to make the sentences as well as the words. Now please read
the passage one last time, this time with a little distortion
added:

How much   of what we read   do we remember?   Not a lot,
I think. It would be   a bit awkward   if we remembered
everything we saw in newspapers,   on television screens,   in

books,   and so on. We'd know so much   when it came to
answering any question,   we wouldn't know   where to start!
    Reading can be   a pleasurable activity.   It can be relaxing
as well as stimulating.   Reading something   you're not really
interested in, however,   can be boring and frustrating.   And
if you're studying,   you're certain to need to read   at least
some things   you don't like much.   Left to instinct, most of us
tend to   read rather passively.   This is partly because we
don't usually expect   an imminent quiz   on what we've just
finished reading.

In that final version of the passage, I've grouped the words into
'clumps' of the sort that the human eye can make sense of in
one 'shot'. In other words, readers who have passed the
'verbalizing' stage 'bounce' along sentences extracting the
sense from clusters of words, rather than looking at every
single word. I should add at once that my division of the above
passage into 'clumps' is only one of very many ways of doing
this, and different readers will structure the passage in their
own ways.

Passive reading

That's the enemy when you're reading to learn. It's all right to
read a newspaper passively. It doesn't then matter that you
forget quickly almost everything you saw. The danger is that
passive reading creeps into your reading to learn, and
swallows vast chunks of valuable time without giving you any
real learning payoff. Most of this chapter is about ways of
avoiding this waste.

Speed reading

As you'll have gathered from that experiment with layout and
clumps of words, it's possible to deliberately shake off the habit
of verbalizing as you read. As with any other kind of skill, the

more you practise it, the better you become. Even when you're reading for pleasure, it's useful to practise speeding up your reading (though you'll spend more time on books as a result!).

With academic reading, it's not always safe to read too fast. Which of the following pieces of reading lend themselves to fast reading, and which do not?

1 A discussion of the main causes of rusting of iron.
2 A case history in law.
3 A mathematical derivation or theorem.
4 A statistical analysis of the risks of smoking.
5 A nineteenth century novel.
6 An examination question.

Here are my comments on each of these.

1 A discussion of the main causes of rusting of iron: probably safe to read it quite quickly at least in the first stage, then maybe go through it once more jotting down key points and turning them into a summary.
2 A case history in law: probably best to read such pieces quickly, as law students have thousands of them to get through.
3 A mathematical derivation or theorem: this doesn't lend itself to speed reading, as quite a lot of thinking may be needed to make sense of each successive line in the argument or proof.
4 A statistical analysis of the risks of smoking: while it's relatively easy to speed read the facts, it's not so easy to speed read the figures.
5 A nineteenth century novel: it's safe to speed read most works of fiction in the 'early' stages of studying them, though you'll probably have to slow read parts of them later, when analysing the writing in depth.
6 An examination question: it's *never* wise to read exam questions quickly. It's vitally important that before putting pen to paper, you have a very clear idea of the exact meaning of every word in the question.

So, in short, speed reading is a very useful technique *when used in appropriate circumstances*. When doing background reading, and when tracking down the most relevant sources, speed reading can save you a great deal of time. We've already looked at one way of speeding up your reading – reading clumps of words rather than one word at a time. There are other useful ways you can speed up your reading (first readings, anyway) of academic materials, including:

- Scanning the whole piece (or book) looking just at main headings, to get a 'feel' for the piece.
- Reading the first sentence of each paragraph only. This will often give a good idea of what the material is about, as the remainder of each paragraph will often simply be an amplification of the first sentence. However, be on your guard: some writers save their important points for the closing sentences of paragraphs – so do a little research and see what sort of writer is involved.
- Looking at the end of the piece for a summary, and reading that first. You're then alerted in advance to the main conclusions, and you can take more notice of them as they come up in the preceding material.
- Reading the introductions and summaries only, until you find material which is so relevant and important that it's clear to you that it's worth slowing down and reading 'more seriously'.
- If it's a long book with running heads changing as the chapters and topics change, simply flicking through the pages, gaining an impression of the way the book is put together, and the key words used in the headings.

Tone and style of textbooks and published materials

Many textbooks and articles tend to be written in a rather impersonal, remote – and boring – style. Much of the language is 'third person passive':

'It is often found that. . .'

'It can therefore be deduced that. . .'

'Taking into account both sides of the picture, it can be concluded that. . .' and so on.

Sentences tend to be long – far longer than we would speak or listen. It's all too easy therefore to grasp only part of the meaning of a sentence.

In printed materials, most of the words are in the same size and weight of print. This means that often important points look just the same as background details. It's often easier to understand the background details – and these may well be what we remember from what we read. The important points may need to be read several times, and thought about, before they start getting home to us.

Because of all this, when we read with the purpose of learning, it's worth consciously examining exactly how we are reading. We need to make reading for learning an *active* process. We need to *organize* the ways we go about our reading. Above all, we need to be *selective* in what we read.

Tracking down materials in libraries

What do you do? Do you wander round the shelves in the library, picking out books or journals which seem, from their titles, to contain the sort of information you're looking for? It's quite enjoyable doing this, but it's a slow way of getting at information. There's no guarantee that the most relevant looking books will actually be the most useful. We may not be able to tell which authors are the most respected or up to date. The attractive, glossy looking book may not be the best. In fact, the best books may not be on the shelves, being already out on loan. Of the books which are on the shelves, it's often the most grubby looking ones which are the most relevant – that's why they're grubby!

Almost all libraries have catalogues. Sometimes these are on computer. Alternatively, card indexes of various sorts may be provided. It is often hard, at first, to use the catalogues efficiently, but library staff are usually only too pleased if you ask them for help in how to use the cataloguing systems. They'd much rather help you to find out how to use the library well, than if you were to ask them to find your books for you!

Computerized catalogues are particularly useful. These allow you to do various kinds of 'search' sitting at a terminal rather than walking miles around the book stacks. For example, you may be able to do searches:

- By author (useful when you already know which are the best authors in your subject, or when you've discovered an author you like, and want to find out what else has come from the same source).
- By title (usually typing in any keyword will yield an on-screen list of books containing that word in the title. To narrow the choice down (you may get hundreds first time) type in two keywords. Library staff will be able to help you decide what are the best keywords to try).
- By subject (again working on the keyword principle).

Computerized databases in libraries can even tell you which stack contains the books you want, date of publication, publisher, how many shelf copies there are of each book, and how many are already out on loan. Even this information is useful in its own right – when a library has 20 copies of a book, and 16 are out on loan, you can be fairly certain that the book is highly relevant to the course – probably yours.

You'll normally have quite a bit of guidance from your lecturers as to what books are most relevant. Many lecturers start their courses by giving out book lists. Don't rush out and purchase all the books! If you buy them all, you'll probably find you simply haven't time to read them all, and in any case, some books will be much less useful than others. So it is important to get to know which books are going to be sufficiently relevant, and frequently needed. These are the ones worth buying for yourself. It's a good idea to ask students who have already done your course (and passed!) which books they found most useful. In fact, you may well be able to buy some of your books second hand from students who have now finished with them.

A checklist for selecting the right books

- Is it recommended by lecturers?
- Is it recommended by library staff? (They often know a lot about which are the most useful books – even more than lecturers.)
- Can you find out what learners who have used the book already (e.g. learners who did the course last year) think are the best books?
- Have you checked the contents pages and made sure that it contains things you really want to find out?

Now you've found a book, how should you use it?

Imagine you've tracked down a relevant textbook, and you're about to use it to write an essay, or get to grips with one of your topics. What would you do? Which of the following options is closest to how you tend to start on your books?

1 Scan quickly through the book, looking for the parts relevant to your immediate purpose.
2 Start on page one and read through the book, trying to take in as much as you can all the way through.
3 Look carefully at the contents pages and the index, and make notes of page numbers where the information you need seems to be centred.

Option (1) is quite sensible. If you're looking for something definite, rather than just taking in all you see, you're less likely to go off on tangents. Option (2) is hardly ever wise. Even if it's an excellent book, and directly relevant to your course from cover to cover, simply ploughing through it is not a good way to get the best out of your reading. Option (3) is the best one. Using the contents pages and the index is a very quick way of finding out several useful things, including:

- whether the book is indeed relevant to your studies;
- where the most relevant chapters are to be found;
- how the book is structured;
- how the presentation of the subject is handled.

Making your own agenda

If you simply read a book in an unenquiring way, it's all too easy for your reading to be passive. It only takes a few minutes to jot down a list of questions you want to find answers to from the book – in other words an 'agenda' for your reading. In fact, it's extremely useful to work out what you want to find out, as this means that when you see the 'answers' to your questions, you are much more receptive to them. When your brain is switched into 'search' mode as soon as you see the information, it is snatched up. If we're not in 'search' mode, even the most useful information can be passed over without anything being captured by our brains. Jotting down the answers to your agenda questions helps make time spent reading really valuable. Of course, you'll think of more questions as you go so don't have a 'fixed' agenda – have an expanding one. Things you read will trigger off more questions that you want to find the answers to.

How can you make reading an active process?

Let's assume that you've found a relevant book and tracked down the relevant information in it. Suppose you're now in the business of studying the book, rather than just reading things in it. We've already looked at the idea of making your own agenda, but let's look at yet more things you can do to ensure that the time you spend reading is well spent.

What's the main danger while reading? It is reading page after page, and just as quickly forgetting all about what you've read. Coupled with this is that when you're reading, you're doing all sorts of other things, such as writing coursework, preparing systematically for exams, and so on. In fact, it is only too easy to make reading a 'work avoidance strategy', kidding yourself that because you've got a book open in front of you that some serious studying is happening!

It's quite easy to read something and understand it at the time, but it can be another matter to be able to recall, discuss and apply the things you've just read. Books tend to be longwinded. You can't possibly 'learn' all your books! So you need to extract from the books things suitable for you to learn.

The secret of active reading is not to simply read! Probably the important thing to decide first is exactly what do you need to learn from each book. It won't be the whole book. The next thing to do is to make 'learning tools'.

What are learning tools?

They are things which help you to make your learning more efficient and effective. They are 'tools' in exactly the same way as sanders, drills, saws, and so on. When you use such tools, imagine how much slower it would be to do the job without any tools at all – just with your hands. Often, it would be impossible. Learning tools are specially designed to tackle the particular task of getting what you need from your books, and storing what you need in your memory. Here are some learning tools.

Summaries: When you read, it's always useful to make 'tight' summaries in your own words of the really important things. Later, when you're preparing for exams, it's far more time efficient to refer to a bank of good summaries, than to have to wade through all the books again. In any case, you'll often need to make summaries of information that you can't take away and put on your shelves – for example from journals and reference-only books. In any case, 'having it on your shelf' is of little real value. You and I have books on our shelves that we've seldom opened!

Question banks: A very efficient method of paving the way to success is to build up a large bank of short questions, which will be useful for you to develop the ability to answer. The best question bank questions are one-liners, along the lines:

- What's a blurgeion?
- Where do you find queeters?
- Who discovered grommit-fluke?
- What's Ellington's Second Law?
- How do you make portogen?
- When can mungling take place?
- Why does parbling happen?

and so on.

Never mind the nonsense words – do you see the point? If you jot down a question every time you notice something worth remembering, you're already more than halfway towards learning it successfully. The questions can mount up into thousands, and can be stored on record cards, or in a pocket book. Being the owner of a question bank allows you to practise answering questions. That's exactly what written exams measure. It's nice to find questions you remember the answers to – but it's even more useful to find questions where you've forgotten the answers. Once you identify exactly what you've forgotten, you can easily re-learn it. The problem is not knowing what you've forgotten, and only finding out too late in the exam room.

Making notes on the book

When you own a book, it's a good thing to make it *really* your own by writing all over it. Among the things that you can write are:

- your own thoughts at the time of reading it;

- questions you would like to find the answers to;
- points where you agree with the author;
- things you disagree with;
- 'I simply don't know what this means' – giving you the chance to find out later, and so on.

You'll often find that you remember the things that you write on books and also that you remember by association the things you were trying to work out as you wrote your comments. Also, when you scan the book again and spot particular comments you jotted onto it, you'll often remember quite a lot of your thinking when you first read it. In other words, stopping now and then to scribble on a book not only helps you avoid the trap of passive reading, but it gives you added learning payoff. It could well be said that active reading is always done with a pen or pencil in the hand. In any case, at the end of the day it's not your reading that's assessed in exams, it's your writing!

Highlighting

This is another way of 'making a book your own'. It's quicker than writing notes and looks rather better usually. But beware, it can become possible to highlight key points rather 'automatically', without engaging your brain to the same extent as would happen if you wrote comments yourself. Also, a book covered with highlighted words and sentences becomes rather tiresome on the eyes. However, it's possible to engage in 'creative highlighting'. What I have in mind takes three or four different colours of highlighting pen, and the application of your own codes. For example:

- yellow for key information, definitions, etc.
- green for facts and figures that may be worth learning;
- pink for key ideas and links between things;
- blue for things you want to find out more about, for example by asking questions in tutorials, or looking up information in other sources.

Photocopies

Libraries increasingly have photocopying facilities. University libraries often have banks of photocopiers, and machines issuing tokens for cash, and long and busy queues of learners waiting to capture key pages from textbooks and journals. When you see a really relevant extract in a book or journal that isn't simply your own property, it's very tempting to 'capture it' in a photocopy. However, simply owning a photocopy is far from enough. There's a danger that the photocopy will get 'filed for later', or lost, or forgotten. It's what you do with the photocopy that matters. When you've got a photocopy you can scribble on it, you can use highlighters and all sorts of things that you can't do to the library stock itself. When you've made a photocopy it's a good basic rule to 'do something with it within 24 hours', i.e. while you still remember why you thought it was important enough to make a copy. In other words, make the copy your own, by personalizing it – and better – making learning tools such as questions and summaries from it. Don't forget that there are legal limitations on what you can photocopy – your librarians can advise you on this.

Quantity versus quality

You'll often get the impression that your tutors expect you to read about three books per hour during a course. Much is said about breadth of reading. Never forget, however, that you're not going to be measured on how much you've read, but rather on what you can do with what you've gained from your reading. This often means that it's much better to read to a modest amount really well, extracting all the key sense from it, than to read a vast amount but not really gain mastery over it. Also, if you read too much, you may well end up in the unfortunate position of knowing so much about a topic that you can't possibly answer a 30-minute exam question in anything less than three hours! Getting a good grip on the basics is always a safer strategy than trying to read everything that's ever been written on your subject.

Group reading

This looks like a contradiction in terms – reading is by definition an individual task. But mastering the information you read can be helped enormously by working with fellow learners. For example, if say you and two colleagues set about reading one each of three different accounts of a topic, making notes or summaries as you go, you can then spend some time explaining each of the three perspectives to each other. Try it. You may be amazed how much you remember of what you explained to the others. The act of preparing some information so that you can explain it to other people is in itself a very useful way of 'sharpening' your reading. Ultimately, of course, you're going to have to 'explain' much of what you read, in writing, to examiners. So the more practice you get at explaining things and putting them into your own words, the better. Working in this sort of way with colleagues is not only really productive, but it's also a lot more fun than burying your head in books in solitary confinement.

Conclusions

You'll soon pick up the skill of being able to track down which parts of a book particularly lend themselves to your purpose of making learning tools. For example, the summary at the end of a chapter might have quite enough detail in it for your purpose and you may only need to glance through most of the chapter itself.

As we have seen, there's quite a difference between reading to learn, and just reading. Reading for the sake of it is still one of your options, of course. The main thing is not to kid yourself that you're actually doing productive work if you're reading passively. Passive reading is a luxury to be enjoyed when you know you've done sufficient work for the day. You'll know your reading skills have really advanced when you find your-self having to fight off the urge to make notes on your newspaper, and write questions and summaries!

To sum up, productive reading is an active process. You need pen and paper to make learning tools as you read. The question 'Do I need to remember this?' should be permanently in your mind when you read. Very often, the answer is 'No', a good clue for you to engage the speed reading mode we talked about earlier. Whenever the answer is 'Yes', a question, or summary, will help you record what you need to remember and give you the chance to test how much you remember.

Action plan

Ten tips for active reading

You've heard the expression 'reading for a degree'? It's rather misleading. Now if it were 'writing for a degree' perhaps it would be nearer the truth. However, reading is something you'll do a lot of in your studies. The suggestions below should help you make your reading more efficient and avoid some of the dangers which can be associated with reading – and I don't mean eyestrain.

1   *Put reading into perspective.* When you read something, how much of it do you actually remember, say, two weeks later? 50 per cent? 10 per cent? 5 per cent? If you're honest with yourself, you'll admit that 'just reading' isn't a very efficient way of studying. Reading has to be made 'active' in one way or another.

2   *'Further Reading. . .'* How often these words come up! Is it assumed that you will go off and read all the books and references suggested to you for 'further reading'? By definition, further reading is not 'central' reading – it's the additional icing on the cake. If you spend all your time doing further reading you'll be away at a tangent to the fundamental things you're meant to be studying – these are often in your own notes or in central books and papers.

3   *Find the really relevant parts before you get sidetracked.* The most useful pages of many books are the contents pages and the index. Use these to track down exactly where the most relevant part of the book is.

4 *Make an 'agenda' before you start reading.* Work out what you need to pick up from each source you use – write some questions you need answers for. Then, as you read, when you come across the answers to your questions, the answers will 'register' because the questions were in your mind already. Without an agenda you'd simply skim right over much of the most valuable information.

5 *If the book belongs to you make it 'your own'.* Write notes on the pages, use a highlighter pen to make the really important parts easy to find again. This allows you to progressively consolidate your work with the book – every time you see things you've already done to the book you're reminded of thinking you've already done. (But don't do any of this to library books – make photocopies first).

6 *Write questions as you read.* When you've just learned something important, jot down a question which will give you the chance to test yourself on it later (with a page reference for when you need to have another look at the book). Build lists of such questions as you go. Active reading is done with a pen – again!

7 *Summarize as you read.* Make notes of the things you think you really need to remember (probably quite a small percentage of the average page). Put page references on your summary points, then a few days later look at your summary and try to mentally reconstruct some of the content of the book – going back to the pages where something has slipped your mind. Active reading is done with a pen – again!

8 *Prioritize your reading list.* This becomes possible as you get to know your books and references rather better. Divide the books and references into categories such as 'essential and useful', 'useful for some things', 'has a very useful chapter 5 – ignore the rest' and so on. Then spend most of your reading time with the books or chapters with 'high learning payoff' – relevant, useful ones.

9 *Balance your reading* with all the other study tasks on your agenda. Don't spend too much time reading – remember it's still not the most efficient way of learning.

10 *Read for pleasure too* but as a reward for doing some useful work, not as a way of putting off the task of starting some real work.

Crosslink chapters

Further reading

Race, P. (1992) *500 Tips for Students*. Oxford: Blackwell Publishers.

4

Creative Problem Solving

Richard Kemp

Many lecturers say that the best students are those who think for themselves and have original ideas. Many students say the same thing about their best lecturers! Creative problem solving is all about tackling problems which have never been solved, or which have lots of different kinds of solutions. Richard Kemp introduces some methods which are popular, successful and above all, enjoyable to use. They can be applied to essays, projects, seminars and presentations, and are guaranteed to produce novel and original outcomes.

Human beings of all ages seem to relish being asked to 'solve' a riddle, a puzzle, conundrum or teaser. They welcome the opportunity to exercise their knowledge, wit and intelligence. Most newspapers, both tabloid and broadsheet, carry crossword puzzles; some also offer 'brainteasers' and other kinds of mental challenge.

Some humour has a distinct kind of 'creative problem solving' feel to it. For example, 'What is green, has six legs and would kill you if it fell on you?' The respondent to this question is expected to reply 'I don't know', whereupon the questioner will reply with an answer which is unexpected and rich in novelty ('A snooker table!'). Generating answers which are unusual and rich in novelty is the essence of creative problem solving. In order to do this, however, it will be necessary to use our imagination in a free and unconstrained way. This will involve an element of risk in that the suggestions we make may seem at the outset to be foolish, frivolous or irrelevant. But it is precisely this state of free association of ideas which is most precious to creativity and to be encouraged in all participants.

Problem solving is a skill highly valued both by academics

and the world of work. But what is meant by 'problem solving'? The academic problem solving environment consists normally of a solitary student grappling with a set problem or piece of coursework which tutors have designed and which will lead to a unique 'solution'. The typical world of work environment contrasts sharply in that the problem is normally one that may be lacking in definition, that often has no unique solution and is approached not by an individual but by a group working together for a common goal – an answer by yesterday!

Individual and group problem solving

All of the problem solving ideas put forward here, with the exception of synectics, can be used by you, either alone or with a group of your fellow students (see also chapter 8). The group approach to problem solving is recommended, not just because two heads are better than one, but because group problem solving is usually more fun and can develop many more interpersonal skills at the same time, such as communication, for example.

A suitable problem

It is necessary first to decide on the particular problem to be solved. Whilst you are aiming at developing skills, instead of applying them to your particular study area, then one of the following problems might be thought suitable:

- Enabling more cars to park on the campus.
- How to get more travellers to use the railways.
- How to get better jobs in the vacations.
- How to improve the catering facilities of the Students Union.

Note that it is useful to choose a problem based on improving something already existing – this helps to provide a common starting point for participants (and reflects the nature of the vast majority of real-life problems).

The group work envisaged in this section will be most productive with groups of no more than eight. Like most rules of thumb it can be safely ignored by experienced practitioners. Within the group it will be useful at the outset if two people could be nominated, one to record the activities of the group and the other to coordinate the activities.

Brainstorming

Brainstorming is a process closely associated with creativity and innovation. Typically, brainstorming is carried out in three phases:

- Firstly, ideas are generated at random and in quick succession for a time – say ten minutes – or until there is a marked slowdown in suggestions.
- Secondly, the ideas generated are then examined and put together in a number of suitable categories or themes.
- Finally, the ideas are then discussed and ranked in order of priority.

Brainstorming the solution to a problem is the recording of the rapid and free expression of thoughts about a problem and possible solutions. Many innovative developments arise from suggestions which may at first seem far-fetched, silly or absurd. Science abounds with illustrations of such discoveries, inventions and processes; from float glass to radio valves.

Creative thought knows no boundaries, so it is essential to encourage participants to give voice to any thought, however irrelevant it might seem. Such an activity is best conducted in an environment free of criticism. Thus the essential rule for brainstorming is that adverse reactions are prohibited. The group will nominate one of their number to write the ideas generated by the group on a flipchart or similar large surface.

Individuals in the group will then call out ideas which are immediately written down on the flipchart. No discussion or comment is permitted, but building on ideas is encouraged, and a speedy turnover of suggestions is ideal. As each page of the flipchart is filled, it is torn off and tacked to a wall where it can be easily seen by the group.

In the second phase of brainstorming, the filled sheets are discussed so that the various ideas can be identified and classified according to categories or themes suggested by the group. The categories and their associated ideas may then be displayed on fresh sheets.

Finally, the group is invited to identify the most promising ideas for further development and to enter these on one or two transparencies.

Rules for brainstorming

- Write down on the flipchart exactly what each person says (don't edit or substitute).
- Don't elaborate at this stage.
- No one is allowed to criticize any idea until the first phase is complete.

Negative brainstorming

Negative brainstorming is similar in process to brainstorming. The crucial difference is that the original problem is inverted. Thus, for example, instead of looking for ways of generating more car parking space on the campus we would take as our task the problem 'How to ensure fewer available car parking spaces on campus'.

Ideas would then be generated and recorded as before. Themes or categories would be identified and the solutions laid out accordingly. The ideas would then be evaluated and the most promising set aside for consideration. At this stage, the most promising ideas would themselves be inverted to provide solutions to the original problem. We might, for example, decide that 'Parking in a fashion which maximizes the space between cars' is a promising solution to the inverted problem. Thus for our solution to the original problem we would arrive at the suggestion 'Parking in a fashion which minimizes the space between cars'.

Negative brainstorming can often reveal new aspects of a problem, and point to corresponding solutions. It is often amusing, when negative brainstorming lists are displayed, to hear the cry 'But that's what things are like now!' A good topic for negative brainstorming is 'How to improve lectures', i.e. brainstorm 'How to make lectures worse'!

Mind mapping

Mind mapping is the setting of the problem in its complete context. It is essentially a diagrammatic representation. All social, technical and psychological aspects are considered. Factors inhibiting or blocking a solution are also elaborated. The mind map of a typical problem is to be found in figure 4.1 of this chapter.

The following can be a very useful subject for most problem solving techniques:

Activity
Mind map the topic of 'Successful study' for your course.

Zwicky's morphology

Zwicky's morphological method consists of identifying all the sub-elements that make up the system or problem under consideration, and varying their relationship with each other.

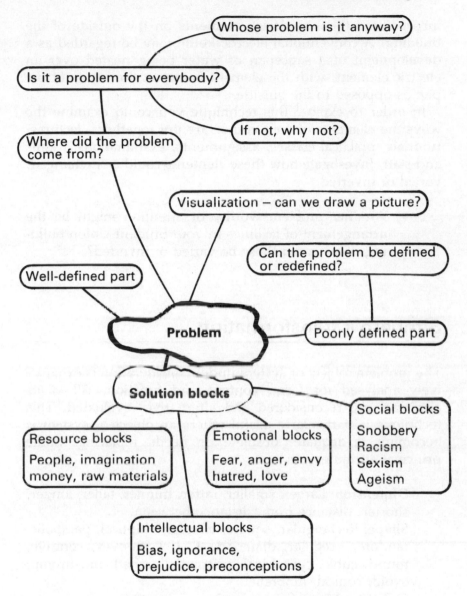

Figure 4.1 A mind map for 'problem'.

For example, the architects of certain modernist buildings have taken some of the elements normally concealed within, such as the structural framework and waste disposal systems, and incorporated them as design elements on the outside of the building. A conventional electric kettle may be regarded as a development of a saucepan of water being heated over an electric element, with the element being on the inside of the pan as opposed to the outside.

In order to explore this technique you could examine the ways the elements of your course are put together – lectures, tutorials, practical classes, assignments, examinations, rooms and staff. Investigate how these elements could be exchanged, varied or inverted.

- Another problem worthy of attention might be the arrangement of facilities in your Student Union building. How could these be varied or inverted?

Simberg's transformation

The problem, object or system under consideration is exhaustively analysed for form, content and function. All of its attributes are reconsidered and alternatives evaluated. This technique is particularly useful where an object or system is becoming inadequate, obsolete or needs replacing. Some principal attributes are:

Dimension: Larger, smaller, fatter, thinner, taller, longer, shorter, distance from, distance between.
Shape: Rectangular, square, circular, elliptical, parabolic, random, irregular, diamond, T, I, L, convex, concave, round, cubic, cylindrical, prismatic, arched, mushroom, ovoid, conical, umbrella.
Quantity: More, fewer, combine, separate.
Material: Wood, paper, plastic, string, stone, wire, glass, foam, organic, inorganic, iron, stainless steel, copper, aluminium, zinc, bronze.
Time: Faster, slower, higher frequency, lower frequency, sporadic, intermittent, pulsing, time-delayed.

Connections: Bond, screw, nail, adhesive, plug, socket, tie, zip, button, pin, staple, clamp.

Texture: Rough, smooth, corrugated, dimpled, serrated, plane, perforated, meshed, stratified.

Character: Strong, weak, wet, dry, damp, hard, soft, brittle, flexible, dense, heavy, light, solid, liquid, opaque, translucent, expensive, cheap, loud, quiet.

Power: Battery, mains, petrol vapour, solid fuel, fire, wind, water, solar, steam, person.

Action: Cutting, boring, winding, planing, rotating, falling, rising, pulling, pushing, pressing, compressing, crushing, exploding, imploding, bending, folding, heating, cooling, shaping, forming, powering, raising, lowering, joining, separating, filtering, mixing, smoothing, abrading, penetrating, closing, opening, clarifying, magnifying, focusing, reflecting, refracting, attracting, repelling.

Environment: Light, dark, hot, cold, humid, arid, clean, polluted, filled, vacuum.

Feelings: Love, hate, affection, fear, loathing, admiration, contempt, anxiety, joy, elation, ecstasy, dread, anticipation, excitement, apprehension, surprise, shock.

Relationships: Blood, marriage, nation, tribe, club, profession, cooperative, hostile, competitive, symbolic, representative, delegate, subordinate, superior, personal, collaborative, supportive.

The attributes above are an adaptation of Simberg's original set. The procedure, which can be individual or group based, entails examining the object or system, and for each of its attributes a set of possible alternatives is considered along the lines of the lists supplied above. It helps if the situation can be sketched or represented diagrammatically. The process is time consuming but can give invaluable insights into ways of altering the makeup of an object, or the operation of a system.

- List the components of an everyday object and investigate how they might be altered using Simberg's transformation.

In increasing order of complexity, the following might be considered suitable:

> Coathanger
> Clothes peg
> Spectacles
> Briefcase
> Bicycle

Kelly's repertory grid

Kelly's Role Construct Repertory Test is adapted here to a problem solving tool. The repertory grid method, or rep grid as it is better known, is a technique for enabling the drawing of comparisons between sets of attributes, people or objects. Similarities and differences are the basis of the technique. It is not in itself a solution generating activity, but it can provide detailed insight into the nature of a problem and thereby help greatly with defining where a solution might be found.

At the outset a list is constructed in which the most important characteristics, attributes or analogies of the problem are written down. The car parking problem, which is used later as an example, could suggest analogous situations like 'books on a bookshelf', 'a maze', 'packing', and so on. The list could be brainstormed and then prioritized to define what those attempting the solution see as being the crucial attributes or analogies. The problem is thus expressed in a language which is determined by those attempting a solution.

The list is now presented in groups of three called triads. Clearly a certain amount of selectivity is called for since out of a list of, say, ten attributes there are 120 ways of selecting three items. In a typical comparison between the problem P and an arbitrary set of three attributes or entities A, B and C we can examine the following:

1 P is like A, but unlike B or C in the following ways:
2 P is like B, but unlike C or A in the following ways:
3 P is like C, but unlike A or B in the following ways:
4 P is like A and B but unlike C in the following ways:
5 P is like A and C but unlike B in the following ways:
6 P is like B and C but unlike A in the following ways:

Clearly, not all possibilities will engender insight into the problem. The most promising combinations are chosen to provide key words and phrases which may assist in the search for a solution.

The rep grid title is derived from the most common way of setting out the method. The set of chosen attributes or analogies forms the columns and in each row a set of three attributes is selected for comparison marked by three circles. A cross is marked in each circle where similarities are felt to occur and the word or phrase which encapsulates the similarity is noted in a similarity column. In a corresponding way a contrast column is also built up. The layout of the grid is shown in figure 4.2. That grid has space for a dozen attributes which could well be reduced in order to facilitate the process.

The similarities and differences can be of any kind. The following is a short list of ways in which things can be distinguished:

- Gender
- Culture
- Organization
- Structure
- Method of communication
- Method of manufacture
- Function

You could list some other characteristics which could distinguish objects, people or systems.

In order to illustrate the technique we choose the car parking problem and express it formally as: 'How to enable more cars to park on the campus'. We then carry out the following steps:

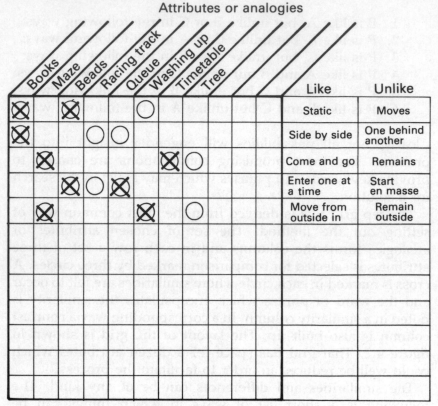

Attributes or analogies

	Books	Maze	Beads	Racing track	Queue	Washing up	Timetable	Tree				Like	Unlike
⊗		⊗			○							Static	Moves
⊗			○	○								Side by side	One behind another
	⊗					⊗	○					Come and go	Remains
		⊗	○	⊗								Enter one at a time	Start en masse
	⊗				⊗		○					Move from outside in	Remain outside

Figure 4.2   Kelly's repertory grid.

1   Generate attributes or analogies.
2   Add unrelated concepts.
3   Produce promising list.
4   Form triads.

1   Generate attributes or analogies

Brainstorming the situation we emerge with the following list:

Analogies

- Books on a bookshelf
- Sardines

- A maze
- Beads on a necklace
- Motorway
- Racing track
- Railway
- Supermarket trolleys
- Queue
- Draughts
- Wheelchair

Attributes

- Size – big, small
- Turning circle
- Access – narrow, wide
- Shape – rectangular
- Space – sought
- Angle – to others
- Time – occupation
- Direction – in, out

2 Add unrelated concepts

We could add concepts or words totally unrelated to the problem which might create a fresh viewpoint, such as:

- Washing up
- Table
- Dressing gown
- Paper bag
- Timetable
- Tree

3 Produce promising list

From the above lists we can select items which seem promising. The attributes list seems distinctly unpromising, but we can return to it if needed. The most promising items might be:

- Books
- Maze
- Beads
- Racing track
- Queue
- Washing up
- Timetable
- Tree

4   Form triads

Items are selected three at a time and comparisons 1–6 are made of the kind outlined on the previous page. Some mental juggling is required to find the best set of comparisons.

Synectics

Synectics is a group approach to the promotion of creativity pioneered by William J J Gordon and his associates in America during the early 1960s. The technique is based on the generation of similes, analogies and the use of metaphor in order to develop insight into problems and their potential solutions. In Britain the Synectics Education Initiative is aimed at developing synectics as a means of improving the management of learning, and the management of education (and the education of education managers!)

In problem solving, key concepts are 'idea development' and the 'ownership' of problems. One person is identified as the owner of the problem and the function of the others in the group is to work collectively with the problem owner to explore the nature of the problem and to assist in creating solution possibilities.

Vincent Nolan, the former Chairman of the UK company, Synectics Ltd, identifies two types of problem, one defined by 'deviation from the norm', referring to everyday problems, like the breakdown and urgent need to repair a car. The second type is defined as 'the gap between where you are and where you want to be', with no known way of getting from one to the other. It is to this second type that creative problem solving techniques can be best applied. Nolan identifies certain characteristics of the creative approach:

- non-logical, random;
- lateral, going beyond or outside the obvious line of thought;
- imaginative, not constrained by known and what exists, considers what might be;
- divergent, expands the problem and areas for solution;
- intuitive, jumps to conclusions without 'proof'.

Much of the above description has been touched on in techniques such as brainstorming and mind mapping, and there are obvious connections with the rep grid method of problem solving. As we pointed out earlier, creativity flourishes best when apparently irrelevant, fantastic, frivolous or childlike ideas are given free reign. We therefore require a supportive atmosphere, in which participants can use the highest levels of their creative imagination:

- The 'owner' of the problem – the client – tries to outline the problem to the remainder of the group using a phrase such as 'I wish that . . .' or 'It would be wonderful if . . .'
- An experienced and trained member of the group – the facilitator – chooses a central aspect of the problem on which to focus through a key word or phrase.
- The group, including the client, is then invited to explore an example of the key word or phrase in a context unconnected with the problem. The facilitator then lists the examples.
- The individual members of the group then choose an example from the list and develop associated ideas, images and connections conjured up by thinking freely about the example.
- The original client wish is now brought back into focus

and the group is asked to develop novel approaches to the problem by suggesting ideas which might at first seem impossible, irrelevant or impractical.

- The more promising of these novel ideas are then developed and elaborated in more realistic detail.
- The original client wish is then compared with the possible solutions suggested by the synectics process.

The range of techniques outlined above should give an indication of the rich possibilities of obtaining novel solutions to problems. We wish you well in your efforts.

Action plan

- Choose a problem to be solved, preferably one based on improving something existing, so you have a starting point.
- Form a creative problem solving group, where members have common knowledge of the problem.
- Ensure all group members have an understanding of the creative problem solving methods to be used.
- Run through one or more of the methods or techniques, ensuring that everyone has a rest between sessions: this can be a very intensive but enjoyable series of activities, so expect people to tire out!
- Keep a record of solutions and suggestions.
- Turn to other problems, perhaps where there is less familiarity or understanding, and repeat the above procedure.

Crosslink chapters

Further reading

Adams, J. L. (1987) *Conceptual Blockbusting*. Harmondsworth: Penguin.
Nolan, V. (1989) *The Innovators Handbook*. London: Sphere.
Svantesson, I. (1989) *Mind Mapping and Memory*. London: Kogan Page.

5
Live Projects

Rod Gunn

> Many projects help to break down the smug 'ivory tower' image of college or university by being based in local communities, businesses or other workplaces. These projects are 'alive' in the sense that they tackle real and current problems, and there is the very real possibility that your research will help somebody 'out there'. Rod Gunn introduces a number of issues associated with doing live projects, including the possibility of getting sponsorship, budgeting and planning, setting objectives, ownership and assessment of your work, and managing your time.

It would be worthwhile to begin this chapter by giving you a description of what I would call a 'live project'. A project is of a 'live' nature when it incorporates some or all of the following issues:

- deals with real problems;
- deals with problems of today;
- involves students directly with a client organization;
- seeks solution(s) feasible and capable of being implemented;
- moves beyond theoretical concepts and produces action plans;
- requires more than desk research to deal with the issues.

My experience of live project work emanated from the marketing modules on the B/TEC Higher National Diploma in Business and Finance, together with some work in this field for the Enterprise Unit at the University of Glamorgan. This experience taught me a number of lessons, the first being that the number of tasks together with the different roles required make it a natural group activity (see also chapter 8). There is far too much work for one person to successfully complete a live project. Second, although it is useful for part-time students, it is better suited to full-time students. The quantity of work and the irregular work schedule make it a very difficult option for part-timers. Also, since it is aimed at introducing students to work based activity it is of limited value to part-timers with their work experience.

Here is a checklist of important objectives for live project work:

- To achieve an understanding of both internal and external group dynamics.
- To gain an appreciation of the importance of personal and group activity scheduling.
- To obtain an awareness of the structure(s) of the host organizations and their cultures.
- To develop an appreciation of the dynamic internal and external environments in which the project is conducted.
- To gain a knowledge of the criteria to be used in submitting a research proposal to a prospective client.
- To experience the process of negotiation.
- To understand the methods employed in cost formulation and the techniques of budgetary control.
- To develop personal and inter-personal communication skills.
- To develop personal organizational skills.
- To gain a knowledge of the sources of secondary data and to appreciate the inherent problems in the accuracy and integrity of such information.
- To appreciate the importance of methodological formulation in the design of primary data collection activities.
- To enhance report writing skills and confidence when undertaking oral presentations to an expert audience.
- To develop the intellectual skills necessary when undertaking strategic formulation recommendations.

- To develop feasibility/implementation testing (costing, time, implications) of any strategic recommendations and to rank recommendations by expected outcomes.
- To become aware of the importance of collective quality assurance monitoring of all group activities.
- To understand the importance of identifying further research as a result of the completed project.

Working with clients

Quality

Clients will accept certain failings in a student report. They realize that what you are producing is not brought about by years of experience and a proven track record combined with the necessary academic background. They appreciate that yours is a learning experience and are often happy to assist you in that learning experience. Every now and again they know that the student live project can and often does produce remarkably valuable and interesting results. What they are not prepared to accept is low quality and non delivery. Consequently, it is important that every effort is made to ensure that the highest quality possible is achieved. In order to do so, it may be necessary to limit the size of the study to manageable proportions.

Reputation

The reputation gained by meeting deadlines and working in a professional way with others seems to be the indicator which decides whether or not clients will continue with their sponsorship. Once a good reputation is lost it appears almost impossible to retrieve it. Members of staff have worked hard to obtain live projects each year. They will have invested time and reputation securing these projects. It has taken a great deal of time and effort to gain this reputation but unfortunately it can be eliminated all so quickly. The students' attitude and performance will make an enormous difference to the outcomes achieved. Any meetings that you have with your client should be of a professional nature with the standard formalities adhered too. Remember that such meetings must be prearranged: do not just turn up and expect to see someone – their time costs money.

I suggest that clients would benefit from having some documentation beforehand. This might only be the objectives of the meeting, or the provision of some form of data. It would then be necessary to place all these agenda items in an appropriate appendix in the back of the report. Please remember that if you are unprofessional in your approach yours could be the last live project from that organization or company. It is commonplace for colleges to follow up live projects by circulating questionnaires asking employers the extent to which they were satisfied with the work carried out by the students.

The process

Live Projects, like many other things, suffer from the same problem: that is, knowing where to begin and where to end. If not enough time and thought is given at the commencement of the project to these seemingly trivial aspects then insurmountable problems may be encountered later.

A few of the questions which need answering are:

- What are the objectives of the project?
- What is the completion date of the project?
- Who are the people that I have to work with?
- How is this work to be assessed?
- Who is involved in the assessment?
- What should be contained in the project?
- How am I to communicate findings to the client?
- I am working in a group. What do I do with the person who continually fails to turn up for the meetings?

There are many other questions that can be asked but these are some of the more common that, in my experience, have cropped up. As with most things in life, many difficulties can be overcome with a little preplanning as well as working to an agreed timetable. The client and the actual project will generally have been found for you already by your tutor.

The budget

The process of following through a live project from beginning to end is one that must be approached in a business like manner. All businesses require that you submit a budget proposal which is scrutinized, then amended and finally agreed. At the end of the project you, the students, should carry out a variance analysis (see below) which is recorded as part of the project. Variance analysis is the analysis of the difference between actual figures and expected figures. It is calculated so as to identify those areas in which actual performance is departing from planned performance with a view to remedying this situation as soon as possible. It is necessary that you undergo these standard business approaches with the live project work. Without doing so, you will miss out on some fundamental business requirements.

You should present the budget proposal in formal financial language, and this must include a breakdown of all likely costs. At the end of this chapter I have included some elementary guidelines for making claims and it is best if you adhere to them at all times. You should obtain prior permission from the person with the necessary authority or else all manner of difficulties can arise.

Suggested budgetary headings

These headings vary from one situation to another. Choose whatever you think are the most appropriate as long as they are agreed between yourselves, your tutor and possibly the sponsoring organization.

Reprographics
Travelling expenses
Subsistence allowances
Telephone, letters

Programme structure

One of the issues which you will have to deal with is the order in which you must proceed with the live project. In the next section I have outlined several stages:

1   Firstly, you should meet with your tutor to indicate the areas of interest that you have in the relevant subject.
2   Your tutor will be involved in initially negotiating with the client the potential project. Once this has been done you should meet as soon as possible with the client and your tutor to discuss the objectives of the project. The method by which the research is to be carried out, as well as the support services that the client's organization can offer, should also be discussed at this point.
3   After this meeting you should be in a position to fill in the Estimated Time Sheet (see p. 95). This will provide your college with a basis to negotiate any fees or expenses that might be incurred. It is to your advantage to have these issues dealt with as soon as possible.
4   Completion of anticipated budget. You will be expected to meet with your tutor to agree to the budget project. *No agreement means that you will be unable to claim any expenses related to the project.*
5   At this stage you must meet again with the client to finalize the timetable and administration of the project. All forms must be signed by the relevant people and handed to your department or sponsor for processing.
6   It is important to remember that as you move through

the project work there is always a possibility that events might occur that require changes to the agreed objectives which then need to be negotiated.

Documentation

We find it worthwhile that for every meeting (between students, students and tutors, students and clients) accurate documentation is achieved through the keeping of minutes. This helps later with your write up as well as providing evidence that you have been meeting regularly and who has been in attendance. In order to do this properly it is a requirement that a Chair, not necessarily the same person for every meeting, and a Secretary be appointed. These minutes should be agreed and signed and form part of the final document, perhaps as an appendix. I suggest that some of the likely headings be:

Chair
Secretary
In attendance
Apologies for absence
Date
Time meeting began
Decisions reached
Date, time and place of next meeting
Chair's signature
Time meeting finished

Stage 1

Clearly, the obvious starting point is to meet with the tutor to discuss the objectives of the project. In my opinion, this first meeting should take place without the representative from the client organization being present. This reduces the chances of any inhibiting factors. The client most certainly should not be aware of any internal difficulties or problems: these should be resolved internally before you meet the client. It is important that students, tutor and client meet as early as possible after this in order to agree the objectives of the project. Although your tutor will have already made an agreement with you on the outcomes of the project by the time that you meet the external organization's representative, there may well be slight changes which could have come about for any number of reasons.

Stage 2

On pp. 92–4 I have included a form that is useful in the formalizing of proceedings. What is agreed in October may not be remembered in precise detail in June. It is to your advantage to ensure that the document is signed by the representative of the client organization. It gives you written evidence of what was agreed. I would suggest that copies of this document are kept by a member of your group as well as with your client and/ or tutor. You will notice that the form allows you to change your objectives as the project develops. This is to allow you to complete the project successfully, because remember that this is primarily a learning process for you and you may well find that experience gained as you go further into the project will cause you to change your ideas. However, any changes that take place must be the subject of negotiation between yourselves (every member of the group must be present), your tutor and the client. Remember to include all of this in the minutes of your meetings as well as the reasons why such changes have been implemented.

Stage 3

At this stage you should deal with all of the nitty gritty issues such as:

- timetable of events;
- who is responsible for what;
- filling in the live project hours and budget section of the form;

- methodology of carrying out the project.

It is worth mentioning that having a timetable is more than just setting a few dates by which certain events should occur. You should spend some time looking at the scientific techniques that are available. A number of commonly used methods are Critical Path Analysis (CPA) combined with a Gantt Chart (Lockyer 1986, Anderson et al. 1985).

Stage 4

Stage 4 is the carrying out of the actual project itself. Remember to keep a diary of events and times, which will assist you enormously later on.

Stage 5

A draft document needs to be produced which should be submitted to your tutor for advice and comment. Once the tutor's advice has been included it is a good idea to arrange a meeting with the client to run through the main findings of the report to see what else should be done in order to satisfy his or her requirements. The chances are that the client will only require an oral report.

Stage 6

It would be worthwhile giving an oral presentation to the client at this point (see also chapter 12). Many of the issues which you think might have been addressed may not have been dealt with to the client's satisfaction. Also new questions might be asked at this stage for which the answers are readily available and so could be included in the final report.

Stage 7

Final write up of the document. Copies are given to client, tutor and any other collaborating unit or department. It is anticipated that you will have to give an oral presentation to a number of people, including the client, and that these people will be involved in the assessment of the project. Chapter 10 gives further details about report writing.

Presentation

It goes without saying that the work contained within the report must be of the highest standard. The quality of the work is the top priority of potential clients. Later on I will indicate a way in which we can use the methods of self and peer assessment to act as a quality control mechanism for projects. I will also suggest likely sections into which most projects can be divided.

The content of the work and the findings may be excellent but unfortunately you are not judged by the content alone. Therefore you must make every effort to ensure that:

- the grammar is correct;
- the style of English does not vary from section to section;
- the spelling is perfect;
- the page layout is professional looking;
- you do not use single spacing (it looks cramped and untidy);
- there is good use of charts/diagrams;
- any cross referencing from one section to another actually works – there is nothing more annoying than being told to refer to page 47, or fig. 5 only to find that it is inaccurate.

Content of the report

All reports must contain an accurate index, an executive summary of the findings, a variety of chapters plus some appendices. The major difference between this type of report and a standard dissertation is in the amount of theoretical background. A typical dissertation will have a rather large amount in the literature search chapter; here we do not expect a great deal. You will need guidance from your tutor on the amount required for your particular piece of work. However, as a guide you are referred to chapter 10.

Quality control

I emphasized earlier the need to produce work of the highest achievable standard. Once work goes outside a college any reasons why something has not been done, deadlines not met, documentation missing, sound like hollow excuses for laziness. So do not fall into this trap.

We are now in the era of the word-processor and so most parts of the documentation can be written up as you go along. This is a must if you are to meet the agreed submission date. One of the most common reasons for lack of standards in the documentation is that too much is left to the end, which is completely unnecessary, (see chapter 1 on time management). After all you are only adding further pressures to yourselves by leaving everything to the end. Please keep more than one copy of the documentation disk. Also ensure that these copies are kept separately with different people. You never know what might occur!

Although different team members will be asked to write up different parts of the report it is essential that you give somebody an editorial role. The major duty here is to check for consistency, language, ambiguity, spelling, repetition, omissions, grammar and, above all, that the whole document reads 'as one'. Obviously you will have a number of meetings about the writing up of the report, but two meetings will be of particular value.

You will require a meeting where everybody has already read the initial draft of the document. The aim of this meeting is to check that all is contained in the report as previously agreed. The next step is to decide if any additional comments should be included or what alterations should be made to the report. Some days later the new report should be discussed and further alterations implemented. This process should overcome some of the problems of quality. To make these meetings successful they should be deemed quality control meetings and previously held roles must be eliminated so that ownership of certain parts of the document by certain individual members does not become paramount in the discussion. It is too large a task for one of you to check accurately the entire document, and anyway it is a group report and group ownership must prevail. However, the authority of the editor should be retained because that person will have to carry out the changes as agreed.

Peer and self assessment

It has proved worthwhile in terms of learning to be involved in the assessment of other projects. The logistics of such a process are fairly simple as long as every group keeps to the agreed timetable (see also chapter 6). The first stage is for each group independently of each other to agree amongst themselves a suitable assessment strategy. This assessment strategy must be applied to all projects and not be altered as they read the other groups' reports. It is quite likely that a group's assessment strategy will be based on its own document, because having worked within the constraints of its own project it will have a form of 'tunnel vision'. It must then work as a team assessing all the projects submitted, including its own. From my experience students are honest about the assessment and will not try to favour their work in comparison to the others. This will be much more successful if the entire group meets with all the different reports in front of them. One of the rules is that the assessment of each group is kept secret from the other groups until the end, when the complete set of assessments is pinned to each report for that group to read.

If each group were to write a paragraph or so explaining

what difficulties they experience in carrying out the process, together with what they learnt, then the procedure would prove to be a most valuable one. Also, this will tend to improve quality as an honest and frank approach by all involved in the project should be beneficial to the final piece of work.

Final comments

It must be emphasized that you will put in a great deal more time than you originally expected, which is the reason for the two time sheets. However, what you will have achieved will be extremely worthwhile and at times not only tremendously exciting but also sometimes very frustrating. The one question that I posed earlier for which no answer has been suggested is the following. What do I do if someone in the group is not pulling their weight? I'm afraid that there is no easy answer to this. You will learn to try to motivate such people in all manner of ways and that is part of the entire learning process. Sacking people is an unlikely solution, so do not rush to this stage.

Time sheet

I have included a time sheet which has a number of uses. It will allow the team involved in live project work to understand the time you actually spend in carrying out the work. We only have our view of how long we think it takes to produce a live project report, and it is quite possible that we do not estimate the time required at all accurately.

It is necessary to submit time sheets in an appendix to your report. They must be signed by all in the group, as they then represent a true and accurate record of the hours required to produce the report.

The reasons for submitting an estimate are as follows:

1 The client will then have some indication when and how much time he or she will have to make available to you for working on the project.

AGREEMENT FORM

STUDENT SPONSORSHIP

NAME OF SPONSORING ORGANIZATION

....

NAME OF REPRESENTATIVE

....

AMOUNT OF SPONSORSHIP

....

50 per cent of the sponsorship money is to be paid at the commencement of the project (this is to help cover the cost of student travel, reprographics, etc.). The other 50 per cent to be paid on completion of the work.

ADDRESS FOR CORRESPONDENCE

....

....

....

....

TEL. ....

MEMBER OF ACADEMIC STAFF

....

COLLEGE/UNIVERSITY DEPARTMENT

....

TEL. EXT. ....

NAMES OF STUDENTS INVOLVED IN THE PROJECT

....

....

....

TITLE OF PROJECT

....

OBJECT OF PROJECT

....

....

....

....

....

....

COMPLETION DATE OF PROJECT

....

ORAL PRESENTATION YES/NO

IF YES, LIKELY DATE OF PRESENTATION

....

We have read the terms of the contract and are in agreement with the information provided.

SIGNATURE OF CLIENT

....

MEMBER OF ACADEMIC STAFF

....

STUDENTS ENGAGED IN THE PROJECT

:

:

:

:

:

:

CHANGES TO AGREEMENT FORM

NEW OBJECTIVES

....

....

....

....

COMPLETION DATE

....

WHO INSTIGATED THE NEED TO CHANGE THE PROJECT

....

REASON FOR CHANGE

....

....

....

....

....

....

....

....

We have all been involved in the discussions concerning the changes to the project, understand the changes and agree to them taking place.

SIGNATURES:
CLIENT　　　　　　　..

ACADEMIC STAFF　　..

STUDENTS　　　　　　..

　　　　　　　　　　　..

　　　　　　　　　　　..

　　　　　............................. DATE ....

TIME SHEET (ESTIMATED) HRS

								SEMESTER 1							
	WEEKS	1	2	3	4	5	6	7	8	9	10	11	12	13	14	15
SPONSORS																
TUTOR																
STUDENTS																
OTHERS (INDICATE WHO)																
TOTAL																
								SEMESTER 2							
	WEEKS	1	2	3	4	5	6	7	8	9	10	11	12	13	14	15
SPONSORS																
TUTOR																
STUDENTS																
OTHERS (INDICATE WHO)																
TOTAL																
OVERALL TOTAL																

TIME SHEET (ACTUAL) HRS

								SEMESTER 1							
	WEEKS	1	2	3	4	5	6	7	8	9	10	11	12	13	14	15
SPONSORS																
TUTOR																
STUDENTS																
OTHERS (INDICATE WHO)																
TOTAL																
								SEMESTER 2							
	WEEKS	1	2	3	4	5	6	7	8	9	10	11	12	13	14	15
SPONSORS																
TUTOR																
STUDENTS																
OTHERS (INDICATE WHO)																
TOTAL																
OVERALL TOTAL																

2   It will cause you to think a little further ahead than you would normally, and forward planning is a useful management skill worth developing.

Action plan

- Decide whether this is to be a group-based or individual activity, and agree the topic to be researched.
- List objectives and probable client(s), make contacts and establish budgets along with possible sponsorship and time commitments from start to finish.
- Ensure agreement of academic staff with project objectives and client group, as well as classifying details about what is to be assessed and who will assess (the client? the lecturer? you? or all these?). Complete relevant proforma.
- Keep a record of all meetings, decisions and outcomes. With group-based projects, go through the seven stages contained in the Documentation section (p. 85).
- Produce the report (if appropriate) as advised in chapter 10 of this book.
- Honour commitments regarding possible self/peer/ client(s).

Crosslink chapters

1   Time Management
8   Working in Teams and Syndicates
10   Writing Reports
12   Giving Presentations
13   Student Tutoring
15   Personal Transferable Skills
16   Employment Profiles
18   The Placement Experience

Further reading

Lockyer, D. (1986) *Critical Path Analysis*, 4th ed. Bath: Pitman.

6

Self and Peer Assessment

Sally Brown and Peter Dove

Many experienced lecturers know that the best way to learn something is to teach and then assess. In recent years students have also been getting involved in active assessing (rather than just 'being assessed') – of each other and of themselves. This activity has won the support of employers, who value graduates with a realistic view of their strengths and weaknesses. At a more cynical level, it has to be said that larger class sizes pose problems for lecturer-only assessment. It is worth adding also that academic staff are assessing themselves and each other: a major part of modern quality assurance procedures. So you are not alone! Sally Brown and Peter Dove define what this kind of activity means and they explain its relevance and importance. Some very useful examples are provided of self and peer assessment procedures, proforma and checklists.

Assessing ourselves?

Students assessing themselves and each other? It sounds almost too good to be true. But nowadays lots of educational institutions are looking at ways of getting students involved in assessing their own and each other's work, because they believe that students who are involved in monitoring and evaluating their own learning tend to take their study more seriously and to learn more effectively.

What is learnt tends to be better integrated into students' existing knowledge patterns and to be retained more deeply when students have a degree of autonomy over the process.

Engaging constructively in your own assessment requires self-discipline, honesty and mature judgement of your own ability, and that is invaluable for all your studying.

The tendency towards involvement of students in assessment is also, in part, a response to the increasing numbers of students being recruited to further and higher education, with no corresponding increase in staff. Tutors are having to re-evaluate radically their working practices with students, and assessment forms a significant part of the overall workload. They are faced with the prospect of choosing between drowning beneath the sheer volume of marking, cutting down on the number of opportunities given to students to present themselves for assessment, reducing the level of feedback they give to the students, or changing the whole system by which they assess students. The one choice they do not have is to carry on as before.

Using self and peer assessment is not an easy option for staff, however, in that it tends to take a great deal of time, vision and effort to set up practical schemes to implement it. In the long term, however, it can eliminate some of the dull routine marking for staff, giving them a more interesting and valuable role moderating the effectiveness of the students' assessments. A method that can help staff reduce their marking workload and bring significant benefits sounds too good to be true, but we believe that, with hard work and good will on the part of all involved, it can be invaluable all round.

The principles are applicable to your lecturers too. You may well find that they are being asked to address these issues themselves in their own working lives. The appraisal process of many universities nowadays requires the application of the principles of self and peer review. Observation of teaching may also include elements of both. We assert that these methods are powerful tools for both students and staff, not forgetting research staff, who often work a great deal on their own. They can benefit greatly from the additional elements of feedback obtained from peers, as well as improved personal skills in evaluating their own performance through using the same kinds of methodologies which we advocate here for the assessment of students.

What are self and peer assessment?

Self and peer assessment are ways in which students can be involved in a meaningful way with their own assessment. They should not be confused with *self* or *peer marking* or *rating*. Most students have at some time or other been given a set of test questions by their tutor. In sophisticated models of self rating, the whole process takes place on a computer, with answers checked against those on a database. In both cases, the process is fairly mechanistic and there is an assumption of correct answers provided by an external agency.

Self and peer assessment are designed to help students to develop their own critical abilities, so that they can evaluate their own or each other's performance against a series of criteria, either provided by the tutor, or generated by a process of negotiation with the tutor. This is much more useful where issues are less clear cut, where students' responses are not so clearly right or wrong and where feedback and evaluation are the most appropriate responses to the assignment.

Inevitably, the level of work undertaken in higher education predicates a greater applicability of self and peer assessment, although they are fairly widely used at all levels of education nowadays. Indeed, a lot of contemporary practice in colleges and universities is based on techniques that have been developed in schools.

How does it work in practice?

There is no single correct way for self and peer assessment to be implemented: different models exist in different contexts, and the techniques may be used separately or in combination. Basically *how* you approach it is in many ways more important than *what* system is actually used. The key is for tutors and students to take an incremental approach, gaining confidence stage by stage at a pace at which all feel comfortable. Some tutors like to start with self assessment and then move on to peer assessment; others prefer to start with peers assessing each other and then move on to the task of evaluating their own performance.

Self assessment tends, at least initially, to involve tutors suggesting a set of criteria upon which the students can assess their own work. This is then followed by discussion so that a shared understanding of what each criterion means can be reached. The student might then go away and do some work and submit the assignment with a personal critique for subsequent discussion with the tutor. The discussion should help the tutor to evaluate the student's achievement and enable the student to appraise his or her own achievement realistically. The process is cumulative, with students eventually developing the skills and judgement to take on quite a high level of responsibility for their own assessment. They are also then in a good position to evaluate the work of their colleagues.

Another model starts with the tutor setting out the criteria for students to assess the work of their peers; this may be in the form of assessing another group's presentation (see chapter 12), display material (see chapter 11), or written report (see chapter 10). When students are practised at this, they can then move on to assessing the work of their colleagues within their own group. The final stage of this model is self assessment as a culmination of other forms of assessment.

You may encounter either of these models (or other models) of self and peer assessment, but a key aspect of each is the requirement to justify your assessment of self or peers by clearly articulating the reasons for your evaluation.

Whether working alone or in a group, self and peer assessment tend to use a four stage process. Having determined the remit or brief of the work to be undertaken, and having clarified exactly what is required of you, you should ask yourself the following questions.

What do I/we know now? What can I/we do already?

This *audit of skills, knowledge and abilities*, performed alone or with guidance from tutors, will allow you to get a realistic overview of your current abilities. Sometimes you will be given proformas by tutors, at other times it will be your responsibility to list what you can do and know, generally expressed as a series of competences. You will need to demonstrate your level of competence and may be required to provide evidence.

What do I/we need to know/do in order to achieve the task?

You should ask yourself what resources do I/we need to consult? What research needs to be done? Who should be consulted? Where are the gaps in my/our knowledge and ability? This forms what is generally termed the *need analysis*.

What plans should be made to achieve this?

You will need to determine realistic deadlines for all parts of the task, setting out clearly what you will achieve by when. It is a good idea to include some consultation with tutors or colleagues to help you foresee problems in advance. This will provide you with an *action plan*.

How will it be possible to show what has been achieved?

In order to make possible evaluation of your work, you will again need to provide evidence of your achievements and a revised demonstration of your competences. It will be important to demonstrate your progression in any particular area and also the level of your achievement.

This four stage process may represent the full extent of the assessment, or it may be developed as a cycle where, after initial evaluation, you re-evaluate your own competences, revise your targets and modify your plans for action. This will depend on the scale of the project you are working on and also your experience in assessing yourself and your colleagues. This may at first sound quite difficult and complicated to achieve, but remember that your tutors will be offering plenty of guidance to you in the early stages; however, as you develop skills, you may be required to take more and more upon yourself.

What's in it for us?

Students who assess themselves tend to be better at evaluating how successful they are for themselves, and so are better able to modify and develop their own learning programmes. You will identify any likely areas of weakness or deficiency for yourself. You are then more competent to develop strategies to remedy any such defects and to avoid the problems that occur when assessment only takes place at the very end of the learning process with the tutor in control.

Self-knowledge achieved through self-profiling, needs analyses, action plans and evaluation of progress in a series of tasks are *enterprise skills* that will stand you in good stead throughout your career rather than just while studying. Similarly, regular evaluation by yourself and your peers of what progress you have made and what needs to be done next forms a perpetual cyclical process to improve and update your competences (see figure 6.1).

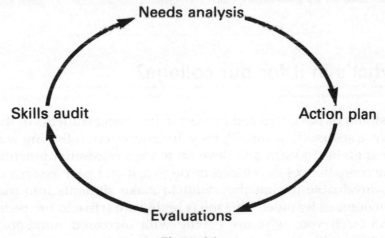

Figure 6.1

What's in it for employers?

Employers value students with skills in assessing themselves and each other because they are relevant to a wide range of employment contexts. They want graduates who can reasonably accurately assess their own and their colleagues' competences in performing tasks. Students who can do this are well placed to take on responsibility and adapt readily to roles in workplaces. A further advantage is that students who have developed an autonomous approach to learning do not expect to stop when they leave college; they are well set up for life-long learning which will continue throughout and beyond their working lives.

Profiles

Where students have produced profiles of their own abilities as part of self and peer assessment, these are valuable to present to potential employers at or before interviews. Many employers will expect graduates to continue with these activities in appraisal of their work.

What's in it for our college?

Institutions have a vested interest in involving students in their own assessment: primarily they are interested in finding ways for students to learn and develop to their maximum potential. The competences developed through self and peer assessment are invaluable in that they tend to make students into more autonomous learners. This too is highly attractive to the people who teach you, who are coping with increased numbers of students with no equivalent increase in resources.

What happens if things go wrong?

If I don't feel good about myself?

For all kinds of reasons, students frequently suffer from low esteem and don't feel able to make fair evaluations of their abilities. By concentrating on the criteria for assessment which have been devised by the tutor or by the student with support from the tutor, many of these problems can be eliminated. If the criteria are sufficiently clear, the student can't say 'Oh, that was useless' without any reference to a scale of competence. You are required by the system to justify why a piece of work is in your opinion good or bad, and this counterbalances to some extent problems of feeling bad about your work.

Remember too that assessment in these models is not a one-off event but part of a continuous process with checks and balances built in. The traditional methods of assessment can be subjective too; at least in this system you can address the issues openly.

If I don't realize my own weaknesses?

This is in fact the reverse problem of the previous one; the same kinds of safeguards apply to students who over-value their work as to those who under-value it. It is actually rather less common, and the ability to gauge accurately your own level of performance is tremendously valuable. Just as the over-confident driver is as dangerous on the road as the under-confident one, so also the student who has an excessively high opinion of his or her work is equally at risk as the student with low self expectations when it comes to exam performance.

If I don't feel I have the experience to rate myself?

You will not be expected to undertake this kind of thing without training and support; normally there will be opportunities for you to have a practice run at assessing yourself and others before you are expected to do it for real! You will be given the chance to evaluate your own achievements with guidance from tutors about what kinds of criteria you should use to judge your own work, and there may be chances for you to see quite a lot of work by other people in the same field, so that you can develop your own critical faculties. In actual fact, what is involved is in many cases merely a development of the kind of self evaluation that you have probably been doing informally already.

In group work particularly, it makes sense that the best people to assess the participants in the group are the other group members; they are actually much better placed than the tutor to assess each other, because they are the only ones who have experienced working in that particular group.

If I don't feel competent to rate my peers?

As you become more confident about your critical faculties, you will feel less nervous about your competence to do this. Again, you have almost certainly been evaluating your colleagues for years on an ad hoc basis. You look at colleagues' essays, drawings, projects and so on, and think 'That's a lot better than mine' or 'Mine looks really much more professional than that'.

It's a fairly short jump from that kind of thinking to the ability to evaluate other people's work against an agreed set of criteria, especially given the support of the tutor and your colleagues. It is unlikely that a fellow student will pass or fail an assignment simply on your assessment. Normally peer assessment will form part of a programme which will include tutor assessment and sometimes self assessment too. Your level of responsibility is therefore relatively limited, at least in the early stages. As you become more expert the weighting given to your assessment may increase.

If I don't trust them to rate me fairly?

Just as there are built-in safeguards to support you in your assessment of colleagues so that they can be sure of fair treatment by you, so these will apply equally to their evaluation of you. There is no question of someone being able to vent their spite on you or to bear grudges against you. The system will be designed to mitigate against this, because the models are based on the use of concrete evidence, just as it prevents you over- or under-valuing your own work. Additionally, where the peer assessment is in groups, the fact that all contribute to a group assessment lessens the likelihood of individual vendettas.

If some of the other lecturers don't understand what is going on?

Any programme which has self and peer assessment built into it will necessarily have to ensure that all staff involved are properly briefed. Public sector institutions will have published documents that set out exactly what is to be taught and how it is to be assessed (the Definitive Course Document (DCD)); ask your course leader to show you the relevant sections of the DCD and refer any queries to him or her. You should also talk to your personal tutor who will normally clear up any problems and sort out any uncertainties.

If I fail an assessment or miss a lot of work through illness or other problems?

Your tutors have thought of this! Just as with traditional assessment, there will be strategies to enable you to redeem failures in all assignments. Your tutor will be required by course regulations in most cases to have inaugurated a system for coping with failed or missed work. There are normally systems in operation to cover the eventuality of you missing exams through illness or problems, and the same kinds of safeguards should apply in the case of self and peer assessed work.

Additionally, the processes invoked in self and peer assessment will tend to be better placed to enable you to foresee failure for yourself and others, and to do something about it before it goes too far. It certainly presents no more problems than conventional assessment.

What about my institution?

Not every course in every college will be implementing self and peer assessment. Although the practices have been around for many years in schools and colleges and have been widely implemented in a number of employment contexts, some consider assessment by any one other than the tutor to be highly radical and even dangerous. This guide sets out to be only mildly evangelical about implementing self and peer assessment, and if your tutor doesn't use these methods, he or she may take some convincing.

Conclusions

We believe that self and peer assessment are valuable tools in the assessment repertoire; it is unlikely that they will ever fully replace tutor assessment, but they can be a useful adjunct to it, having numerous advantages for tutors and students alike. We suggest if you are asked to participate in assessing yourself and others, that you enter into it with an open mind and a willingness to make the most of the opportunity.

Action plan

- Establish the reasons for doing self/peer assessment with academic staff.
- Identify implications: how much does this assessment count towards end of year or level marks, and where

possible negotiate the topic, question or assignment so that you 'own' the problem to be solved.
- Agree the assessment criteria.
- Select and/or design assessment proforma to be used, and rehearse solutions to queries contained under *What happens if things go wrong?*
- Assess, and obtain feedback from all concerned.

Crosslink chapters

Further reading

Brown, S. and Dove, P. (1991) *Self and Peer Assessment*, paper no. 63. Birmingham: SEDA (Staff and Educational Development Association, formerly SCED).

Brown, S. and Knight, K. (1994) *Assessing Learners in Higher Education*. London: Kogan Page.

Cowan, J. (1988) Struggling with self assessment. In D. J. Boud (ed.), *Developing Student Autonomy in Learning*, 2nd ed. London: Kogan Page.

7

Tackling Exams

Robert Purvis

Whilst there are lots of new developments in further and higher education, the unseen examination paper which has to be answered in a limited period of time retains its foremost position as a method of assessment. The examination challenges students in academic as well as psychological ways, and Robert Purvis gives some invaluable advice about how to succeed through using revision strategies and exam techniques. His comments will help you to calm those nerves!

The formal examination is still the most commonly used form of assessment in further and higher education. Students are expected to solve a problem in a short space of time and then start to solve another one immediately afterwards. The object of the exercise would appear to be to test whether you can do this in a stressful situation, without sources of reference and, simultaneously, write coherently in a limited time period.

Examinations are a fact of student life and your aim is to make the best possible use of the limited time at your disposal. You have to show that you possess the ability to sort out the facts you have learned and apply them to answer the examination questions. It must be remembered that, in further and higher education, examinations do not normally require you merely to regurgitate memorized facts. You are expected to *use* these facts to answer specific questions or to solve set problems. Your first and most important task on opening the examination paper, therefore, is to read over the questions very carefully to find out exactly what you are required to do. Possibly the most crucial mistakes examination candidates make are:

- failing to read and follow instructions;
- failing to read and answer the questions properly;

- writing lots of irrelevant material.

In their book *53 Interesting Ways of Helping Your Students to Study* Habeshaw, Habeshaw and Gibbs say that very poor answers in exam papers give the impression that candidates were following a set of instructions such as:

> Write down whatever you can think of about this topic, in the order in which you remember things. Do not structure your answer. Include irrelevant material if you can't think of anything better. Abandon all intellectual rigour. Draw no conclusions. (Habeshaw, Habeshaw and Gibbs, 1987, p. 195.)

Much of this is due to inadequate preparation and the resulting panic to write down hastily-learned material before the memory fades!

Although it may be possible to pass an examination after very little revision by using the question answering techniques described later, the most effective way is to formulate and follow a revision timetable well before the examination.

Revision

Revision should be an *active* process involving the recall and sorting of material gathered during your course. Revision should *not* be:

- learning new material (apart from updates and filling in gaps);
- a massive memorizing task;
- something to be done just before exams.

As you are being tested on your ability to answer examination questions, a large proportion of your revision should include practice in analysing typical questions and planning appropriate answers. Your first priority, then, is to make sure you have access to former examination papers.

Sort out your material

Look over your course objectives (if you have them), sets of notes and handouts. Make out a plan of which objectives you feel you can and cannot satisfy and list your strong and weak areas. Use this plan to decide the proportion of time you allocate to your revision topics and ensure that you do not neglect difficult or disliked subjects. Decide on which materials you are going to use for your revision – lecture and personal reading notes, handouts, sections of books and journals, your assignments, past examination papers, etc.

Make up a revision timetable. . . and stick to it

1 Examine your present use of time and work out the number of hours you can make available for revision purposes. See if you can detect periods of time you would normally waste and try to make use of them. Consider the value of enduring some temporary changes in your day-to-day pattern to accommodate your revision timetable – but don't be *too* radical or your efforts to adapt to change may interfere with your work.

2 Do not neglect normal coursework and assignments but include them within your timetable.

3 The timetable should be made up at times which suit *you*.

4 It should consist of short periods (ideally no more than an hour) involving only one topic at a time. These blocks of time can, of course, follow one another within a larger block.

5 In most cases, avoid allocating large blocks of time to only one subject – vary your subjects to keep up your interest. However, if you find that you would rather pursue a particular subject in depth, be prepared to break your set timetable but allocate another time for the displaced subject.

6 Review your progress regularly and be prepared to amend your timetable as necessary.

7   Allow yourself breaks between each session – don't plough straight on with the next subject. Walk around a bit, have a cup of tea, read a newspaper – anything to give your mind a bit of variety.
8   Ensure that you timetable regular periods for leisure, social contact, relaxation and exercise.
9   Try to develop some simple relaxation techniques or use one of the special tapes which are readily available.

Revise factual material

Whilst it is true that the *use* of facts takes priority over mere knowledge of them, you are still expected to *know* the facts necessary to enable you to answer the examination questions adequately.

You will be wasting valuable time if you try to revise by simply repeatedly reading over your notes. This will only result in your brain ticking over rather than fixing information into your memory. You will probably find yourself turning pages without remembering that you actually read them and you may realize that you have switched to 'automatic pilot' while actually thinking of other things. Above all, you will not be able to check whether or not you have retained the essential points – or *any* points!

'Active' revision

First of all, when doing formal revision, work on one subject or topic at a time and put out of sight any materials that do not relate to the topic in hand.

Try to clear your mind of distractions and/or worries that you have not revised long enough, started late, don't have enough time to complete your revision programme, etc.

Assemble your revision materials, scrap paper and a pencil. You can use a highlighting pen on your own notes, handouts or photocopies but do not fall into the trap of turning your notes and handouts into large areas of bright green, yellow, etc! Highlighting everything is counter-productive. You may find it useful to use different colours to highlight certain categories of facts but be consistent with your colour scheme. Use a pencil (lightly) when highlighting items in books and journals so that the marks can be rubbed out later.

There is little point in setting down hard and fast ground rules for how you are going to commit factual material to memory because what works for some people (or topics) may not work for others. Try two or three different methods and see which one works best for you and for the topic concerned. Above all, remember that doing things is the best way of learning and remembering. Techniques include:

1 Highlight or underline key points and write your own comments about them on a piece of paper.
2 Make up topic sheets summarizing essential information. Try to make each one look different in some way so that you can trigger your memory of each sheet.
3 Study a section of your notes and try to commit the essential points to memory. Put the notes out of sight and write down the essential points on a piece of paper. Check what you have written for content and accuracy. Note any missing or incorrect points and concentrate on committing these to memory.
4 If the topic concerns processes or procedures, try to draw a plan of the stages involved.
5 Write out essential points in a different form to your original notes; for example, pictorial or diagrammatic instead of words, or words instead of diagrammatic.
6 Make up cards or sheets of paper of related key points and refer to them at odd moments; for example, travelling, waiting for a bus or train, waiting for a class to begin. You could also use them as self-test cards.
7 Write down important single topics on cards or small squares of paper and use them as 'flash' cards. Deal yourself a card every now and then in spare moments to test your knowledge and this should give you an idea of what areas are giving you most problems. This

can be even more valuable and stimulating if done with a colleague.

8 Relate your notes to past examination questions and see if they would help you to answer them (see next section). If they don't, try to fill in the gaps.

9 Set your own short questions and attempt to answer them. Check that your answers would be adequate.

10 Choose key topics and compile short notes intended to assist you to explain them to a friend or colleague. If possible, use these notes to give your explanation and see if it is understood.

11 Form a revision group (see below).

You will find chapters 1 and 2 very useful as a backup for drawing up a revision timetable and memorizing material.

Study past examination papers

As stressed previously, it is important to recognize that effective examination revision should not be confined to learning factual material. Remember that the questions will assume you know the essential facts and will be testing your ability to apply them.

The careful study of past examination papers will tune you in to the style of both the make up of the paper and the questions. However, you should be wary of trying to 'spot' questions. Familiarize yourself with the normal layout of the paper, the timing, the number of questions to be answered, whether there are compulsory questions and what combination of choice is allowed. Analyse the wording of the questions and ask:

- What does the question actually want me to do? Underline the key words.
- To what part of the course does the question relate?
- What facts, evidence, examples are required? Jot down the main points.

Try jotting down outline answers and check to see that they would actually answer the questions *as set*. It would also be a useful exercise to think up some questions of your own and jot down outline answers to them. If you have the time available, try to answer one or two questions fully within the time normally allocated.

Group revision

Many students have discovered that group revision can be most rewarding. If you have one or two friends who are willing to revise together, do try to organize regular sessions. Discussion is a stimulating, active aid to remembering and widening knowledge. All members of the group will benefit from the experience, even if there are only two of you. You can use various techniques here, such as:

- asking each other questions;
- explaining topics to the others, as described above;
- using flash cards to test each other;
- individually analysing an examination question and then all comparing notes and discussing the results;
- discussing each other's problems and trying to solve them – but keep the discussion positive and don't let it degenerate into a worry session!

It is wise to limit the number of topics dealt with during each session and take a break if it begins to get tedious. It helps things along if each member is made responsible for leading a topic.

Too little time?

Often, a big worry is the overall scale of the task in hand – the amount involved, the time remaining, guilty feelings about not making an earlier start. My own advice, which I have seen give gratifying results with very relieved students, is to try to ignore the global picture and concentrate on revising those topics you are actually able to cover in the time available. In this way, you will have revised at least part of the course properly and, if you are lucky, the examination questions may match what you have learned. In any case, examination performance does depend on a certain amount of luck even where you have revised thoroughly.

I know that it is easy for me to say 'ignore the global picture' and that it requires a good deal of will power (or bravery!), but it is surely better than spending so much time worrying that you end up revising nothing at all.

The examination

First priority: compose yourself

It is important to settle yourself into the examination situation as quickly as possible so that you are in the right state of mind to sort out which questions you should answer and write suitable responses without getting in a state of panic.

Arrive early and, unless you prefer to compose yourself quietly, join in the usual chit-chat and jokes with your colleagues (without taking much notice of those exuding super confidence or claiming that they haven't done any revision) before entering the examination room. Sit down at the desk allocated to you and arrange your things conveniently, including any lucky mascot you may have! Make sure that your watch is in clear view.

Although it may sound like a cliché, spending a minute or so taking regular deep breaths actually does have a calming influence. Look around the room and carry out any relaxation techniques you may have developed, such as alternately tensing and relaxing muscles (especially those in your writing hand). Don't worry about being nervous or keyed-up as the adrenalin produced will keep you alert! All the best performers expect to feel nervous before they begin.

Second priority: follow instructions

When you open the examination paper, carefully read through all the instructions to check exactly what you have to do. You should, of course, already be familiar with what you are required to do but it is always wise to double check to ensure that you answer the correct number and combination of questions – and parts of questions. Any extra questions you answer will not be marked.

Third priority: understand the question

Spend at least the first five minutes reading through all the questions and choosing those which you think you can answer best. Mark the questions you have chosen and re-read them to make sure that you *really* understand what they mean.

Remember that any fool can *read* a question; what you have to do is *understand* its exact requirements. Look especially at the direction words and underline them – for example, 'compare', 'illustrate', 'describe', 'discuss' – and prepare to write the kind of answer that each question requires. For instance, if a question says 'explain', do not 'describe'. The question '*Explain* the development of the Second World War' demands an entirely different approach to what is required for '*Describe* the development of the Second World War'.

Always remember that you must answer the questions as they are asked, not what you would have liked them to be! The examiner will only give marks for information directed specifically to the topic of the question.

Fourth priority: allocate your time

Keep a close watch on the time. Divide your time according to the number of questions to be answered – you may be advised of this on the question paper. Stick as closely as possible to the allocation for each question as you cannot gain more than maximum marks for any of them. It is rare, anyway, for maximum marks to be awarded! It is always a great temptation to go well over time on the first – or your favourite – question.

It is comparatively easy to obtain the first few marks for an answer but it becomes progressively harder to gain the higher marks! Therefore, time is better spent – and marks more easily

Activity   It doesn't matter at all if these questions have nothing to do with your own subject. In fact, it may be an advantage as it will illustrate how good technique can help you gain at least a few marks for a question you thought you couldn't possibly answer!

Underline the words which you think give the key to the proper understanding of each question. When you have done this, turn to p. 123 to see whether you agree with the suggestions.

1   How do you think the British public sphere would be affected by a move to broadcasting dominated by market forces?

2   Discuss the advantages and limitations of the use of computer-mediated communication in higher education.

3   Predicted changes in the number of elderly persons likely to need health care in the 1990s has implications for society in general and nurses in particular. Explore this statement.

4   Patient teaching may be seen as a prime aspect of professional nursing. Discuss this role in relation to a patient with a chronic leg ulcer.

5   a)   Briefly describe how the structure of the small intestine is adapted for the maximum absorption of nutrients. (4 marks)

   b)   Give an account of the digestion and absorption of protein. (16 marks)

obtained – by tackling all the required questions than by exhaustively completing only a few answers.

Remember that some examination questions have the marks allocation indicated beside certain sections and that you must concentrate on those sections bearing the higher marks. *Never* be tempted to write more than necessary on a section bearing very few marks.

Technique

1   Carry out the process of underlining the key words as described earlier.

2 Check again that you *fully* understand what the question requires you to do and, if applicable, which parts of the question carry the most marks.

3 Jot down the main ideas and any important details that occur to you, despite the fact that not all will be equally useful. While your mind is fully occupied as you write your answer it is all too easy to forget some points. However, if you do think of something important while writing, quickly jot it down to remind you. If scrap paper is not available, you can always cross out your jottings later.

4 Sort out the points you have noted into a skeleton outline of your answer. In the limited time available during an examination you need to have a firm guide to your writing. This should give you a better chance of impressing the examiner with a logical, well organized argument rather than a rag-bag of jumbled outpourings! Sometimes, a clear outline can gain substantial marks on occasions when time has run out.

5 It may be a good idea to choose first the question you are most confident with. This would give you a start and get you into the swing of things. However, you must avoid the temptation of going well over the time you have allocated for each question. Alternatively, you may prefer to start with the next question on your confidence list.

6 When actually writing your answer, concentrate on saying only what is most worth saying. Be concise, get the main ideas down simply, directly and to the point. Very often, 50 per cent of the words could be cut from an answer without losing marks!

7 Always try to check your answer for errors, missing information or ideas, spelling and grammatical errors. This advice is rarely taken during the stress of an exam, but checking it over is probably more useful than frantic writing of paragraphs at the end of your final answer. The examiner has probably decided on the quality of your work by then and so the refining of earlier answers would be much more valuable to you.

8   However, despite what has just been said, if you are running out of time you must make an attempt at the last question, even if you have to write it in summary form. As stated previously, it is easier to gain the first 25 per cent or so of marks on a question than it is to gain the higher marks. If you are really pushed, jot down some notes in a logical order. *Some* marks are better than none!

9   Easier said than done, but try not to panic! If you really feel that some of the questions are beyond you, concentrate on doing the best you can. If you use the limited amount of knowledge you may have logically, you will at least gain some marks.

Key to success: make your impact quickly

In normal circumstances, an experienced marker will aim to deal with an average of four or five scripts in an hour! This means that you will have about 15 minutes of his or her time to make your quality count. With a small group, the marker may be able to devote more time to the marking but you still need to make your impact in a limited time.

Legibility

This is of paramount importance. However brilliant and inspired your answers may be, if the examiner cannot read the words, he or she cannot possibly give you the credit you would otherwise deserve. Moreover, you will start off at a disadvantage as the examiner cannot help but be irritated.

Administration

Fill in all the details requested fully and accurately. Number the answers to the questions clearly and boldly. This may seem of little importance but *you* do not have to mark the papers. Anything which helps the marker will help you.

Don't hang about

Grab your examiner's attention by getting straight into the substance of your argument. It is a waste of time and effort writing needless introductions: the examiner already knows what the subject is!

Conclusions

Show that you can relate what you have written to the main point of the question by finishing each answer with a valid conclusion.

Question analysis activity: suggested solutions

How do <u>you</u> think the <u>British public</u> sphere would be <u>affected</u> by a move to broadcasting <u>dominated by market forces</u>?

You are required to give your own thoughts on how the British public would be affected if broadcasting had to rely on commercial interests; for example, sponsorships and advertising. Would only the most popular programmes survive because they brought in most money? Would programmes be dominated by advertising? What about minority interests?

<u>Discuss</u> the <u>advantages</u> and <u>limitations</u> of the use of <u>computer-mediated</u> communication in <u>higher education</u>.

You have to consider ways in which computers can be used for transmitting messages within *higher* education – *not* other sectors. You are required to say how communications may be improved by the use of methods such as electronic mail, bulletin boards and electronic conferencing. Are these methods actually improvements over traditional methods, such as memos and telephones, or do they have drawbacks?

> Predicted changes in the <u>number</u> of <u>elderly</u> persons likely to need <u>health care</u> in the 1990s has implications for <u>society in general</u> and <u>nurses in particular</u>. Explore this statement.

You must confine yourself to the predicted numbers of *elderly* persons and how *their* demands for health care will affect everyone; for example, taxation, demands on health care resources. You must then consider the special ways in which *nurses* would be affected; for example, changes in type of work.

> <u>Patient teaching</u> may be seen as a <u>prime aspect</u> of <u>professional nursing</u>. Discuss this role in <u>relation</u> to a patient with a <u>chronic leg ulcer</u>.

You are expected to say how important the nurse's role is in teaching patients why they are receiving their specific treatments and/or how to cope with their afflictions and possibly assist with their own treatment. You must illustrate your argument by taking your major examples from the treatment regime of a patient with a chronic leg ulcer.

> a)   <u>Briefly describe</u> how the <u>structure</u> of the <u>small</u> intestine is adapted for the <u>maximum absorption</u> of nutrients. (4 marks)

Only four marks are given here so be brief and to the point, preferably using a simple sketch. Confine yourself to the small intestine, its structure and how it provides for maximum absorption.

> b)   Give an <u>account</u> of the <u>digestion and absorption</u> of <u>protein</u>. (16 marks)

This is the main part of the question. Remember to deal with *both* digestion and absorption. Note especially that the question asks about *protein* – it would be a waste of time dealing with starches, fats and the rest.

Action plan

Before the examination:

- Work through previous papers to get the 'flavour' of the style of the questions and the type of answers required.
- Attend final lectures to pick up any clues about what aspects of the subject the paper may contain.
- Revise carefully and prepare yourself properly for the occasion.

During the examination:

- Compose yourself and make sure that everything is to hand.
- Carefully read through the instructions and the questions.
- Make sure that you understand the questions and exactly what they require you to do.
- Mark off those questions you feel that you can answer.
- Read them again, jot down ideas and make your choice.
- Select the question you will answer first.
- Construct a skeleton outline.
- Write directly, clearly and concisely, keeping to your outline and avoiding all irrelevant waffle.
- Keep a careful check on the time and avoid overrunning.
- Check your answers and cross out your jottings.

Crosslink chapters

1 Time Management
2 Making Notes in Lectures
3 Active Reading
14 Making the Most of Seminars

Further reading

Brown, M. (1990) *How to Study Successfully for Better Exam Results*. London: Sheldon Press.

Habeshaw, T., Habeshaw S. and Gibbs, G. (1987) *53 Interesting Ways of Helping Your Students to Study*. Bristol: Technical and Educational Services Ltd.

Rowntree, D. (1991) *Learn How To Study: A Guide for Students of all Ages*. London: Sphere.

8

Working in Teams and Syndicates

Danny Saunders and Phil Race

As student numbers increase and resources become more stretched it is essential that a spirit of co-operation emerges for the establishment of teams and learning syndicates along with the sharing of resources and workloads. The skill of working with others is highly valued by employers, and so team-based project work has become a major element of any vocational course. In this chapter we argue for an awareness of the need to be part of a team, rather than just a collection of individuals within a group. We also highlight the importance of groundrules, of roles played by team members (and roles which should be periodically changed around within the team), and of stages associated with team-based problem solving.

All courses require teamwork. But being part of a team, at first glance, runs against the tradition of being 'an individual' at college. The notion of being top of the class is deeply ingrained throughout education, and with some justification when crucial exam boards operate a quota system (x per cent of candidates receive top grades, y per cent receive middling grades and z per cent receive low grades).

It is easy to assume that this system operates at college as well. The difference is that for most courses the lecturers who teach also mark, and those marks contribute towards your final qualification; there is more freedom to reward everyone – or nobody! Lecturers will often talk (amongst themselves) of good years and bad years. In other words, you are now competing with lecturers' standards rather than with one another.

Couple this realization with a sad fact: further and higher education is seriously under-resourced. You are probably operating on a tight budget, there are not enough books or journals in the library, there may not even be enough seats in the lecture theatre. Limited resources can result in even more competition, but by establishing an atmosphere of co-operation resources can be shared (we will be arguing that a learning syndicate can be very cost effective) and everyone can benefit. From business and sport we have learned that teamwork leads to more success.

Employers

Employers value team work above everything else. Admittedly, employers like good exam results as well. As long as we have exams, the results will be used as part (at least) of the basis for selecting people for employment. But does a brilliant record of achievement in exams make a good employee? Not necessarily! Here are some further things highly valued by employers:

- ability to get on with other people;
- ability to be an effective member of a team;
- ability to support a leader;
- ability to lead other people.

A brilliant exam record may get you your first job, but the abilities to work with other people are likely to be very important in getting your later appointments (more important in career terms). In five years time it will not matter so much whether you got an upper or lower second class degree – a recent glowing reference enthusing about your popularity and support for your colleagues will count for much more. In short, ability to work with other people is a key ingredient in those good references you need to move along your career path.

Here are some quotes from the British Petroleum sponsored survey of various employers, all of whom were asked about the effectiveness of British graduates:

More and more these days we find that if we promote specialists, the absolute specialist, the one-discipline man [*sic*] who cannot deal with people, we get an immediate response. He sorts out all the specialists and then comes up against a brick wall – that he cannot deal with people, he cannot take a relaxed view, he cannot accept that the more open, participative management structures that are very relevant today actually do work.

You have a good project that is actually run by people none of whom are actually the tops at anything in particular, but you put the whole lot together and they form a very effective operation.

(Cowie and Ruddock, 1988)

Groups versus teams

Jot down the differences between groups and teams. This helps us to distinguish between mere collectives of people who happen to be together, and something more purposeful and fascinating. Perhaps you identified the following:

A group	**A team**
Has a variety of objectives not shared by all	Has a common set of objectives
Members work independently	Members rely on each other and share tasks
Some conflict of interests	Unity and coherence
No power sharing	Power sharing and delegation
Inflexibility and dogmatism	Creativity and adaptability
Trust and respect for some members	Trust and respect for all
Fear and preoccupation with emergencies	Emergency as a challenge, often anticipated

| No definite desire to work together again | A *need* to work together again |
| No consistent help for other members | Consistent help for other members |

Groups and teams can of course overlap. Consider a queue of people at a bus stop. After ten minutes of waiting one or two start chatting, and after 20 minutes it starts to look as though something has gone wrong. One person suggests calling a taxi and another suggests sharing the fare. They get to their destination and agree to meet again in two hours' time in order to share a return ride. This is an example of how a group is transformed into a team – often when faced with a crisis!

Things to avoid

So what are the qualities we look for in effective teams? It's easier to ask what causes the rest of a team to ignore you! Not every attempt to form a team is successful. Here are some ways to cause a team to discard you:

- have too much to say;
- don't do your share;
- put other people down;
- keep people waiting for you;
- go on the defensive if criticized.

Working with fellow students

There's quite a lot of resistance to this idea. It's worse in some disciplines than in others. We've already argued that this is because (sadly) the British school tradition often seems to favour individual achievement, with the sheep being distinguished from the lambs by a sacred exam which officially or unofficially produces a 'league table' of students. This leads to people who:

- hide how much work they are doing;
- try to get one-up on their fellow students;
- feel that they are competing with their fellow students;
- spend a lot of time on their own.

And there are the recurring complaints at course and exam boards about books being hidden on other shelves in the library, chapters being ripped out, assignments being stolen and copied and the originals destroyed. A system which produces these outcomes has to be changed because it is a system which actually encourages such behaviour.

The priority is therefore to encourage a crucial team quality: putting the team first and *you* second, and this is not seemingly self destructive once the overall objectives for the team coincide with your own. Early discussions with other people are therefore crucial if your interests are to be represented.

Team roles

Here is a list of qualities considered important for effective teamwork; tick those that you are good at:

- leading ideas and arguments
- resolving disputes
- making friends
- helping other friendships
- being reliable
- communicating well
- being adventurous

- working hard

- making people laugh
- speaking your mind
- listening to others

- having original ideas
- organizing
- finishing a task

You can see how people will vary in their personal qualities;

the beauty with teams is that such variety is welcomed. The most effective performance will reflect our entire checklist, with individual students shifting between qualities. Sometimes this is called 'role playing'. Consider a team you have been part of and select your favourite role:

- leader of ideas
- leader of people
- follower
- comedian
- worker
- scapegoat
- researcher

- technician
- devil's advocate
- listener
- councillor
- secretary/administrator
- finisher
- tough guy

As with the earlier qualities, all of these roles are important and members can shift from one role to another. One of the above is however very different from the rest because it allows the team to channel anger, scorn and cruelty onto a victim. You have probably guessed that this is the scapegoat. The danger is when one person is made a scapegoat all of the time: if it's you, reconsider whether the team's objectives are still fulfilling your own self interests!

Team reflection

A lot of teamwork in further and higher education centres on projects, the writing of a report and giving a presentation. It is important to reflect on how you operated as a team – perhaps through keeping a log, journal or diary – and to offer this information to your lecturers. For example:

- Who was the chairperson, the minutes secretary, the technician?
- How and when did your team make crucial decisions?
- When did you become a team rather than a group?

Teams often move through four stages of decision making and

performance, and again it's useful if you make links with your personal experience:

Forming
: Anxiety, looking for help, what are the rules, who are the members, shyness and curiosity.

Storming
: Conflict, diverse opinions, creative thought, humour, evaluation of the tasks, subgroups emerge, authority and leadership challenged, anarchy!

Norming
: Unity and co-operation, roles are agreed, expectations of each member formulated, plans are made, communication of views and feelings develop.

Performing
: Constructive group action emerges and feedback is provided, a group structure is seen, physical activity and the collection of materials, actions fit together like jigsaw pieces.

Teams can reverse these stages depending on success or failure. For example, plan A may be agreed and implemented (norming and performing) but it quickly becomes apparent that it will not work – back to the drawing board for more forming and storming!

Team presentations

Whilst the written report can show such detail, it is a group presentation (see chapter 12) that really shows off effective teamwork. A far better performance is achieved if presenters have roles than if they have 'sections' to talk about. Thus a 'link person', 'academic', 'visual aids technician' and 'critic' can operate throughout a presentation as opposed to the usual uninspired format: person A stands up, talks, sits down; person B does the same, as do persons C and D, finishing with person A again who briefly summarizes and asks for questions.

Be part of a learning syndicate

We have talked about teamwork as formally asked for by your lecturers. We'll conclude this chapter with a simple suggestion which, if implemented, will save you a lot of time, money and boredom. This suggestion rests on two decisions: that other people studying the same course can help you succeed, and you can help them do the same. The aims of a learning syndicate are:

- to do things that can be done better by a group of people than by individuals;
- to be a resource to each of its members, and maximize everyone's potential to succeed.

There has got to be something in it for everyone, or it won't last. Making sure each of you benefits should be the basis for your groundrules. Here are a few you can choose from and adapt to your own circumstances (better still, formulate improved ones):

- don't do other people's work for them – help them to do it;
- be constructive and positive – and honest;
- operate a principle of equal input, overall;
- make the syndicate task oriented: every meeting with something to do;
- meet regularly and briefly (a one hour meeting achieves as much as a two hour one!);
- share out the chores (for example, tracking down reference material);
- rotate the leadership – each of you take charge for different tasks;

- revise the groundrules as tasks and needs change.

Finally, when syndicates form they are usually based on expertise (each person already has a specialism, or aims to develop that area) and convenience (living close to one another). They are not based on friendship, but instead are clearly geared towards working relationships. This does not rule out friendship, it's just that work is the priority.

Action plan

- Identify an area of study where you can get involved in teamwork or a learning syndicate, along with other students you are likely to work with.
- When you are all together, establish whether you are a group or a team. If it is the former, decide on how you can move into a team-based framework.
- Get everyone to meet regularly and have clearly defined objectives for each meeting.
- Identify and agree resources to be shared, and groundrules.
- Periodically review team roles as viewed by each person about each other person, and give people a chance to change roles.
- Review also the stages of teamwork referred to under 'Team reflection', especially when the team has to write a report on a document based on their meetings.

Crosslink chapters

Further reading

Adair, J. (1986) *Effective Teambuilding*. Aldershot: Gower.
Cowie, H. and Ruddock, J. (1988) *Cooperative Groupwork*. Education Service, Sheffield University.
Glassman, U. and Kates, L. (1990) *Group Work*. London: Sage.
Johnson, D.P. and Johnson, F. (1990) *Joining Together*. London: Prentice Hall.

Part II

Getting Your Message Across

9
Writing Essays

Robert Purvis

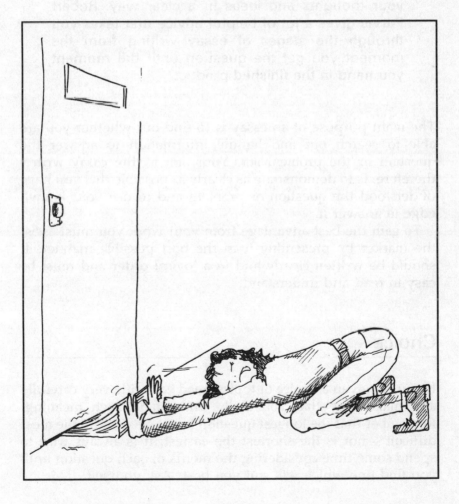

Essay writing is one of the most important skills to be assessed by the lecturer. It involves managing your time in order to meet a deadline, gaining access to references and resources, interpreting and analysing information, and communicating your thoughts and ideas in a clear way. Robert Purvis gives a lot of helpful advice that takes you through the stages of essay writing from the moment you get the question until the moment you hand in the finished product.

The main purpose of an essay is to find out whether you are able to search out and handle information to answer the question or the problem set. Your aim as the essay writer, therefore, is to demonstrate as clearly as possible that you have understood the question or problem and to use your knowledge to answer it.

To gain the best advantage from your work you must assist the marker by presenting it in the best possible manner. It should be written clearly and in a logical order and must be easy to read and understand.

Choice

If you are given a choice of topics, read each title very carefully and make sure that you really understand each meaning. Remember that the longest question is not necessarily the most difficult – nor is the shortest the easiest. It is always wise to spend some time considering the merits of each question until you find one which will suit you best. Ask yourself:

- Do you really understand the question or topic?
- Do you have, or will you have access to or knowledge of, a topic?
- Do you have a special interest in, or knowledge of, a topic?
- Is your main purpose to increase your area of knowledge or to gain the best mark you can?
- Are you better dealing with abstract concepts or practical matters?

Remember that you are representing yourself and need to make the best possible impression. A bad choice could cause you lots of extra work, a good deal of frustration or damage your chances of success.

Understand the question

Once you have chosen the question, it is essential to understand *exactly* what you are required to do. Look for the *key words* in the title. However, remember that those who set essay questions may not always be rigorous in their choice of wording. If you ever have doubts as to the exact meaning of the question, you would be wise to consult the person who set it. Here is a selection of some of the more common key words and what they should mean:

Account for	Give the reason for something or give evidence to support a statement. Do not confuse with 'give an account of' which is really asking for description.
Analyse	Examine and explain the relationships between various parts of a topic.
Argue	Use evidence to prove or disprove a point of view. Set it out logically and try to disprove other points of view.

Assess	Use evidence to estimate the value or importance of something.
Comment on	Unfortunately, a very commonly used 'coverall' phrase which is rather vague. The person who sets the question probably really wants you to analyse or assess.
Compare	Concentrate on those aspects which two or more things have in common – although it would be wise to deal with any differences as well.
Contrast	Concentrate on the differences – but do mention any similarities.
Criticize	Try to find fault with the value of something or the truth of a statement. You must state the evidence upon which you base your judgement.
Define	State precisely the meaning of something.
Describe	Relate what something looks (or sounds, feels, smells) like, how a sequence of events happened or what are the main characteristics of a topic.
Discuss	Another word open to various interpretations – similar to 'comment on' but you are usually expected to write a logical argument about the subject.
Evaluate	This is similar to 'assess' but, in this case, you should be weighing up the performance of something which has already happened.
Explain	Relate how things work, how something happened or give reasons for certain actions.

How far . . .? *To what* *extent . . .?*	These phrases invite you to assess a situation or the truth of a statement.
Identify	Single out the main features of something.
Illustrate	You are required to give examples, statistics, diagrams, sketches, etc. to support your statements.
Indicate	Point out the main features of something (may be used instead of 'identify').
Justify	State valid evidence for accepting a statement or conclusion (similar to 'argue').
List	An item-by-item record of relevant items. This would normally be in note form without any need to describe – but do check if you are unsure.
Outline	Point out the main features of a topic or sequence of events.
Prove	Establish the truth of something by offering indisputable evidence or a logical sequence of steps or statements that establishes the truth.
Relate	Depending upon the working of the question, this means either give an account of how things happened or compare and contrast.
Review	Look back on or survey a topic and estimate its value (may be used instead of 'evaluate').
State	Write down the main points of something.
Summarize	Give the main points of an idea or argument, leaving out all the unnecessary detail.

Trace	Outline the main connections between one thing and another or describe the development of something.

When you have identified the key word(s), carefully and thoughtfully read over the question again and decide whether or not you will be able to do it justice. The importance of reading the question carefully and understanding its exact meaning cannot be over-emphasized. You must always answer the question as it is set, *not* as you would like it to have been!

Title

Apart from examination questions, it is always a good idea to write out the full title of an essay, even if you are not asked to do so. This should act as a reminder to keep you focused on the actual question rather than straying away from its specifications. Never alter or shorten the wording of an essay title! This is another way in which you can easily be diverted from the real meaning of the question.

Preparation

Ideally, start your preparation as early as possible. Obviously the first thing to do after choosing the question is to start collecting material. Facts, evidence, your own ideas, other people's ideas and anything relevant from magazines, newspapers, television or radio should be noted. Jot down immediately anything useful that occurs to you from time to time – you will surely forget if you don't. It is advisable to keep all your material together, so keep a special notebook for the purpose or transfer all jottings to a file as soon as you can.

Read around the topic and remember to note down all references so that you can return to them later. Failure to do this will result in frustration as you try to search through your

memory for where you read 'that priceless piece of information'.

Look first at your lecture notes, then consult any journals or
books which have been recommended. This will attune you to
the expectations of the person who is going to mark the essay.
Having done this, look at the journals and books which are
referred to in the recommended texts. Check the publication
and revision dates to ensure that the material is up to date.
Again, bear in mind that you should select only the relevant
bits to read through.

Remember that preparatory reading of journals and books
should be done quickly and economically. Develop the ability
to skim through material using lists of contents, indexes,
chapter summaries and by sampling paragraphs. Concentrate
only on the passages having direct relevance to your particular
topic. Look especially to see whether different authors have
come to a general consensus or if there are disagreements or
different points of view. Carefully weigh up the evidence and
come to your own conclusions – but be prepared to justify them.

Sort out material

Look through the material you have collected and discard
anything which proves to be irrelevant. Try to arrange the
retained material in such a way that it forms a clear line of
argument. This should indicate how you will order your
paragraphs and will help you to spread the information
throughout your essay.

References

Decide on which references you are going to use and where.
Note them carefully in case the books and journals are not
available later (this could well be the case if several colleagues
are working on the same assignment). The most convenient

way of quoting references is the author-date/Harvard system where the author and date is stated (in brackets) within the text and the full reference is given in the bibliography at the end. However, do check which referencing system is used in your own course.

Making a plan

The idea of making a plan is to help you view your essay as a whole. The plan need be no more than a summary of headings indicating what you are going to say in the order in which you intend to say it. This will help you to:

- set out the material in a logical sequence;
- check whether you have included all relevant ideas;
- avoid needless repetition;
- identify the positions of examples, quotations and references.
- compose more fluently once you start writing.

Remember that the plan is there to help you, not hinder you. It is not meant to be inflexible and should not prevent you changing your approach if you think of better ideas as you write. A convenient method is to use separate sheets for notes on the main stages or topics of the essay. This will allow you to shuffle your work around if necessary. When you are planning, bear in mind that:

- a good start *creates* a favourable impression;
- a good ending *confirms* a favourable impression.

This implies that you should concentrate on composing an introduction which will impress the reader and encourage him or her to read on, together with a conclusion which leaves the reader in no doubt as to what you have said and how it has all been drawn together.

Structure

1 Introduction

Define the topic, say what you understand by it, state the main issues and give a general idea of how you are going to deal with them.

2 Main body

This is where you state your facts, your evidence, examples, illustrations and develop your argument. It is essential that they are all in an easy-to-follow logical sequence.

3 Conclusion

Here you sum up your main ideas and state any firm conclusions you have come to as a result of these ideas. Say whether you consider that there are any possible wider implications, future trends or scope for further investigations.

Before writing check the instructions!

- Re-read the question to check that you have not strayed from the point.
- Is there a word limit? This could make a big difference to the way you tackle the question.
- If it can be handwritten, has ink colour been specified (usually black to aid possible photocopying)?
- Has paper size been specified? It is wise to stick to A4.
- Has layout been specified (for example, double spacing or minimum margin size)?

Writing

At last, the actual writing of the essay! If you have gone through all the stages described above, you should be ready to write out at least the first draft of your essay. It doesn't really matter if you cannot decide how to start. Begin writing at any stage rather than wasting time fretting over an opening sentence – the important thing is to make a start somewhere!

Once you have started the flow, you will normally find that writing becomes easier and you can sort out the proper order later, using your plan. If you are writing on paper, you can always cut up the paragraphs and clip them together in the correct order later. If you are using a word processor, you can do this 'cutting and pasting' on the screen. If you have made a good plan, you may be able to write the draft straight off without needing to make many re-arrangements.

Warning! A word processor is a very convenient tool for writing assignments, but it can be a dangerous one, as many students (and tutors) who lost whole assignments can verify! When working on a computer you must *save* your work on disc periodically and *always* at the end of each session. It is always wise to save the work on two discs and store them separately.

Coherence

Structure

You want the person marking the essay to be able to find his or her way easily through your work. A good structure is the first essential for this and here is where good planning plays its part.

As stressed previously, make sure that your introduction illustrates your understanding of the topic and states clearly how you are going to tackle it. Try to make a positive impact in the critical opening sentences.

Paragraphs help the reader by indicating when the text is moving on to a new point. They also break up the appearance of a page, making it appear more readable. Try to keep to one topic or main idea per paragraph. However, avoid making each paragraph totally independent with each idea becoming isolated and unrelated to your general argument.

To help the marker retain concentration and interest, link your ideas in a logical order so that one idea leads naturally to the next. Use headings and subheadings where you think they will assist clarity. Make sure that you have covered all possible arguments and have included the evidence to support them. Use simple instructions and clear examples wherever they will make your work easier to understand. Cut out all irrelevant material, particularly wordy and unnecessary 'waffle'.

Originality

It is a great temptation to use other people's material and pass it off as your own, sometimes by changing the wording slightly. This is plagiarism, which is a serious offence and can result in stern action. It is usually obvious when you have copied material from books – it rarely matches your own style of writing, even if you have made some alterations. Remember that the person who reads your work probably knows the literature better than you and will have a good idea where your borrowed ideas came from. Credit is given for the correct use of sources rather than for a jumbled version of someone else's work.

If you do use the exact words of another person, enclose them in quotation marks and acknowledge the source. Similarly, if you paraphrase another person's work or use his or her ideas or interpretations, credit must be given.

Format

It is sensible to ensure that your work is presented as attractively as possible. It is by no means unknown for markers to give more credit to a neatly presented essay than to an untidy one. Pay special attention to any instructions you are given on presentation. If none are given, it is usual to use A4 paper with wide feint lines for handwriting and plain A4 paper for typing or word-processing. Make sure that your typewriter or printer has a good ribbon. If you are writing the essay by hand, use black or blue ink.

Your name and the title of the essay should be clearly printed, preferably on a separate title page. Always date your work and number the pages. Some markers prefer it if only one side of the paper is used.

Lay out the text with good margins on both sides and at the top and bottom. The left hand margin must be wide enough to allow for the method of binding you intend to use (for example, punched holes, sliding bar or spring clip), as well as providing space for remarks written in by the marker.

Typing should be double spaced to allow for written remarks. A clear space should be left between paragraphs. Place any diagrams, sketches or tables adjacent to the text to which they relate.

Legibility

It is a waste of everyone's time if your writing cannot be deciphered. Just imagine how you would feel if you had to mark a piece of work where you had to spend time and effort struggling to make out the words. If your writing is not easy to read, either take steps to improve it or use a typewriter or word-processor.

Before handing in your work

Read it over carefully and critically, using the action plan below. If you can, ask a friend to read it over to see if he or she finds it easy to understand. Often, your tutor may be willing to read over the final draft – indeed this is desirable, but some may not be too keen on adding to their workload. If you have one, your study skills adviser may be willing to read your work and help to sort out any shortcomings in style, layout and so on – but not content.

Be sure that you make the necessary alterations. Where possible, obtain a receipt for work handed in: sometimes essays go missing!

Action plan

- Understand the question and identify the fundamental issues.
- State how you are going to deal with the issues and clarify your ideas.
- Ensure your facts are correct and up to date, and use sufficient evidence to support arguments.
- Set down work in a logical manner, making sure it is readable and easy to follow.
- Correct all spelling, punctuation and grammatical errors.
- Cut out all irrelevant material
- Illustrate work with relevant examples and/or illustrations and acknowledge all sources and give all references.
- Provide a logical conclusion based on arguments.
- Ensure you have carried out all the instructions (for example, length, style, layout).
- Ask yourself whether you are *really* happy with it.

Crosslink chapters

1   Time Management
3   Active Reading
10 Writing Reports
17 Portfolios

Further reading

Fairburn, J. and Winch, C. (1991) *'Reading, Writing and Reason: a guide for students.* Buckingham: Society for Research into Higher Education and Open University Press.

Rowntree, D. (1991) *'Learn How to Study: a guide for students of all ages'.* London: Sphere.

10
Writing Reports

Christine Sinclair and Jim McNally

Report writing is becoming increasingly popular as an assessed activity, given how much later employment depends on this skill. It requires structure, a summary and attractive presentation of an order which is different from the more indulgent essay. Christine Sinclair and Jim McNally have written this chapter as a report in itself, and provided a model which helps you to understand exactly what is expected.

Terms of reference: This report is the result of an investigation into the requirements of academic staff and industrialists, and contains recommendations for structuring reports. It was written in response to a wish expressed by students for help with report writing.

Contents	**Page number**
Executive summary	156
Introduction	156
Skills in report writing: an operational skills model	157
The purpose of the report: what are your terms of reference?	161
The main text: find, select and arrange your information.	162
How the report should appear on the page	164
Conclusions	168
Recommendations – an action plan	168

Executive summary

This chapter has been deliberately written as a report to demonstrate a possible structure for a report. It is based on the finding that staff and employers are looking for an ability to structure a report and provide properly constituted evidence for what is written. It considers the skill you will use in writing reports, based on an operational skills model. A key skill is the ability to use the structure as a tool for writing the report, and this is further broken down into the skills of ascertaining purpose, gathering, evaluating and arranging information, presenting it coherently and finishing the report with the appropriate conclusions. Recommendations are given throughout, but the report concludes with a checklist against which you can assess your own progress.

Introduction

Students are often requested to write a report – on an event, on a project, on a piece of research. Some students are concerned to know the difference between a report and an essay; others simply do not know what is expected of them. The following definition indicates the key features of a report:

> A technical report is a written statement of the facts of a situation, project, process or test; how these facts were ascertained; their significance; conclusions that have been drawn from them; the recommendations that are being made.
> (Mitchell 1974)

The report you are currently reading seeks to demonstrate:

- through its layout, how a report is a stylized piece of writing;
- through its content, how successful report writers approach their task.

The information is based on observations by academic staff and educationalists, research into the educational benefits of report writing and other guides to report writing. Like any report, it could only be written after:

- consideration for whom it was to be written and why;
- gathering of information;
- careful structuring.

The first draft of the report in this case did not take much more time than these other activities. Once they were done, the report practically wrote itself. Then additional time was needed to 'polish' it and discuss it with colleagues.

We have asked academics and employers about the pitfalls students face in report writing. Academics tend to the view that inadequate preparation and planning leads to careless writing, where the point the student is trying to make is lost. Employers are concerned about the lack of concise writing in graduates, some of whom seem only able to write in great quantity. On a more positive note, students who practise a structured approach are believed to make better progress both in learning and report writing.

Skills in report writing: an operational skills model

The operational skills model described below can be applied to all student learning, but here we concentrate on its application to report writing. Academic staff ask students to write reports:

- to discover what students have learned from reading or experience;
- so that students gain experience of a skill they will need in the workplace.

We hope to show that these aims are not mutually exclusive and in fact draw on the same types of skill. Research shows that students do indeed learn *through* writing (as exemplified in the work of the 'Writing Across the Curriculum Movement' in the United States). Thus, you are not so much writing about what you have learned, you are using the process of writing to *do* the learning.

How learning relates to report writing

It seems that what students have to learn is continually expanding, with the result that the curriculum becomes piecemeal and fractured. Is it possible to bring a coherent approach to such an expanding curriculum? One attempt to do this – and provide a tool which has practical application in a range of student activities – is the operational skills model. This is a coherent, comprehensive and hierarchical set of activities used by students (and everyone else) to make progress in their learning – moving from simple observation to application of what has been learned. How it can be used in report writing will be expanded throughout this report: for an overview, we will consider its use in terms of a disaster report.

An operational model

Skills hierarchy	Example
Observation	Witnesses can be asked what they noticed, e.g. saw, heard, smelled, felt, even tasted.
Discrimination	Witnesses will probably offer significant distinctions . . .
Conceptualization	. . . such distinctions will be shown by the concepts used, e.g. fire, inferno, fireball.
Classification	Witnesses may be classified by the evidence offered, as above, on their 'view'.

Speculation	Expert witnesses will speculate on causes, consequences, cures of the disaster.
Validation	Evidence must be consolidated as to which speculation is most valid.
Explanation	An explanation can be provided for the disaster.
Prediction	A fault may be identified which could lead to further disasters.
Application	The outcome of the enquiry may be to use the knowledge gained to act to prevent a further, similar disaster.

Reports students write are evidence that they have undertaken a piece of work. It is therefore important to do the appropriate work and to *show* that you have done it. A question at the forefront of your mind throughout the structuring and writing of the report is 'How will I be able to justify what I am doing?' As writing a report is a purposeful activity, some consideration of the purpose is the only starting point which is likely to work. *Don't start writing the report until you have done this*. (We can justify this piece of advice with reference to the frequently heard staff complaint: 'They never answer the question!')

The report structure which follows, exemplified in the report you are currently reading, provides a starting point. This has been distilled from our experience of different reports and also from advice given in textbooks on report writing. One word of caution: reports are written in many different formats and the suggestions here are drawn from those held in the literature to be the most common. However, different organizations may employ particular house styles and you could be obliged to follow a different pattern from the one given here. It is a good idea to get hold of as many different reports as you can to see what styles are used and what ideas you could adapt for your own purposes. Whatever its style, a report should provide clear and concise information: if it does not then you are well advised not to emulate it.

The structure of a report

	Example
Title page	A report into the ―― Disaster in 19 ――.
Terms of reference	On the request of Her Majesty's Government to ascertain the causes of the disaster and the associated responsibilities and to make recommendations for the avoidance or recurrence. Sources of information were expert witnesses, eyewitness accounts, video recordings, documentation . . . etc.
Contents	1 Summary 2 Introduction to the company 3 . . . etc.
Summary	This report seeks to provide an accurate account of the events of (*date*) and to infer the causes of the disaster. It does this by. . . etc.
Introduction	―― Ltd is a major multinational company specializing in. . . etc.
Main text	Section 1: Events according to eyewitness accounts and other evidence. Section 2: Some of the hypotheses as to the causes of the disaster. It does this by. . . etc.
Conclusions	After weighing up all the evidence as detailed in the body of the report, we have come to the conclusion that the likely cause was. . .
Recommendations	It is recommended that Her Majesty's Government. . .
Appendices	Appendix 1: Transcript of main eyewitness account. Appendix 2: . . . etc.

In addition, the report might contain graphs, acknowledgements, a glossary of technical terms, references, a bibliography, a list of committee members and an index. Not all these headings will be necessary, especially in short reports. Some of them may also appear in a different sequence.

The purpose of the report: what are your terms of reference?

Not only can the report writer not start work on the report without knowing the terms of reference, some formulation of the terms of reference is likely to constitute the first part of the report. In this report, we did this overtly as well as in the title. Sometimes, the terms of reference are only contained in the title, or perhaps a subtitle, or they might be found in the introduction. They will probably appear somewhere in a well written report. So what are the terms of reference? Look again at the example at the beginning of this report. It answers the questions:

- Who will read the report?
- Why will they read it?
- Why was it written?
- How was it written?

The answer to a further question, 'Who wrote it?' is given in the subtitle. The title attempts to sum up the terms of reference, so that if it is just quoted in a list people can quickly see its relevance to their needs. If they follow it up further, the terms of reference as spelled out should finally determine whether they want to read the full report (or even just the executive summary).

Often, students are *given* the terms of reference. If this is the case, then don't change them to suit your own circumstances. If you have been asked for a report with recommendations, then a simple eyewitness account will not do. When you're asked to write a report, consider your terms of reference in relation to the skills model outlined earlier. Which skills are you being asked to employ? Are you being asked to explain or predict, for instance?

The main text: find, select and arrange your information

Finding sources

A clear statement of the terms of reference should provide at least some guidance to the sources of information which will make up the main body of the report. Different disciplines will require different sources of information to be used. Some of the following might be considered:

- *written material:* books, journals, newspapers, reports, questionnaires, letters;
- *information technology:* databases, spreadsheets, multi-media packages, microfiche readers, electronic mail;
- *pictures:* graphs, videos/films, sketches, maps, television;
- *sound:* discussions, interviews, radio, television, tape recordings.

These are all examples of searches for already existing information. In addition, information can be gathered from:

- *research:* experimentation, investigation.

This list is not exclusive, but is designed to show the range of sources of information. Report writers frequently draw on several different types.

Evaluating information

Again this depends on the subject matter, but there are a number of questions the researcher can ask at the data gathering stage. Inevitably more information than can be used will be gathered, and while you don't want to waste time on superfluous information, you do want a reasonable source from which to select. Some useful questions are:

- Is it relevant to the purpose of the report?
- Is it accurate? What evidence or justification is there?
- Is it up to date?
- What do other commentators think?

Arranging information

The same questions are asked again at the stage of sorting information with a view to discarding some of it and structuring other information under various levels of headings. Figure 10.1 shows the sort of notes a researcher might make just before starting to draft the report. (Don't worry if this does not fit in with your own style; it is only a suggestion.) Additional questions at the sorting stage are:

- What information can be grouped together?
- Are there clear points for and against particular views?
- Is there a natural sequence? For example, time, location, importance, logic.
- Which pieces of data are fact and which are opinions?

As you evaluate and arrange your information, various parts of the structure of the report should start to emerge. For example, headings, subheadings and ideas about conclusions and recommendations if any are required. It is worth thinking about your conclusion before starting to write, so that the evidence you present leads logically to that conclusion. This is not to say that you should not include any relevant counter-evidence – a report is not usually a piece of propaganda.

Activity

We acknowledge that it is unusual to come across a self-test activity in the middle of a report! However, you might find it useful to look at figure 10.1 in terms of the skills hierarchy on p. 158. For example, where is the potential author using observation, discrimination, conceptualization, classification, speculation, validation, explanation, prediction, application?

How the report should appear on the page

Structuring

Presentation of reports is probably what worries students – and graduates – the most. Yet if the structured approach to report writing is taken, a large part of the presentation should slot into place easily. Our sample structure – or similar versions drawn up by report writers for their own use – can be used as a guide for the main headings. It is quite likely that the main text will also need to be divided up for ease of understanding. Consider themes and sub-themes and create headings to suit them. If there are a lot of subdivisions, some form of numbering system might be helpful.

Activity

Go over this report and list the main headings and subsequent subheadings. In your opinion, is this a sensible structure for this report? Note how the headings are distinguished by uses of capitals, bold, italic, position on the page, etc.

Consistency

Not only should the headings be easily recognizable as main, subheading, sub-subheadings, etc. but everything else should

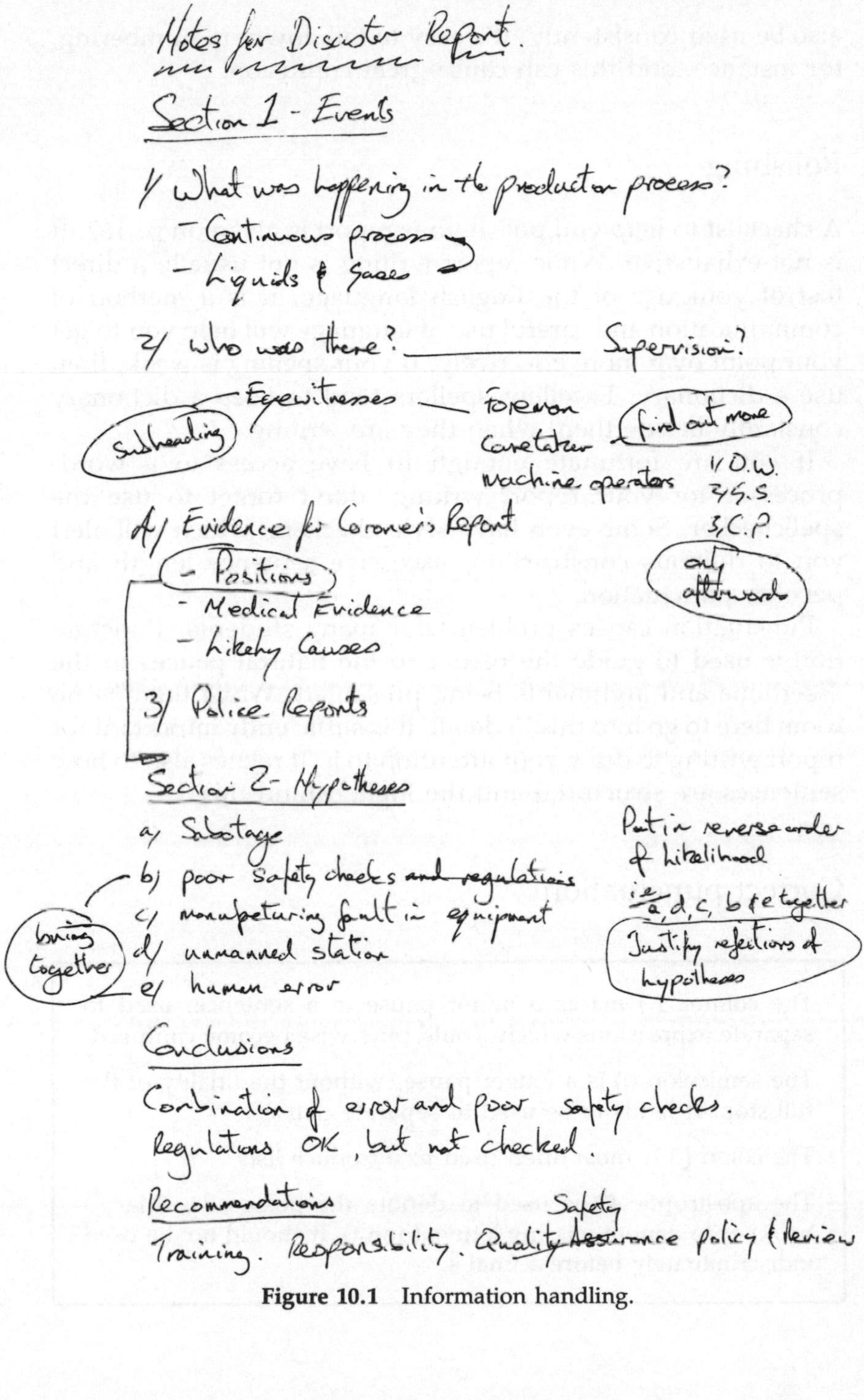

Notes for Disaster Report.

<u>Section 1 - Events</u>

1/ What was happening in the production process?
- Continuous process
- Liquids & Gases

2/ who was there? _____ Supervision?

Eyewitnesses — foreman
(Subheading)   Caretaker — (find out more)
                                machine operators   1/ O.W.
                                                     2/ S.S.
A/ Evidence for Coroner's Report   3/ C.P.
  - (Positions)   only
  - Medical Evidence   afterwards
  - Likely Causes

3/ Police Reports

<u>Section 2 - Hypotheses</u>

a) Sabotage   Put in reverse order
b) poor safety checks and regulations   of likelihood
c) manufacturing fault in equipment i.e. a, d, c, b re together
d) unmanned station   (Justify rejections of
e) human error   hypotheses)

(bring together)

<u>Conclusions</u>

Combination of error and poor safety checks.
Regulations OK, but not checked.

<u>Recommendations</u>
                                          Safety
Training. Responsibility. Quality Assurance policy & Review

Figure 10.1 Information handling.

also be used consistently. It's easy to fall down on numbering, for instance, and this can cause great confusion.

Polishing

A checklist to help you polish your report is given on p. 167. It is not exhaustive. While report writing is not usually a direct test of your use of the English language, it is a method of communication and careful use of language will help you to get your point over more effectively. If your spelling is weak, then use a dictionary. Excellent spellers tend to keep a dictionary constantly beside them when they are writing.

If you are fortunate enough to have access to a word-processor for your report writing, don't forget to use the spellchecker. Some even have style checkers, which will alert you to dubious construction, excessive sentence length and peculiar punctuation.

Punctuation causes problems for many students. Punctuation is used to guide the reader to the natural pauses in the assertions and arguments being presented. While there is no room here to go into this in detail, it is sufficiently important for report writing to draw your attention to it. It relates also to how sentences are structured and the logic behind this.

Correct punctuation

The comma (,) marks a minor pause in a sentence, used to separate expressions which would otherwise become confused.

The semicolon (;) is a longer pause, without the finality of the full stop. It tends to be used to separate clauses.

The colon (:) is most often used to introduce lists.

The apostrophe (') is used to denote the possessive (Mary's book) or to denote missing letters (don't). It should not be used indiscriminately before a final s.

Polishing your report

Have you clearly distinguished between different levels of heading?

Are all numbered lists in the correct sequence?

Have you checked the spelling/meaning of all unfamiliar words?

Are spellings, punctuation and grammar correct?

Are spellings, punctuation and grammar consistent?

If there is a summary, does it contain all the key points?

Are instructions to the typist/printer clear?

Has the copy been proofread?

Is there a house style to be observed?

Is the style of writing appropriate for the reader?

Is there any extraneous material?

Has any important evidence been missed out?

Do any statements have legal implications which have to be checked?

Do you need permission to use any material?

Have you obeyed the copyright laws?

Have you justified your conclusions?

Are your recommendations workable?

You might like to use this checklist to help you write a report during a placement or project.

Typing

A typed report is much easier to read and gives you more flexibility with layout. If you do ask someone else to type it for you, check it carefully when it comes back – they might not be aware of all the important underlying structure. Many students are unable to get their work typed; it goes without saying that handwriting should be legible and as neat as possible. Underlining, capitals and judicious use of spaces can help you distinguish between headings.

Conclusions

People prefer students to take a structured approach to report writing because:

- the messages the students are trying to get over are much clearer and it is easier to see whether or not they have understood what they are supposed to have been learning;
- when the information being presented is justified and evidence provided for it, there is less likely to be extraneous material;
- the skills of structuring the report are closely linked to the skills of learning.

The structured approach is also a more satisfying one for the student. Used in conjunction with the operational skills model, it leads to a more coherent way of learning and provides a skill which can be used throughout life.

Recommendations: an action plan

When you are asked to write a report, ask yourself the following questions:

1   *What is the purpose of the report?* (Eyewitness account, recommendation, information, etc. – this can relate to the operational skills model; for example, you might be asked to speculate or utilize, but you might simply be asked to observe and discriminate).

2 *Who will read the report?* (Your tutor, industrial contacts, etc? What assumptions can you make about them?)
3 *Why is the report being written?* (As part of your formal assessment, in response to a request, because of a perceived need?)

Action: Write the terms of reference

4 *Where will the information come from?* (The library, something someone does, a questionnaire, an experiment?)
5 *When is the report needed?* (What information will be available by that date, how much time is available to gather and sort information before writing the report?)

Action: Plan the report – and your own time

6 *How will you gather the data?* (Notes, books, other reports, computer printouts, graphs, etc.)
7 *How much detail is required?* (Relate this to purpose, select information which looks as though it may be relevant.)

Action: Gather the data

8 *Which data will you include?* (Criteria for selecting and discarding data, conflicting data, justification for inclusion, evaluating data.)
9 *In what sequence should the data be presented?* (Top headings, time sequence, logical sequence, for and against.)
10 *What conclusions can be drawn from the data?* (Depends on purpose – for example, summary recommendations.)

Action: Organize the data and create a rough draft

11 *How should the report be presented?* (Main headings, subheadings, summary, layout, spelling, punctuation, sentence structure, tone.)
12 *How will the report read to other people?* (Test out, proofread, ambiguity, justifications.)

Action: Write/polish your report

Action: Present/submit your report (see chapter 12)

Crosslink chapters

Further reading

Mitchell, J. (1974) *How to Write Reports*. Glasgow: Fontana/Collins.
Wheatley, D. (1988) *Report Writing*. Harmondsworth: Penguin.

11

Conveying Your Message by a Poster

Alan Jenkins

Poster presentations have become a very successful way of communicating research projects at
conferences. Their use has now reached students
in further and higher education and they provide an
attractive, imaginative and simple means of por-
traying your work to a very wide audience. Some
courses or modules have an exhibition of students'
posters mounted on the walls of corridors, foyers
or lecture theatres. A combination of text,
diagrams, photographs and miscellaneous material – which varies in complexity, detail and wall-
space! – allows other people to browse at leisure.
Sometimes you might be standing by your poster,
prepared to explain anything which interests
viewers. Alan Jenkins explains the mechanics of
poster presentations and provides some examples
which show how imaginative and effective this
form of communication can be.

What is a poster?

You see them advertising anything and everything. If you
consult the Concise Oxford Dictionary it defines a poster as a
'placard displayed in a public place'. This commonsense
knowledge and dictionary definition are a useful starting point
for considering whether and how you can use posters.
However, posters in an educational setting, while often using
pictures and graphics, will also convey much of their message
through words. Indeed in some cases words alone are used.

Perhaps a better way of attempting to convey what is a
poster is to show you one. Figure 11.1 is a poster designed to
encourage teachers to use posters. Looking at the example

Figure 11.1

should give you a clearer idea of what I mean by 'poster', but also start to give you ideas on how as a student you could use them.

If the word 'poster' conjures up the arts alone, I want to assert that it is appropriate to all disciplines. At the professional meetings of scientists, for example, poster sessions are often used to convey and discuss current research findings.

Why use them?

The advantages of posters are as follows:

- By being limited to only one sheet of paper, one is forced to think through what is really important to tell others. Too often when we try to convey information we forget how much people can take in, we fail to signal to them (and to ourselves!) what is really important. The size of the poster starts to impose that discipline upon us.
- The use of words, pictures and graphics can effectively convey your message – sometimes more effectively than by a written or spoken presentation. Furthermore, posters tend to be memorable.
- Those 'reading' the poster have more control over what to attend to than when listening to a speech. They can feel more involved in your message, partly because a poster session generally allows people to move around. (While they are moving around they are unlikely to fall asleep!)
- They can add variety to a session.

How to design them

Work within stated guidelines

If your lecturer has given instructions on the design and stated criteria for assessment, you work within those instructions. But if not, what follows should help.

Decide what is really worth saying

Think through what is the 'guts' of what you have to convey to others. What of this will really interest them? What do they really need to know? One way to get towards this is to imagine sending them a 30–60 word telegram and use that restricted information as a basis for designing your poster.

Decide on the best size of paper

Depending on the size of the room, the complexity of your message, the nature (if any) of visuals to be used, decide on an appropriate size of paper. A1 is often used.

Make sure it can be seen and read

Think through how the poster will be used in the session (see later discussion) and also from what distance your poster will be viewed. This will determine the size of diagrams and lettering. What you have written/drawn must be easily read and seen by those viewing. Generally this means placing it on a wall (or board) at head height.

Recognize your skills and limitations

Be realistic about your graphic skills. Some of you may be good at drawing and design – indeed one advantage of the poster is it enables all of us to develop these skills and gain 'credit' for them. It may be that you are doing this as a separate group. If so divide your labour on the project to gain maximum benefit from your different talents.

You can also work with your present range of skills and just use words. You can decide to use photographs or any other published graphics if you think they help convey your message.

Take care – your poster can be too visual

A predominantly visual poster can be ineffective. To return to the earlier definition, 'a placard displayed in a public place' may have no or few words. There they may do their job. But posters in an educational setting will require far more 'information' and may be better conveyed mainly or entirely by words.

Use words carefully and to best effect

A poster is not an essay. It is 'read' in a different way. It may be helpful to think of yourself as writing and laying out a page of a newspaper that conveys complex and interesting ideas in a direct and accessible manner. The use of headlines, subheads and the layout of text (with relevant graphics) powerfully shapes your audience's ability to assimilate (and question) your message. But first you have to have something worth saying.

Decide on what is worth saying to this audience

To repeat, the advantage of a poster is that it helps you think through what is worth saying to this particular group of people. Do ensure that this is what is on the poster. Do *not* allow the visual, eye catching elements of the poster to so dominate that it appears a slick (or poor) import from the advertising world.

When and how to use them

Is it in your control?

Evidently this may well have been decided by your lecturer. If so, work within the guidelines provided. But if the decision as to when and how to use them is yours, here are some points you should bear in mind.

Some possible uses

Posters are appropriate as a way of giving a presentation (see chapter 12) of what has been learned outside class (for example, a group project on a field course). If you are simply required to report your findings to a small group session you can of course give a spoken presentation. You may decide that a poster session might be more appropriate (particularly if you know that other groups are all giving spoken presentations, or if you think this better demonstrates your skills and what you have to report).

If you are required to do a classroom seminar you may decide that posters are an effective way of giving directions to the seminar. They can convey information for people to discuss and can tell them what to discuss and what to do. It may be appropriate to do all this on one poster. Alternatively, two or three posters placed at various locations around the room can provide variety and direction to your session.

If a number of you are required to report at one session then why not decide (with your lecturer's agreement and help) to report by poster? In many ways this is an ideal way of using posters educationally as it enables a lot of ideas to be discussed and conveyed in an interesting way.

Think carefully about the choice and layout of the room

The choice of room is probably outside your control but ideally the room should be level (rather than tiered), with plenty of wall space or boards on which to hang the posters. Do check whether you can use blu-tac, drawing pins or sellotape to stick up the posters.

Generally, you need plenty of clear space immediately in front of the posters, so that people can see and discuss them. It may also be appropriate to have small groups of chairs away from the posters (but from where they are still visible) so that after they have viewed the posters you can direct people to discuss certain issues.

Structure the sessions so that all are involved

The poster is a central part of the session but you need to create a structure that ensures readers look carefully and central themes are discussed. I can only offer some suggestions which you will probably have to adapt to your circumstances.

- Get the poster up quickly at (or before) the beginning of the session.
- Make clear what are the aims of the session: tell people at the beginning of the session what you want them to have gained by the end.
- Get them to look carefully at the poster(s). The poster(s) by itself should have picked out key issues and not either included too much or too little information, but you may need to give people signposts about what to consider. For example, you can have an OHP or a handout specifying questions for them to consider as they look at the posters.
- One way to get them to look carefully is to place blank sheets of paper and marker pens by each poster. You can ask participants to comment on particular issues you have specified. You can encourage them to comment or ask questions as they think appropriate. Calling the blank sheets graffiti sheets might set the right tone.
- Decide on where you want the poster designers. One way – as is done at academic conferences – is to have them standing by their poster for a fixed time, answering questions. If they are to see other posters you may need to have some sort of rota for this activity.
- Decide on what you want participants to do after looking at the posters. The posters can provide key information and issues for people to discuss, but you probably need to define what are those issues and how to structure the discussion.
- One way to involve everybody in the sessions is to get them to evaluate or even assess the posters (again, this

may not be in your control). But you may decide that the one way of getting participants to look carefully at the content of the posters is to ask them to complete an assessment sheet.

Go beyond these instructions

I hope these suggestions give you useful ideas for making your classes more enjoyable and effective. I created them not by reading but by reflecting on my experience of participating in poster sessions. As you try these ideas out, I hope you will go beyond them in devising your own effective poster sessions.

Action plan

- Agree with the lecturers that a poster presentation is appropriate for a project or seminar activity.
- Agree the groundrules – for example, size of display, permissible content, assessment criteria.
- Balance the visual with the textual context.
- Identify place and time for poster display, and exact position in order to recognize possible constraints.
- Ensure that the aims and the outcomes of the topic are evident in the display.
- Be available, or provide information about who to contact and where, during viewing periods.

Crosslink chapters

12

Giving Presentations

Danny Saunders

Speaking in public is rarely a popular activity, and many students dread the experience. Yet presentations are often a valued memory for graduates who think back to their college days. It is the presentation that recurs in much later employment, rather than the unseen examination or the discursive essay! It is worth noting that there is no 'perfect' presentation, everyone has their own style and this is to be encouraged. However, in this chapter, I have tried to pinpoint some of the common problems with giving presentations, along with some advice and strategies for overcoming difficulties.

Presentations usually refer to formal occasions where one or more people speak to an audience. The onus is on one-sided communication where there is a verbal summary of a topic, issue, debate or research programme. Whilst presenters invariably do a lot of talking, they usually use visual aids and handouts to help with their delivery.

Presentations have always been used in further and higher education. The traditional delivery of the curriculum has been 'the lecture' where students are experienced audiences, having to sit through many lectures during the course of their studies. In recent years an increasingly popular requirement involves asking students to make their own presentations to the rest of the class, and even to other lecturers. These presentations are typically short – ranging from ten to 30 minutes in most instances. In some cases a team of presenters is required, where (for example) each of four students will make a specialized contribution to an overall topic of discussion.

Such presentations often provide invaluable experience that

can be transferred to later employment situations. In many areas of work, brief oral presentations (backed up by written reports) are a necessity. Examples include:

- presenting a case study on a client at a monthly conference meeting within the social services;
- presenting a bid for a contract;
- presenting the case for your appointment at a job interview;
- presenting a research paper at a conference (and often you can get sent to a conference or have reduced fees if you give a presentation).

The thought of speaking to an audience when 'under pressure' – especially when being assessed – can be very threatening. The best way of helping people to overcome fears and anxieties is to provide opportunities for rehearsal and practice within a supportive setting (video recording and playback is very popular here). We have all seen or heard about the 'natural speaker', but it should be emphasized that most good presenters learn the necessary skills through making mistakes, and learning from those mistakes.

What follows are comments for helping novice presenters. These notes do not offer mandatory advice. It has to be recognized that there are no universal rules because so much depends on the context for the presentation, the background of the presenter and the audience itself. You will also find chapters 4, 13 and 14 of value.

Thinking about your audience

A crucial reminder: if you are relatively inexperienced, and the audience knows this, then they are from the outset on *your* side. Usually they will also have to give presentations to the same group of people, and they will appreciate the difficulties facing you.

Forget about the detailed content of what you are going to say – that is an academic concern which we will return to shortly. Instead, focus on these questions:

1 How many other presentations will there be on the same topic? (If lots, then think about presenting it in an unusual or original way; if few, then focus on a general overview.)

2 Is there also a written report to accompany your presentation? (If so, then the need to 'show off' academically to the audience is not so great.)

3 When will you be speaking? (If you are scheduled towards the end of a series of speakers, there is a danger of the audience being tired, bored or impatient – in which case there should be an emphasis on picking up on things that have been said by the other presenters, or on 'doing the unexpected' in order to regain an audience's attention.)

4 How many people are you speaking to? (The general rule is that if it is under 12 or so people, it is easier to provide more in-depth analysis and to be more informal.)

5 How 'expert' is the audience? (Usually the safest ploy is to keep it simple and clear – although this does not always apply to conference papers and research seminars!)

Activity

Try filling in the following checklist (based on Mandel 1987) about your audience. If possible, ask a few colleagues or even your lecturer or supervisor about some of the questions. The answers will help you to estimate the appropriateness of some of the content and style of delivery.

Time limit: ☐

Number of other presentations before mine: ☐

Number of other presentations after mine: ☐

Size of audience: Under 12   12–30   30+

Their level of understanding:	introductory, varied, advanced, unknown
Their special needs:	knowledge, sort out confusion, humour, varied, unknown
Willingness to accept my ideas:	high, varied, low, unknown
Audience's views about me as a speaker:	good, poor, erratic, unknown

Examples of supporting ideas and arguments which may work well:

Examples of supporting ideas and arguments which probably won't work well:

Preparing your presentation

The plan

The following sequence is usually preferred:

>   Introduction
>   Preview (say what you're going to say)
>   Main content
>   Pros and cons of this content
>   Summary (say what you've said)
>   Conclusion
>   Recommendations for further work
>   Questions

Be creative

Identify your objectives (no more than three, as a long list is boring as well as difficult to remember): what is your presentation hoping to achieve? Go into the central idea or topic and think creatively about it. If you have the chance to talk to a few friends, try a bit of 'brainstorming' (see chapter 4). This is where you think about imaginative and wild ideas that somehow (even if you cannot explain why) link up with the gist of your presentation. Such brainstorming is especially useful in groups – the old saying of two heads being better than one is very appropriate.

Once you have a list of these ideas, select one or two that 'appeal' and contain a bit of humour or surprise. It helps at this stage if you draw a diagram and develop the plan for your talk on a large piece of paper. You are encouraged to use pictures, cartoons, phrases, colours, symbols and anything else in order to make the diagram more imaginative. Sometimes this is called mindmapping, as outlined by Buzan (1974). An example of a mindmap is given in chapter 4.

Many experienced presenters will actually use the map as a memory aid: the sheer variety of images and words make it easy to recall key sections of your speech (as opposed to 30 sides of notes), and easy to summarize your talk to an audience that needs an overview of the entire area.

By now, the key features of your presentation will have been identified, and hopefully you will know which areas (if any) require more background research. You will also have a clear idea about whether it is possible to include everything within the time limit – key editing decisions have to be made at this early stage.

Beginnings and the end

Above all, the introduction has to be clear and needs to set the scene for the audience. You have identified up to three objectives, so use these in order to explain the title of your presentation. Give a brief overview of your talk, and suggest that you hope to answer a particular query. This is always a useful strategy because by setting up a question you get the audience thinking about the answers: the trick is to get them to think along the same lines as yourself, but for you to be one step ahead and leading the search. If your presentation follows on from a number of others, the introduction is always that little bit more effective if you comment on previous discussion: you hope to *develop* issues, debates and ideas.

The ending is relatively straightforward should a descriptive summary be offered. It has more impact if in addition to drawing together previous discussions it also returns to the initial query and the objectives that were outlined in the introduction. A very good ending concludes with a provocative query about the next question that needs to be addressed.

In general, introductions and conclusions are crucial when it comes to an audience's memory of what has been said. The well documented 'primacy and recency effects' state that we remember first and last events but that we forget about the middle. A common error is that the beginnings are extended at the expense of the endings: the speaker then runs out of time and is forced to cut the conclusion. In this situation the audience remembers the last event: an unfinished and incomplete presentation. Timekeeping is crucial!

Develop presentation aids

Visual aids undoubtedly help most presenters but using them effectively requires planning and preparation. Six common errors are listed:

1   *Being dependent on only one kind of visual aid* – usually overhead projection, slides or transparencies (OHPs). This ties you down and prevents you from varying your style of communication. It is very effective, for example, to use two or three of the following: OHP, board, flipchart, video, slides, tape recorder – provided, of course, that you have the time and the facilities.

2 *Crowding* – having too much material to present in too short a time period. You should, for example, aim for a maximum of eight OHPs in a 30 minute period. Audiences get fed up with an endless stream of transparencies being flashed at them.

3 *Monotony* – all of the visual aids look the same. A combination of different print fonts, diagrams, text and colours is most effective – but be careful about using light colours (especially yellow or brown) on OHP transparencies: they are difficult to see from even a short distance.

4 *Lack of clarity and relevance* – As Mandel (1987) says:

Use Visual Aids when you have to:

1 Focus the audience's attention
2 Reinforce your verbal message (but do not repeat it verbatim)
3 Stimulate interest
4 Illustrate factors that are hard to visualise

Don't use Visual Aids to:

1 Impress your audience with excessively detailed tables or graphs
2 Avoid interaction with your audience
3 Make more than one point
4 Present simple ideas that can be stated verbally

Ultimately, the advice is to KISS – keep it short and simple. The table shown on p. 188 is an example of bad practice, based on the use of OHP transparencies:

Table 1 Gross annual turnover for on, off and tote betting contexts

Financial year	Number of betting offices	Amount staked million £	Amount staked million £	Amount staked million £
		Tote	Off-course	On-course
1971	14462	84	1161	112
1976	13865	105	1859	190
1977	13254	104	2165	221
1978	12812	95	2266	239
1979	12475	105	2820	321
1980	12248	107	3094	350
1981	11993	96	3045	329
1982	11774	87*	3185	362
1983	11237	85	3184	343
1984	10856	87	3432	375
1985	10633	94	3706	405

* After 1982, all TOTE turnover recorded at on-course contexts only.
Sources: *Gambling Statistics of Great Britain 1968–78; 1979 Report of the Gaming Board for Great Britain; 1986 Customs and Excise Report; Betting Licenses Statistics: Great Britain.*

Note that whenever you present an OHP transparency you ask an audience to work with new information and that some members will feel obliged to take notes. It is much better to give this information via a handout, and so summarize the data with this example of good practice:

YEAR	NUMBER OF BETTING OFFICES	AMOUNT STAKED (millions £)		
		Tote	Off-course	On-course
1971	14,462	84	1161	112
1985	10,633	94	3706	405

Similarly, lots of blocked text can be more attractively presented. An example of bad practice:

The greatest density of betting offices is, not surprisingly, associated with the present and former industrial heartland of Cardiff, which includes residential areas that are adjacent to the major factories, steelworks, docks and trading markets. Such betting offices are and were conveniently positioned within easy walking distances of pubs, bars and clubs. Some of these are single office establishments while others are part of larger chains. . .

This can be presented more clearly:

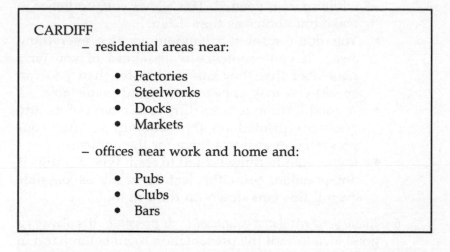

CARDIFF
    – residential areas near:

- Factories
- Steelworks
- Docks
- Markets

    – offices near work and home and:

- Pubs
- Clubs
- Bars

This kind of presentation is not totally self explanatory: it forces the speaker to work with the material and make it meaningful – ultimately, to fill in the gaps. If done well the audience is actually grateful to the speaker for resolving what is really a puzzle.

    5   *Too much paper* Whilst a lot of valuable information can be conveyed via handouts, too many sheets of paper effectively force audiences to look down at the printed material (thereby making it much harder for you to communicate with them, as people). They will often ask one another for information about which page to look at, or give up and gaze out of the window! Ideally, one or two sheets of paper will suffice, although a reassuring offer for the compulsive note-takers often succeeds:

    'Detailed handouts about the content of my presentation will be available afterwards'.

Race (1989) emphasizes the following points about using handouts:

- If you are very nervous about 'being looked at' handouts force an audience to look elsewhere.

- Make sure that the text is not too solid – lots of white space is needed. This allows your audience to make brief notes as they listen.
- You don't want the handout to give everything away. If your audience reads ahead of you (and remember that they can read faster than you can speak) you may appear boring and predictable.
- A good technique is to turn your main points into questions printed on the handout, so that your presentation answers them for the audience.
- If your handwriting is hard to read, type it. If this is not possible, print the text as neatly as possible even if this cuts down on the length.

6 *Know your room and equipment* If possible, it's always a good idea to visit the presentation room beforehand in order to check for sound quality, lighting, seating arrangements and any 'unexpected features' about the venue. It's also worthwhile practising with the equipment you plan to use, although be wary of things disappearing or breaking at the last moment. It is not unknown for some experienced presenters to carry spare OHP bulbs, video leads, flipchart markers, chalk, blu-tac (to stick flipchart sheets up on the wall) or to even use their own equipment entirely.

It is also wise to practise voice control and voice projection within the presentation room. Again if possible, ask a friend to stand at the back of the room and then speak to him or her from the front – by simply saying 'louder' or 'quieter' he or she will give you feedback about the correct volume. One problem here concerns the need to speak a little more loudly when the room is packed: all of the bodies physically absorb sound. If in any doubt, speak a little too loudly rather than too quietly.

A final check concerns the visibility of visual aids from the back of the room. Ensure that your transparencies, slides, graphs, board writing and videos can be seen by everyone. Be careful about level (rather than tiered) rooms – people at the back may get frustrated because the front rows block their view. In these situations you can:

- ask people to move into empty seating at the front and explain that this is because they will have a better view;
- reposition the machines, flipcharts etc. so that they are near the middle of a side wall, instead of at the front of the room;
- project transparencies and slides to the top of the wall so that the top edge is bordering the ceiling.

Unfortunately, there are some situations where there is no answer: with very large, crowded, level rooms you might have to give up using visual aids and concentrate on other techniques – including interactive exercises that break up audiences into smaller groups. A popular technique is 'snow-balling' where people form pairs, and then fours, in order to discuss something that you have suggested. Here are some examples of 'impossible rooms':

- adjacent to a busy road or railway;
- sporadic and unpredictable loud noises from a ventilator, banging door, a noisy meeting next door;
- pillars every five yards near the front of the room, obscuring vision;
- sunlight making it difficult to see OHP screen or television;
- inaccessible power points;
- not enough seats.

In these instances, it really helps if you at least know about the problems and have a few humorous comments lined up. If such difficulties surprise you at the last moment, it is often easy to feel as though everything's going against you, leading to fatalistically giving up or to anger and irritation. It is also worth noting that audiences are impressed if you cope well with such difficulties.

Nerves and overcoming them

Being a little nervous will actually help your presentation. Having that small amount of anxiety helps you to anticipate awkward moments and to plan your reaction; it also sharpens your concentration and ensures you do not underestimate your audience. An audience actually respects a slightly nervous speaker: it shows that you care, and that you are taking them and the presentation seriously.

It is worth quoting some useful comments from Race (1989) about overcoming nervousness. Here are some key questions to ask yourself:

My feelings about the prospect of giving a presentation are:

(a) *Absolute panic!*
You're not alone – many people feel this first time around, and some continue to feel this despite many years of experience! But it is very rarely as bad as you think it will be – and why cross all of your bridges before you come to them?

(b) *It's not the content that worries me, it's the idea of people watching me and listening to me talking*
Put this in perspective. People are usually on your side, especially when they know it's a new experience for you – and when they themselves know that they have to do exactly the same thing – possibly just after you have finished! In fact, people who are waiting their turn will only half listen to what you are saying – they are too busy worrying about what they are going to do!

(c) *My main fear is 'drying' up*
Who isn't afraid of this? Remember that unlike actors or broadcasters who usually have to stick to a script, you are allowed much more room. If things go wrong you can switch to another part of your talk – and very often people won't even notice that you are having difficulties. A visual aid will keep the audience busy while you collect your thoughts. Even if you say very little overall, you will get credit for being brave enough to stand up in front of people, having prepared some visual aids and any handouts.

(d) *I've given a few presentations already, so don't feel nervous about the prospect*
The first time is usually the most taxing – but not always! There is a danger of being too casual and losing 'the edge'. When you have gained a little experience in this

kind of activity, it is worthwhile changing your objectives: not simply to give a presentation, but to add a few professional touches and stretch yourself.

(e) *I like performing, so I look forward to it*
Marvellous! Take a few risks!!

(f) *I'm worried about how many marks may be given for the presentation*
Gaining marks or grades may not be as difficult as you imagine – indeed by simply turning up and trying you will have earned much credit. You can also ask your lecturers about the criteria they use for giving marks – indeed this is your right.

Having said all of this, excessive nervousness will obviously interfere with your delivery of the material. Here are some examples of disrupted performance:

A dry mouth.   This can lead to drying up half way through your talk, or to a ticklish cough (have a glass of water nearby, suck a sweet beforehand!)

Stuttering, tripping over words, rushed speech.   This is often caused by feeling that you have too much material to cover and not enough time. (The solution to this problem is first of all to speak aloud the entire presentation, word for word, beforehand. You may feel silly doing this on your own but it helps you to time the presentation and to realize what is and isn't possible).

Fumbling with equipment and furniture.   Apart from practising with the use of equipment beforehand, it helps if at the very beginning you clear a space for your performance. Many novice presenters feel that the arrangement of furniture and equipment is somehow sacred and that it is improper to make changes. In fact, it helps to put your stamp on the presentation if you change the physical layout, reposition equipment, and even ask the audience to move seats (especially effective if there's an empty front row).

Excessive gesturing and exaggerated mannerisms.   This sometimes results from 'overcompensation', where presenters play-act and put on a front. Sometimes this leads to a very effective performance, but only if it is done well and appears to be 'you'. If it appears to be a contrived attempt to impress, the audience might be sympathetic because they can see at least you are trying to make the presentation interesting. But there is always the risk of an audience getting irritated by what is essentially an insincere and self-conscious performance.

Repetitive fillers.   We all have our favourite conversational fillers and 'linguistic habits': little phrases, words or sounds that help us to express our ideas and arguments. The problem is that sometimes we can become aware of nervous repetitions as we are speaking, which then interferes with the delivery of the presentation. Here are some examples that could be cut out of speech altogether:

'etcetera etcetera'
'you know'
'and so on and so forth'
'and I really mean this'
'fundamentally'
'umm'
'err'
'obviously'
'of course'
'this is really interesting'
'in some senses'
'and things like that'

Many presenters feel they have to say something all of the time: in fact silence can be a very effective part of communication, and helps the audience to digest information.

Runaway speech.   Nervousness also produces 'racing thoughts' which cause distractions. Presenters may suddenly wander away from their planned speech and explore tangential themes or subject areas. In effect the presentation goes off the rails because there's so much happening to the presenter. Often an initial anxiety is followed by relief or confidence once the talk 'gets going' – and this is the danger point! Speakers can get excited about what they are saying and have a new found confidence in their subject matter. A new idea emerges, and off they go! Audiences hate this, unless they are very knowledge-able about the subject matter and can see a relevance about what is being said. Even so, the presenter is often viewed as comical and self-indulgent.

An alternative cause of 'runaway' is a question from the audience – or just the presence of one or two people whom the presenter is especially trying to impress. Here the speaker tries to 'taylor make' the presentation to their needs and interests at the last moment. Whatever the cause of runaways, the advice is simple:

1 Draw up a full plan, with keywords to remind you about the main parts of your speech, on one side of A4.
2 Reduce and simplify this to a visual aid for the audience.
3 Stick to both of these! The audience is guided through the visual aid as you work through your plan.

Apologizing. It is a myth that saying sorry is a sign of weakness; instead it shows respect for an audience's expectations and points of view. But it is fair to say that excessive apologizing along the lines of saying sorry all of the time leads to irritation and despair: often the presenter is seen as having the need to be liked. When necessary, apologies should:

• be brief;
• be at the beginning, to say that (for example) certain research findings were not available, that some of the audience may find some of the material upsetting, or that the OHP is not working;
• be at the end of a presentation, to recognize and acknowledge that certain areas or issues have not been covered, or to state that you have exceeded the time limit;
• be followed by very brief advice about what alternative information is available, if appropriate.

Just being too edgy. Ultimately, the problem with excessive nervousness is that it is unpleasant, and you don't enjoy the learning experience of giving a presentation. Here are some strategies that can help calm the nerves:

- Get some perspective on the task confronting you: what if the worst happens? What are the consequences? Remember that you are still learning how to do this, that your audience knows it and that you are supposed to learn from your mistakes.
- Think positive: now consider the best possible scenario, with an enthralled audience that welcomes your every word – it often happens!
- Think about *your presentation* rather than *you*. The audience wants to know about the topic being discussed and will appreciate a clear delivery. They are not there to judge your personality or character – if they try to do this it is *their* problem not yours!
- Before you get to the lecture theatre or classroom do something enjoyable and don't cram at the last moment. It's much more difficult keeping that calmness when you have to wait for your turn to speak. Some helpful strategies include:
  - Taking notes on other presentations, partly to pick up on what's being said but also simply to give yourself something to do.
  - Completing some deep breathing exercises which can be quietly achieved with no one else noticing: sit up, breathe in for a count of one and out for a count of four; keep it going for five minutes whilst concentrating on the counting and rhythm of your breathing. Continue for another five minutes but thinking 'I am' as you breathe in, 'relaxed' as you breathe slowly out.
  - Relaxing: all of the physical tension can lead to shaking of limbs and voice once you stand up for the presentation. A simple technique allows you to physically relax your body, and can be accomplished in public without other people noticing. Working from the bottom of the body to the top, tighten (for a count of three) and relax (for a count

of ten) your muscles. Toes first, then ankles and arches, then calves, thighs, stomach, hands, forearms, biceps, shoulders, neck and jaw.

The presentation itself

Judging by the amount of material in this chapter devoted to the preparation of a presentation, it would seem that the actual delivery is a matter of routine. If planning and preparation are extensive and complete, this is exactly the case: the presentation itself cannot go wrong barring a few unlucky or conspiratorial events! Here are some comments about actually facing an audience.

Some interaction rules

Some experts suggest things to avoid:

Don't wear casual clothes.
Don't frown.
Don't continually look at the floor, ceiling or walls.
Don't sit down whilst you are talking.
Don't fold your arms, place hands in pockets or behind your back.
Don't fiddle with OHP, twiddle chalk or pens, constantly rearrange your clothing or notes.
Don't stand in one place for the entire presentation.
Don't pace up and down.

So what can you do? There is the very real danger of being so constrained by these rules that you become 'a clone' without originality and character and style. The final product may be a very false and formal delivery which never 'gets going' or a highly polished and professional presentation which an audience regards as insincere.

Perhaps the most important thing is to be yourself but to cut out anything which interferes with what you are saying as regards holding an audience's attention.

Visual aids or obstacles?

Presentation aids can hinder rather than help a presentation. For example, a common error is the overhead projector which is left on for the entire talk. The background noise interferes with the speaker's voice and provides a monotonous and even sleepy effect on those people sitting near the machine. The solution is to provide short clips of visual support: the projector should be turned off after use, a short sequence of audio or video tape should be played, the board or flipchart should be briefly visited.

A final comment concerns the danger of presenters hiding behind machines, and again the OHP is the main problem. Try to keep the projector at a 45 degree angle, rather than standing directly behind it (in which case only your head and shoulders can be seen) or in front of it (in which case you are forced to turn your back on the audience). Your position in relation to an OHP is also important (see figure 12.1).

Other hints about the OHP:

- Don't just read out the content of the transparencies; your audience can read. Your job is to *fill in the gaps*.
- Use a pointer and keep facing the audience as much as possible.
- Use a piece of paper to cover parts of the transparency you have not yet reached, slide the paper down the screen as you work through 'chunks' on the transparency (but not line by line, which audiences find patronizing).
- Speak to the audience and not the screen or OHP.

Notice that by pointing to the screen and covering up a part of the transparency you are forced to move around and interact with the equipment rather than just use it.

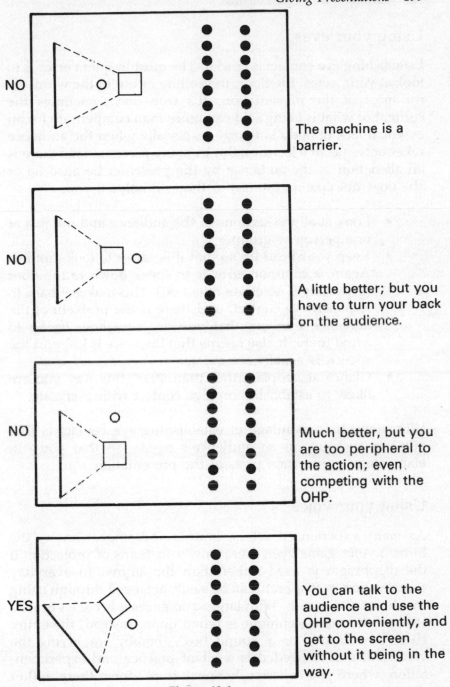

The machine is a barrier.

A little better; but you have to turn your back on the audience.

Much better, but you are too peripheral to the action; even competing with the OHP.

You can talk to the audience and use the OHP conveniently, and get to the screen without it being in the way.

Figure 12.1

Using your eyes

Establishing eye contact is crucial. The most frequent error is to look at your notes, the floor, the ceiling or out of the windows for most of the presentation. It's true that sometimes the content of what is being said can more than compensate for an essential lack of body language, especially when the audience takes notes (as in a lecture). But in many presentations there is an alienation of the audience by the presenter because he or she does not take an interest in them. It helps if you:

- Look at all the sections of the audience and not just at one person or group.
- Keep your head up so that it is easier to look around. Again, a common error is to speak down to the floor (especially if notes are relied on). This makes it hard to establish eye contact, and there is the problem of the audience thinking that you are somehow trying to avoid them. It also means that the voice is lost and the speech is usually too quiet.
- Glance at people rather than stare; this way you are likely to establish more eye contact with everyone.

Ultimately, the advantage of establishing eye contact is that you can pick up on an audience's needs, so that you can elaborate or edit certain parts of the presentation.

Using your voice

As many experienced actors, orators and singers know, the human voice gains even more power in terms of projection if the diaphragm is used rather than the larynx. In everyday conversation 'soft speech' can be easily achieved through using the throat and mouth. With larger audiences it becomes quite a strain if the same technique is relied upon. Instead, the entire chest can be used as a 'sound box', thereby amplifying the voice. All that is needed is a bit of practice and experimentation, where you consciously speak from '**down there**' rather than 'up here'!

Notes

It takes a lot of courage to put your notes on the table or lectern, and to then move away and talk to your audience (whilst occasionally returning for reference). But in terms of effective presentation skills this is the best method: only speak to the audience when you have established eye contact, so this means that your notes have to be peripheral. When having to write something on the board or flipchart, remain silent. Once you have finished writing, turn back to the audience and speak again. You will see the value of rehearsal, preparation and visual aids in this respect. The only time that you should read directly from your notes is when you are quoting someone else.

Three-dimensional

Much of the previous discussion about visual aids has assumed that paper, transparencies, a board or even video is used. Ultimately this is a *flat* medium for communication, especially with the use of screens. More variety can be introduced by bringing along objects or even people to illustrate your speech, arguments or review. Examples include:

- holding up and opening a particularly important book or report;
- uncovering a piece of equipment (if it's difficult to guess what it is, put it on display at the outset so the audience gets curious about it);
- introducing another team member and asking them to say a few (and only a few) words;
- getting the audience to pass around some photographs or documents;
- demonstrating an activity (especially with role play, or in explaining apparatus).

Moving around

There's some debate as to whether it's important to always stand up during the delivery of a presentation, especially when only two or three people constitute the audience. If a chair has already been provided within the presentation area then you are justified in sitting down occasionally. But with larger audiences, and obviously whenever you use OHPs or flip-charts, you should stand up. Once standing it is important to move around (but not to 'dance'!) so that you have a chance to get closer to people. A very confident presenter will actually expand their 'territory' by using access zones: walking down the aisles, or up and down the steps alongside the lecture theatre. Audiences will accept this provided there is a reason. For example:

- if the presenter asks a question;
- when the presenter answers a question from the other side or back of the room;
- if the presenter sets a short task for audience involvement.

Continuity and teamwork

This applies especially to team presentations where perhaps four people will contribute something to the event. It is very effective if each speaker introduces the next presenter and establishes some link for the audience, in order to avoid a disjointed performance. Furthermore, it is crucial that all of the team members look attentive to what their colleagues are saying, rather than adopt a detached attitude because 'it is not their turn'.

When teamwork is needed during presentations, try to play to one another's strengths and adopt roles you are relatively comfortable with. For example, one person can be the 'link' and introduce everyone else as well as summarizing what they have said throughout the presentation (rather than simply at the very beginning and the very end). One person may be a 'comedian', another may be 'the intellectual', whilst another may be 'the performer'. If you have enough people, and one or two of you are particularly anxious about speaking in public, then there is always the role of 'technician', where people can operate visual aids used by the rest of the group during the presentation.

Continuity is also important for individual presentations, especially when video or slide sequences are used. At the end, it is most effective if the speaker provides a mini-summary and reminds the audience of how this fits in with what has gone before and what is about to be discussed.

Questions

Making it interactive

Experienced presenters can ask questions of their audience and respond to them throughout a presentation whilst still managing to follow a coherent plan, and not getting distracted by runaway issues (or people). When learning to give presentations for the first time, or when you have a very short time limit, it's best to play safe and leave a minute or two for questions at the end.

If, on the other hand, you have a long presentation, it is possible to include interactive tasks which encourage individual members of the audience to converse with the others and to reflect on what you have just said. In many cases these activities involve 'time outs' from the presentation and are extremely effective in getting a presenter – or team of presenters – to give a series of short and sharp deliveries. There is a lot to be said for breaking up a presentation in this way, especially because the audience's attention drops away dramatically during the middle of a long talk. More information on interactive methods in lectures and presentations is available in Gibbs and Habershaw (1988).

Question time

Another form of interaction is to invite questions from the audience – provided that your timekeeping has been strict.

Sometimes a chairperson will co-ordinate this for you, but at other times you will be expected to continue with your leading role. If the chair takes over:

- sit down as she or he asks for questions;
- stand up again when the first questioner has finished speaking;
- remain standing until all of the questions have been completed.

If you have to co-ordinate questions yourself, state exactly how much time is left and say something along the lines of:

'We have a few minutes left. I would be pleased to answer any questions you might have about part or all of what I have said, either now or more informally afterwards. Perhaps somebody would like to start us off?'

This is very polite and cautious, because if there are no questions you have covered yourself by the 'informal' invitation. Effective and more aggressive statements would be:

'Do you have any questions for me?'
'I can now take (three) questions from you.'
'We have (five) minutes for questions – who is first?'

It is especially useful at this point to step forward with a smile and establish as much eye contact as possible. There will often be a silence to begin with so see it through for about one minute – don't retreat behind the lectern, start gathering together your notes or start tying up your shoelace! If the silence continues do not force the issue but accept the response with humour and thank the audience for their company and patience. A lack of questions does not necessarily reflect a poor presentation.

Should questions follow, it is vital that you have prepared beforehand by anticipating key queries. As the question is being asked, do not interrupt, but concentrate on what is being said. This concentration is difficult because you will be relieved and tired as you are nearing the end, and in the back of your mind you may already be evaluating your performance. The error is to think that question time is something extra, whilst it is still very much a part of your presentation.

Repeat the question if you think anyone in the audience missed it, or if it's complicated or confused. Repeating the question also provides a few more seconds within which to plan an answer. If you genuinely do not know the answer, or cannot understand the question, then say so.

Usually the question time concludes the presentation event, although there can be many variations. For example, sometimes three or four presentations follow on without interruption but with a question plenary at the very end. At other times the speaker will want to evaluate the entire session and ask the audience to fill in a proforma which she or he has supplied. Whatever happens, it is usually a polite move to generally thank the audience and to say how much *you* have learned from the experience!

Assessment

Presentations are intuitively assessed by your audience and/or tutors, in the same way as an art critic might appraise a painting or sculpture. A checklist approach can also be used. It is worthwhile finding out the criteria your tutors use before you give your final presentation.

Action plan

1 Thinking about your audience:

- determine the level of understanding;
- what are their expectations?
- ask around.

2 Preparing your presentation:

- draw up a plan, with time limits, and identify objects (max. of 3);
- be creative – brainstorming and mindmap;
- KISS: keep it short and simple;
- use a variety of visual aids – but not too many;
- know your room and equipment.

3 Overcoming nerves:

- rehearse beforehand;
- don't have too much material;
- practise with equipment;
- get perspective, think positive, use relaxation exercises;
- be yourself!

4 The presentation itself:

- stand up, move around, establish eye contact;
- don't be note-bound;
- avoid fillers, runaways and apologies;
- make it three dimensional;
- project your voice;
- if it is a long presentation, make it interactive.

5 Questions:

- anticipate questions and formulate answers beforehand;
- don't gather up notes and lose concentration;
- ask for clarification if confused, repeat it for benefit of whole audience;
- provide short sharp answers;
- speak to entire audience and not one questioner.

Crosslink chapters

Further reading

Buzan, T. (1974) *Use Your Head*. London: BBC.
Gibbs, G. and Habershaw, T. (1988) *253 Ideas for Your Teaching*. Bristol: Technical Education Services Ltd (TES).
Gibbs, G. and Habershaw, T. (1988) *53 Interesting Things to do in Your Lecture*. Bristol: Technical & Educational Services Ltd (TES).
Mandel, S. (1987) *Effective Presentation Skills*. London: Kogan Page.
Race, P. (1989) *Giving a Seminar*. Aberdeen: CICED, Robert Gordon University.
Turk, C. (1985) *Effective Speaking*. London: Spon Publishers.

13

Student Tutoring

John Hughes and Roland Metcalfe

An activity which develops communication skills quickly and effectively is tutoring less advanced learners. This involves helping with project work, one-to-one activity (such as reading or terminal/PC work) and facilitating various kinds of problem solving. It should never be teaching *per se*, which is the domain of your lecturer! In this chapter John Hughes outlines the introduction of student tutoring in schools. Roland Metcalfe then gives details of tutoring which involves final year undergraduates working with first or second years within university.

Tutoring in schools

'There is something compelling about it, I found myself looking forward to it every week.'

'An excellent scheme; ought to be mandatory for all research scientists.'

'I enjoyed the challenge of explaining my subject to young children.'

'Easily the most rewarding part of the course.'

These are just some of the comments from students in further and higher education across the country about their involvement in tutoring. They do it because it is rewarding, stimulating and enjoyable. Research shows that they gain organizational, problem solving and communication skills, at the same time as increasing their self-confidence. In addition, they act as positive role models to school children to help increase their aspirations and motivation for post-16 education and training. Many children have never heard of a college or university, let alone actually met someone who is studying in one. A student tutor can break down some of these barriers, helping them to see the relevance of post-16 education and training and assisting them with their studies.

There are now over 154 institutions involved with running tutoring schemes and the number is increasing every semester. One of the biggest factors in its favour is that it is great fun. Tutoring is supported by people from all sides of education including the National Union of Teachers and the National Union of Students.

British Petroleum's Aiming for a College Education programme has supported the promotion of tutoring across the UK. In 1991 we produced, with Toni Beardon of Cambridge University, Allen Flinn of Salford University, Lucy Green of BP Oil/Industrial Society, Ron Sims of Nottingham Trent University and many students, pupils and teachers, a resource pack. One section is devoted to informing students about how to be tutors – some of these sheets are specially reproduced below. As you will see, the important point is that the teacher remains in charge legally, morally and educationally. The tutor acts as a type of resource in the classroom, helping 1 : 1 or with small groups. BP is now working to support the development of student tutoring world-wide with its International Restoring and Tutoring Project. Look at the pages below to read more about what is involved.

Student tutors in schools

Tutoring is an enjoyable activity but it is also serious and requires a commitment on the part of the student for the length of the programme. Pupils in particular get very upset when 'their tutor' stops coming – they might think it's because you didn't like them. Their self-confidence can be badly affected. Tutoring gives you the opportunity to:

- increase your communication and interpersonal skills, and patience;
- practise problem solving and time management;

- reinforce your knowledge of fundamentals in your subject;
- reflect on others' understanding of your subject;
- develop an insight into the teaching/learning experience;
- increase your self-confidence;
- have a welcome break from the rigours of studying!
- get to know people who are often from a different social background than your own;
- relate your subject to the outside world;
- impart your enthusiasm and knowledge of your subject to pupils;
- gain a feeling of satisfaction through helping to play an influential part in the lives of young people;
- participate in valuable community services that are great fun;
- gain experience that will help in making a choice of career;
- develop skills that are valued by employers.

Tutoring: what, why and how?

What? Volunteer students assist teachers in local secondary and primary schools. Typically the student tutors help for one afternoon or morning session per week for between one and two semesters.

Why? Tutoring has been found to be an excellent way of providing extra stimulus to pupils of all abilities. It makes lessons more interesting for pupils by providing student tutors from further or higher education institutions. It raises pupils' aspirations and motivation for staying on in education and training beyond 16 by providing positive role models through which they find out more about their subjects, the outside world and student life.

Further and higher education students are given the opportunity to develop their social, organizational, problem solving and communication skills in a practical context.

How?   Tutors work individually or in small teams, under the supervision and direction of a teacher, helping pupils with their work and discussing the relationship of the subject being studied to everyday life.

Benefits of tutoring

College

Lecturers

- Enable students to develop interpersonal skills.
- Increase quality of education provision for local schools.
- Provide for skills and competence development in line with the requirements for work and life.
- Learn about changes in the Education Service (e.g. National Curriculum).
- Excitement of taking part in a new initiative.
- Increase applications to their institution due to higher local profile.
- Build on links with local community.
- Provide work experience.

Students

- Feel they are doing something useful.

School

Teachers

- Lessons more enjoyable.
- Lessons easier to handle.
- Learn more about FE/HE students and courses.
- More learning activities made possible.
- Freer to manage conditions of learning.
- More opportunities for oral and practical work.
- Free classroom assistance.
- More efficient learning.

Pupils

- More individual tuition and attention.
- Lessons more fun and interesting.
- Learn more than usual.
- Sympathetic help from another young person.

College	School
Students cont.'d	Pupils cont.'d
<ul><li>Increase communication skills.</li><li>Enhance problem solving and organizational skills.</li><li>Reinforce their knowledge of fundamentals.</li><li>Reflect on others' understanding of own subject.</li><li>Develop sense of personal adequacy.</li><li>Experience of being productive.</li><li>Develop insight into the teaching/learning process.</li><li>Increase self confidence.</li><li>Valuable community service.</li><li>It is enjoyable!</li></ul>	<ul><li>Increases aspiration to further training and education.</li><li>Provided with a positive role.</li></ul> General <ul><li>Excellent liaison between institutions.</li><li>Participate in popular initiative.</li><li>Greater appreciation of each other's perspectives.</li><li>Increased pupil uptake of post-16 training and education.</li></ul>

Classroom tutoring

In the classroom you may meet pupils of any age from 5 to 18 and of all ability levels. The following pointers, drawn from the experience of tutors and teachers in the classroom, should help you.

- Tell the pupils your name and show it in writing (a badge can help to remind them). Tell them who you are, why you are there and for how long.
- You must gain the pupils' trust and respect, so that they feel relaxed and confident with you. Always try to seem relaxed, no matter what the situation. It is a great help to learn the pupils' first names.

- Praise and encouragement are the best ways to get pupils working. You will find that many of the pupils you encounter are very short of self-confidence. It is helpful for the pupils to gain confidence in finding their own way to the solution, rather than being led to it by you or the teacher. Proceed by asking questions rather than making statements.

- In some cases you may be asked to lead a small group of pupils in an activity, in which case be sure to explain clearly what you are going to do and remember to summarize at the end (better still ask a pupil to summarize).

- When working with pupils, it is very easy to find yourself doing all the work for them. It is important that you avoid this, and instead lead the pupil along through the work by suitable hints and questions.

- Do not discriminate or show favouritism. Be aware of the pupils' sensitivities; ethnic, social class, gender and religious beliefs.

- Some of the pupils you will encounter may be unreceptive to book work and to written work in general. Such pupils will respond much better and learn more if they can be involved in some practical activity.

- In the same way, where it is appropriate (as in a language or practical class) pupils enjoy interaction with other pupils. This may for example take the form of role playing or group investigations.

- If you have detailed knowledge of the subject being taught, you will naturally feel more confident and more in control of the situation. Even where the work is new to you, however, you can still play a role, learning alongside the pupils and letting them see how you tackle the learning process.

- Should you have trouble with a pupil, hand over the situation to the teacher. The teacher is trained and experienced in dealing with such situations and remains in charge of the class at all times. You are not there to act as a disciplinarian.

- Have patience and persevere.
- Try to find *simple* relationships between the task in hand and the everyday world.
- Smile! It is the fastest ice breaker!

Proctoring

A proctor is a student who helps one or more less advanced students within the same higher education institution to learn under the guidance of an academic. At Nottingham Trent University a form of proctoring was introduced in 1985 by arranging for final year Mechanical Engineering students to be available to first year Engineering Application groups. Each proctor was given responsibility for the management of a group of eight students carrying out a design-and-make project. Twelve hours of contact time were scheduled for this activity which replaced one of the design projects in the final year. Assessment was therefore based on the marks that were already available for that project, which was 5 per cent of the total assessment for an honours degree.

Proctors were required to submit a report with the following contents:

1 Project title.
2 Group membership.
3 General description of the project.
4 A detailed description of the more important technical problems.
5 The individual roles of the members of the group, their reactions and contributions.
6 Personal problems that were encountered and how they were dealt with.
7 Any comments the proctor may wish to make regarding personal experience and any future changes that could enhance the experience.

Students were not assessed on their effectiveness as proctors, but rather the quality of their report. At the same time, in order to obtain some measure of effectiveness, questionnaires were given to both the proctored students and the proctors. The questionnaires also gave the opportunity to give personal comments on any aspect relating to the proctoring experience. As would be expected, there was a wide variation in the comments which generally reflected on the proctors' ability to lead, organize or plan. They ranged from dominant and bossy to ineffective. This was reassuring in that although not all proctors reacted to the management experience in the most ideal way, the students who were proctored were unlikely to be worse off for the experience, however poor the proctoring.

Development

In subsequent years, proctoring has been extended to second year Engineering Design project groups, second year Computing, first year HND in Mechanical and Production Engineering and first year Furniture Design. Assessment methods have been refined to give a more accurate measure of the activity. It has since emerged in many other colleges in Britain as well as America.

Reason behind assessment

In attempting to measure the effectiveness of proctoring it must be borne in mind that the experience is primarily for the benefit of the proctors. These aims give a clear statement of what it is hoped to achieve:

- to give students practical experience in professional activity by providing them with the opportunity of running a team doing a project (in our case, engineering);
- to enable students to act as 'section leaders' in an industrial sense;

- to develop the skills of communication, planning and organization in managing a team;
- to develop leadership and team building skills.

Objectives

We now expand our earlier list of benefits for student tutors by focusing on management skills. Four areas of effective management have been popularly listed – note that employers are often looking for these skills when shortlisting and interviewing!

Communication

- To communicate effectively with tutors, students and other involved parties.
- To initiate group discussions and to listen, learn, act, react and modify actions accordingly.
- To issue instructions.
- To explain technical data.

Organization and planning

- To plan projects and tasks, timetable the developments and maintain time schedules.
- To adapt to developments and changing circumstances.
- To be able to refer to and utilize technical information.
- To have factual knowledge of the subject matter.
- To be familiar with the standard procedures.
- To be able to assess the problems as a whole and develop alternative strategies and procedures.
- To delegate effectively.
- To provide solutions.
- To relate experience to a problem.
- To record and report.

Leadership

- To promote teamwork.

- To be approachable and helpful.
- To recognize the abilities of team members and to utilize members' strengths.
- To delegate.
- To be enthusiastic and to prompt without dominating.
- To take command when required.
- To be open to suggestions.
- To make decisions.

Attitudes and values

- To value other people and to appreciate one's dependence on them.
- To be able to value oneself and one's work.

These qualities may need to be further analysed into more specific tasks and activities which can be identified and measured.

Assessment

Assessment must, therefore, reflect the areas of communication, organization and planning, leadership, attitudes and values. Staff achieve this by attempting to measure the following three criteria:

- the report of the proctoring experience;
- reflection upon the experience;
- the performance of a proctor;

each being awarded a third of the available marks. In order to make this assessment the following can be evaluated:

- written documentation such as interim and final reports and log books;
- observed performance;
- success of the project;

- input from proctored students using, for example, questionnaires;
- self assessment;
- oral presentation.

The report of the proctoring experience should include:

1 The way the group worked, for example:
   - How it achieved cohesion (or otherwise).
   - Did it work together or form sub-groups?
   - Did the appointed leader maintain leadership or did other leaders emerge?
   - Did the group members work to their predetermined roles?
   - Actions that motivated and de-motivated.
2 The behaviour of each individual group member (for example, their contributions and reactions).
3 The interface between the group and its members, the lecturer and other staff members, and yourself.
4 A description of the design, the technical problems encountered and any recommendations on the projects.
5 How you dealt with problems (even relevant personal problems), and whether you met group members outside timetabled hours to discuss matters not associated with the project.
6 Your planning techniques.

The account reflecting upon the proctoring experience may include:

1 What the experience has taught you.
2 What changes you would make to your approach if you repeated the exercise.
3 Actions that achieved positive outcomes and those that did not and your understanding and reasoning of these results.
4 The value of planning – was it effective?
5 Recommendations you would make on proctoring.
6 Any other relevant points.

Proforma feedback checklist for teachers

Teacher ————————————————————————

Proctor ————————————————————————

Please indicate your personal assessment of the student on the centre scale.

	5	4	3	2	1	
Understanding and practice of what was asked. With vigour and full understanding.						Had little idea.
Creativity. Fertile with good ideas.						Could only see one solution.
Comprehensive in thinking. Thinks to a complete solution.						Thinks of little detail. No reference to concept.
Systematic in approach. Organized.						Wild and erratic.
Leadership. Guides others well.						Favours anyone's suggestions uncritically.
Self reliance. Confident.						Has to be pushed. Afraid of consequences.
Co-operation. Helpful to others.						Does not refer to others.
Communicates clearly and concisely						Difficult to understand.
Effectiveness. Produces good results with economy of effort.						Works hard to no purpose.
Demonstrates engineering skills and knowledge clearly.						Hardly at all.
Personal image. Character and charisma.						Slovenly.

Thank you for your help and support in this proctoring venture.

Proforma questionnaire for gathering class feedback

Instructions

Please use the numbers to indicate the extent to which you agree or disagree with the following statements. For example, if you wish to express your complete disagreement with a statement, then circle −3 as shown.

True for me	**Not true for me**
+3 +2 +1	−1 −2 −3

Please feel free to make any additional comments at the end of the questionnaire.

		True for me	Not true for me
1	Proctoring was helpful.	+3 +2 +1	−1 −2 −3
2	I prefer to work with a proctor.	+3 +2 +1	−1 −2 −3
3	I would have preferred more time with a proctor.	+3 +2 +1	−1 −2 −3
4	I talked with the proctor about other topics.	+3 +2 +1	−1 −2 −3
5	The proctor was friendly.	+3 +2 +1	−1 −2 −3
6	The proctor was caring.	+3 +2 +1	−1 −2 −3
7	Anything you particularly liked about proctoring?		
8	Anything you particularly disliked about proctoring?		
9	Any other comment:		
10	Year _____ Subject _____		

Thank you very much for filling in this form.

Conclusions

In addition to requiring a report, questionnaires can be given to staff, students and pupils. The examples on pp. 220–1 are of a proforma used with teachers in school tutoring, and a proforma for use with pupils.

You may encounter other terminology which includes aspects of student tutoring. Growing in popularity is the phrase *supplemental instruction*, which encourages students who are more advanced in their studies to help other students (especially first years) to find their own solutions to various problems. In this way supplemental instructors are not actually giving the solutions themselves. Another term is *mentoring*, which refers to a much closer one-to-one relationship based on trust and the giving of advice: often the less advanced learner is encouraged to choose the mentor or adviser and all the meetings and discussions are treated as confidential.

A final comment concerns the added value of student tutoring – however it is defined – in helping you to prepare for a career which involves guiding, training or educating others. Everyone who encourages mentoring, proctoring, student tutoring or supplemental instruction emphasizes that you never actually 'teach', but nonetheless you often observe teachers in action and you have a wonderful chance to observe how others learn. This counts for much if you are thinking of applying for later teacher training.

Action plan

- Find out what schemes are available at your college, who runs them and what terminology is favoured.
- Establish whether it is assessed or not, and if it is ensure that such assessment is compatible with the rest of your studies.

- Attend briefing and/or training sessions and establish groundrules, especially the fact that you will never 'teach': at the most you will help the teacher or lecturers.
- Establish contact with the people you will be working with and define curriculum areas to be covered along with other administrative details (for example, dates, times and places of students tutoring activities).
- Begin gradually; 'shadowing' learners, teachers or lecturers is a popular initial activity.
- Keep a log or journal of activities and outcomes for each student tutoring session, and if possible get teachers or lecturers to provide confirmation (for example, by signing alongside each entry) or give more detailed feedback at the end of the programme.
- Obtain and summarize feedback from students, pupils, teachers or lecturers and submit appropriate coursework.

Crosslink chapters

Further reading

Goodlad, S. and Hirst, B. (eds) (1990) *Exploration in Peer Tutoring*. Oxford: Blackwell Education.
Hughes, J. (1991) *Tutoring: Students as Tutors in Schools*. London: BP Educational Service (for free copy tel. 0202 669940).

14

Making the Most of Seminars

Hannah Cowie

Seminars usually involve student led discussions in relatively large groups. All too often they can 'go wrong' – perhaps through an over-dominant and talkative individual, or because a lecturer chooses to give another lecture, or when no one wants to speak. These outcomes waste an invaluable opportunity to clarify and understand difficult parts of the course, and in this chapter Hannah Cowie identifies a variety of roles which can be played in order to make seminars work. In all cases it is essential that the lecturer does not 'lead' except by giving information when requested to do so, or when arbitrating between arguers. This means that you have to do more talking as well as actively listening – but the time flies by and you'll get more out of it!

What do we mean by the term 'seminar'?

It is an accepted term and we talk about it as though everyone means the same thing. And yet I know from talking to lecturers and students that we mean a myriad of different things. Sometimes it involves the lecturer making a presentation to a group of students to stimulate a discussion. Sometimes it is a student who will make a presentation and lead a discussion. Sometimes there is no presentation and a discussion is expected to develop. Some lecturers require pre-reading, others do not. Sometimes the role of the lecturer is the focus, at other times she or he may not be present. Whatever the definition, many lecturers and students are dissatisfied with the seminars that they attend. This chapter will help you to make more of seminars.

What is my role in a seminar?

There are a number of roles that participants in seminars undertake whatever their format. This chapter looks at these different roles and the skills they demand. The skills are transferable to many other roles and situations too. Being aware of them, or better still, taking the time to practise them, increases the benefits you gain from a range of situations, including seminars.

An important concept: process balanced with content

There are two broad aspects to any activity; there is the content and there is the process. So, for example, the content of the seminar may be religion in modern Spain. This is the aspect that we concentrate on, and feel most comfortable discussing. It may help to think of the content side of it as the technical or factual side.

The process is how the seminar is to take place; for example, a presentation followed by a discussion chaired by an individual. There will be other processes happening all the time; for example, the presentation process may be made by lecturers with slides, or by mime, graphics, audio tapes or video. The discussion may involve processes such as group dynamics, leadership, conflict, oral communication, non-verbal communication. This is the aspect that we rarely discuss, and is certainly the aspect with which we feel least comfortable. The process involves us thinking more about the human side of our work.

The value of the content is determined by the effectiveness of the processes employed, yet usually we think of our studies purely in terms of content ('I'm writing an essay on. . .'). Sometimes we are given guidance on the process of essay writing, private study or revision. These are principally solitary exercises. I want to use this chapter to give you guidance on some of the less solitary processes that take place in higher education today.

An important question

Who is responsible for the success of the seminar? The lecturer/tutor? The presenter? The Chair? The answer is none of these; instead, 'you are' and 'we all are'. If the seminar is a waste of time, everyone in the seminar is to blame! If you want it to go well, if you don't want your time wasted, you must take responsibility for the success of the seminar. This means thinking about both processes and content before, during and after.

What are the roles involved?

1 Preparing and giving a presentation.
2 Observing and listening to a discussion.
3 Chairing/leading a discussion.
4 Participating in a discussion.
5 Assessing ourselves and others.

Each of these sections that follow is presented as a checklist. If you find yourself expected to perform one of these roles, run through the checklist to make sure you have covered everything.

Preparing and giving a presentation

What is the aim of my presentation? (Key: Be aware of *what* and *how* you speak)	To persuade? To perform? To challenge? To enthuse?

Who is my audience? What is their level of understanding?	Aim for high or low complexity? Avoid jargon.
What will interest them?	Think equally about what they want to hear, and about what you wish to say.
What visual aids would be useful? (Key: KIPS: Keep It Pertinent and Simple)	Slides Overhead transparencies Models Graphics Video
What techniques shall I use?	Standing lecture Seated lecture Handouts Audience participation
Have I collected my material systematically?	Make a plan for collecting information, including what sort of information and in what location it can be found.
Have I collected the right amount? (Key: A little goes a long way)	Too little or too much detail. Too little or too much quantity.
Have I thought about the order and sequence of the material? (Model: News – headlines announced, details given, headlines repeated)	Beginning/middle/end. Important points emphasized and summarized. End with a bang not a whimper.
Am I confident with my content?	Use key notes/pointers or overhead transparencies as prompts. Do *not* read from notes.
Have I prepared my environment?	Prevent external interruptions. Remove

distracting posters. Wipe down chalk/white boards. Informal or formal seating? Comfortable position for self. Access to materials you need.

Do I allow myself a moment of silence when I need it?	Take time to breathe, organize yourself, respond to questions, find necessary items.
Have I prepared myself? (See chapter 12)	General appearance. Eye contact, tone of voice. Relaxed breathing. Clarity and audibility of speech. Posture, movement, relate to audience.
Do I maintain equal concentration and interest during ensuing discussions and questions?	Promote discussion and questions. Show interest. Wait until end of seminar for personal feedback and reassurance.

Observing and listening to a presentation

This is a vital role. What is the point of a presentation without the observers, the receivers, the listeners? How much do you value your time? How much would you charge an employer for an hour's labour? Now multiply this sum by the number of people in the seminar and then ask yourself why we continue to have unsatisfactory seminars and meetings.

What do I want out of this seminar?	Facts? Interest? Ideas? Social interaction?
What do I want to contribute to this seminar?	Discussion? Humour? Peer support? Interest? Analysis? Ideas?

What do I need to achieve these things?	Concentration, pre-reading, physical comfort.
What equipment do I need to achieve these things?	Paper and pen? Articles? Books? Own work, notes?
Am I helping myself to concentrate?	Enough sleep? Not overeating just before? Active listening?
Am I doing anything to prevent others from feeling at ease or making the most of the time, including the presenter and the Chair?	Body language, posture? Eye contact? Private conversations? Poor listening? Feeling negative (angry, disruptive, low).

Chairing and leading a discussion

The role of the Chair particularly concerns itself with processes. Your role is like that of an orchestral conductor, or the circus ringleader; that is, you must make the most of the participants and the topic before you. It is said that a good Chair need know nothing of the topic, because the Chair's role is to facilitate impartially the contribution of others. It is important to be assertive without being aggressive. Chapter 8 will be useful to you in this role. To improve your chairing ability run through this checklist before and after the event and review your performance.

What is the purpose of the seminar?	To inform? To enthuse? To increase understanding?
Do I know what others want to achieve through it?	If so, clarify, reiterate the goals. If not, ask.

Can I achieve all these different objectives?	If not, say so.
How shall I achieve the set objectives?	Formulate an agenda. Pose open questions (Why? How? What?) to stimulate responses. Highlight key discussion points. Bring individuals in to comment. Operate a 'brainstorm' session (see chapter 4).
Is the group too big to work well?	Eight is ideal usually. If too large review what can be done; for example, break group into smaller groups to report back to large group.
Do notes need to be taken?	The Chair cannot chair and take notes. Allocate a note taker.
Is anyone dominating?	Handle them firmly and politely.
Am I dominating?	If so, stop! Your oral contribution should be minimal. Ask for the views/ opinions of others, keep your own comments clear and concise.
Has anyone not contributed?	Invite their contribution. Bring them in.
Has the seminar wandered pointlessly?	If so, say so, then summarize, consolidate, set a new agenda and invite contributions.
Has the discussion become exclusive/ cornered amongst two or three participants?	If so, re-direct the discussion to the wider group.

Have I control over the participants? Are they talking across me? Are they talking across each other?	Make sure participants know that their contributions must be made 'through the Chair'. This means asking you before they speak.
Are anyone's comments being ignored or rejected?	Provide support, and bring them in by asserting yourself over less attentive participants.
Am I aware of the time and how it is being used?	Keep a check on time, reviewing how much time you need to cover the agenda by the end of the time period. Remind participants of time boundaries.
Have I allowed time to summarize periodically and at the end? Ask for participants to give me feedback on how they feel about the seminar.	These are vitally important. Make sure you allow time.
Am I aware of the atmosphere in the room?	Poor understanding and listening. Tensions, cliques, ambience, physical atmosphere.

Participating in a discussion

Chapter 8, on working in teams and syndicates, will be invaluable here. Again, review your performance by running through this checklist before and after the event.

Do I arrive on time?	This makes a big difference to how the whole seminar goes for

all the participants, not just yourself. Make it a priority.

What do I want my contributions to achieve?	To persuade? To inform? To enthuse? To challenge? To compete or put others down?
Do I put others at ease?	Be part of the whole group. Discourage cornered discussion. Don't have separate discussions with neighbours.
Are my contributions clear and concise?	People will be more likely to listen to and appreciate your contribution.
How do I respond to others' comments	Avoid rejecting or ignoring others' comments. Be supportive.
Am I dominating the discussions?	By doing this, you are preventing others from making equally valuable contributions.
Do I accept responsibility for the discussion?	Participants sometimes feel they can opt out. This changes the atmosphere in a negative way for everyone else. Also, the roles of Chair, presenter and debater are pointless without the other two roles. You are,

therefore, as responsible for the success of the seminar as anyone else.

Am I waiting for others to lead?

If so, why? Try and identify the reasons, overcome shyness and abdication of responsibility (see above).

Assessing ourselves and others

Please refer to chapter 6, 'Self and Peer Assessment'. Try building up your own checklist of criteria: 'What features will make this a good or bad presentation/chairship/discussion?'

Action plan

- Clarify with your lecturer what she or he expects a seminar to involve, and draw up a list of expectations and groundrules as agreed by all participants.
- Ensure that everyone knows when they are expected to adopt a leading or chairing role, and when they are expected to give some kind of presentation.
- Where possible, allocate preparation workloads to individuals who then share their research within the actual seminar.
- Try to link each seminar with pending coursework assignments and lecture topics.
- After the first few seminars, try a 'stop-start-continue' activity where everyone writes down:

  - things we must stop doing in this series of seminars;
  - things we should try to start doing;
  - things we are currently doing and should continue with.

Comments are then read out – anonymously!
- Use a variety of methods for presenting information – if everyone reads through their notes each week it will be very boring. Creative problem solving (especially brainstorming and mind mapping), giving presentations, and posters are examples that could be used.

Crosslink chapters

Further reading

Hind, D. (1989) *Transferable Personal Skills – A Student Guide*. Sunderland: Business Education Publishers.
Race, P. (1992) *500 Tips for Students*. Oxford: Blackwell Publishers.

15

Personal Transferable Skills

Lin Thorley

In this chapter Lin Thorley introduces a very wide range of skills which 'transfer' from one situation to another, including from college or university to later employment. Much of this discussion emphasizes the value of realistic self assessment (itself a transferable skill) in terms of getting messages across to yourself as well as to other people, and Lin also includes a very popular and detailed questionnaire to help you diagnose your own skills development needs.

This is a practical guide to skills development. It includes what is meant by Personal Transferable Skills, how to diagnose your skills development needs and how to go about improving your skills independently. This process will be especially useful if you are keeping a self-reflective log or portfolio (see chapter 17) for your work placement, or if you are working on a profile or careers folder (see chapter 16).

Personal transferable skills

What are Personal Transferable Skills (PTS)? This is something of a catch-all phrase which includes a long list of skills, qualities and capabilities. These are the things which enable you to be more effective in what you do and to use your knowledge and understanding to best advantage, so that you can realize your potential. For example, communication skills: you may have a good deal of knowledge about something but you'll be less effective if you can't communicate it to others when you need to. Accordingly, you will sometimes find these skills called Personal Effectiveness Skills.

Although there are certain core skills that always seem to appear, everyone's full list of PTS is slightly different. You'll find mine in the questionnaire on pp. 251–9. You might like to look ahead to see the kinds of thing I include. As I have listed a large number of skills, I've grouped them under headings like 'Interpersonal skills' and 'Self-management skills', to make it easier to see relationships between them. Once you start working on PTS you may find you want to change and individualize both the list and groupings, so that it reflects your own needs and attitudes.

In order to find out more, dissect the name Personal Transferable Skills and see what it tells you about them. These skills are 'personal' in the sense that they are owned by and are part of you. The way you use them reveals – or is – your personal style. So this is more than – and different to – just 'head stuff' (such as the knowledge and understanding you possess). It's about how you operate, and includes your social skills, your personal behaviour patterns and even aspects of your personality.

These skills are 'transferable' in the sense that they can be acquired (or developed) in one arena and used in another. Financial skills you have learnt on a Business course could help you in your private life. Alternatively, having been a treasurer of a sports club could help you in your Business course. Being able to transfer your capabilities from one context or role to another is an essential skill in itself and like the other skills it can be cultivated.

Now the word 'skills'. This is something of a problem, for me at least, because I don't see all these things as skills in the usual sense of the word (that is, as a special proficiency or dexterity in something). There's more than just plain skills in this list. I find it easiest to see them ranged along a spectrum.

The skills spectrum

At one end of the spectrum are what I would call 'true' skills: possessing them means you can do these things, are skilled or proficient or dexterous at performing tasks involving them. Examples of these include numeracy and written communication. Somewhere in the middle I would put things like social competence and teamwork, which although still skills (and someone could be described as being 'skilled at' them) seem to have more to do with the way you operate as a person than did the former group. At the far end of the spectrum we're into things which I'd see as not being skills at all, but being qualities or attitudes, such as self-confidence and being willing and able to change. Going along the spectrum in this way the 'skills' become increasingly personal. Where a skill lies on the spectrum has important implications when it comes to the development process. I'll say more about this later.

The reason all PTS are described as skills is that special ability in them can be acquired and developed by training or practice. This is something that is common to them all wherever they fall on the spectrum, even the qualities. You're not just stuck with what you've got (like the nose you inherit); you can change, learn and improve. This takes choice, effort and practice. More on this later, too.

PTS are also non-subject specific. That is, none of them are special to any one academic discipline. They are all relevant whatever subject you are studying, although some are more important in certain areas. For example, listening is especially necessary for counselling, keyboard skills for journalism and oral skills for law. Where they are especially important in this way they become part of the content of the course concerned, and you can expect them to be developed on the course. Some of the other skills listed, such as critical/analytical thinking, written and information skills will also be given direct attention on most if not all higher education courses. But many skills will not. Which brings me to the crucial issue.

Why self development?

I'm suggesting in this chapter that you should do something about developing your own PTS by taking things into your own hands. It won't have escaped your notice that this will mean making an extra effort, over and above what you already have to do for the rest of your course! So what's in it for you? And if it's so important, why won't it be done for you on your course?

The benefits of self-development of PTS

To start with, taking control of your own learning and development has special benefits in terms of ownership of the learning involved. To become self-motivated and self-directed in your learning helps you to become more 'you'. You'll be going where you want to go, not where someone else wants you to go. And when you've got there you'll be able to express the 'you' more fully. Developing skills is part of personal growth. But if it's your personal style you're affecting then it's more than usually important that you take responsibility for your own development of these areas and steer yourself in the direction that you feel is most appropriate for you. Taking control of your own learning is also likely to spill over into the way you learn in other areas, such as when you're acquiring knowledge. You'll become more of an independent and self-directed learner all round. In addition – and this is especially neat and convenient – the process of self-development itself develops skills.

Then again, well-developed PTS will improve your life chances. This doesn't just mean it will improve your career and employment prospects and performance. These skills are crucial for all life roles: employment, home life, social life, voluntary work and so on. The general rule is you'll need capability in most of these areas if you are to realize your potential across a wide spectrum of life roles.

It has been said that the proper outcomes of higher education are an increase in knowledge, skills and understanding, and that of these the skills area is usually the least successful. Employers, particularly, feel that many graduates are deficient in these areas. In fact, the Enterprise in Higher Education

Initiative originated in the realization that more help should be given to students in these skills. Enterprise activities generally include the chance to practise skills, so if you get the opportunity to participate in them do take it. But a large part of it will still be up to you.

Finally, don't just leave skills development till later. Your time at college is an excellent one to work on PTS, especially as you are in a learning environment and you'll have all the necessary resources around you, plus a chance to experiment without the outcome being too much of a risk! Use college as a practice ground.

The self-development process

The process I outline here is designed to help you get into your own skills development in an informal yet structured way. It provides you with a sequence or pathway you can follow which parallels that organized for you by your tutors for the more formal part of your course. It will be especially useful for those skills not 'covered' by the course you are on.

In essence, the process is extremely simple. You need to decide:

Where do I want to go?
How am I going to get there?
How will I know when I have got there?

If you look now at the self-development process on p. 243 you will find this sequence set out in a more usable fashion. I'll talk you through the stages and refer back to the diagram as we go. If you're set to take the process seriously it's probably best to read through the whole chapter first, to get the gist of it, then come back and read each stage again as you get to work on it. When you come to working on an individual skill there's also a Skills Development Form that you can use to help you keep track of your progress.

Stage 1: self-assess your current skill level (questionnaire)

The first stage of the process involves self assessment. The PTS questionnaire printed here is a tool you can use for this. It comprises a list of 40 skill areas, each named and then defined in a bit more detail, to help clarify the area the skill covers and give some suggestions as to its nature. The list is intended to be relatively comprehensive but at the end of each section you're invited to add your own ideas of similar skills, and score them as usual (check first to see if they appear in another section). Read these definitions carefully.

For each skill two questions are asked. First 'How *important* do you think it is that you should possess/acquire this skill?' Notice that you are asked about yourself not about people in general. Your answer here will depend on several things. Important in relation to what? What perspective are you using? Are you looking at now, or later in your life? Is it for employment generally, for a specific type of employment or for life as a whole? Does the level at which you imagine yourself operating have any effect – student or future managing director? You could usefully answer from any of these perspectives, but do be clear which it is.

The second question asks the 'extent to which you think you *already possess* this skill (i.e. your *self assessment* of your present skill level)'. Even more than for the first question your answers here will depend on your perspective. Who are you comparing yourself with? Someone you admire? Your present student group, your wider social group or what seemed usual in the company you worked in last summer? How are you measuring yourself? Against what criteria? Do you have an idea of some external standard, or even some 'absolute' standard, against which to compare yourself?

Scoring the questionnaire

Even more important than this, though, is that you are really honest with yourself in answering. It won't help you to claim

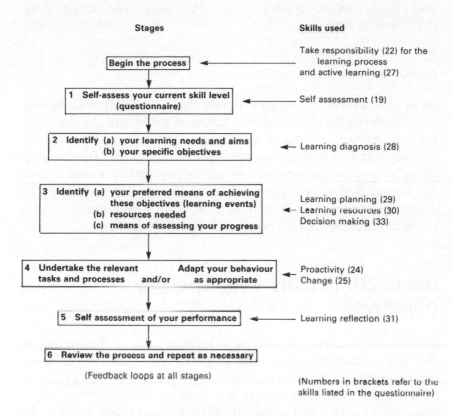

Figure 15.1 The self-development process.

you're capable when you're not. Equally, nothing is gained by being overly self critical. It's very difficult to be objective about yourself in this way. In fact, your answers here are most likely to be subjective (i.e. based on your opinion, what you think you can do, as against what you can actually do), but are nonetheless useful for that.

Self assessment and self confidence are especially important skills in the context of the questionnaire, as your capability in these areas is likely to affect competence at self assessment – which is what the questionnaire is all about. These skills may also be modelled by staff and others you come into contact with: the qualities and attitudes of a professional engineer or health practitioner, for example, may be shown through the way staff operate and in the way they talk about their professional area.

Making your choice

So now you have it. You can choose things at the true skills end – possibly those which don't happen to be taught on your particular course (perhaps numeracy if you're on a Humanities course). Or you can go for something in the middle – where you may get the chance for on-course practice, but which may not be coached or concentrated on or assessed in any way (for example, teamwork). When you've made your choice put a mark against the skills you aim to develop.

Stage 2b: identify your specific objectives

While your general aim will be to improve the skill in question this will probably be too large and too vague an area to work on. Be more specific. For example, if you marked 'management of resources' you may decide it's financial skills that are most important to you, and within that the bit you really want to do something about is learning to cope with a balance sheet. This narrower and more concrete area becomes your objective.

Writing objectives

Writing objectives is quite a skill in itself. Perhaps it will help here to clarify the way I am using the words 'aim' and 'objective', and to give another example. For me, an aim is like a goal, something to reach. It might be quite large and vague, like giving good oral presentations. However hard and well I work on this I will never really get there. There will always be something to improve. An objective, on the other hand, is something smaller, clearer and more concrete, which I will be able to achieve or attain, hopefully quite soon and without too much difficulty. There may be many (even an infinite number) of possible objectives going towards one aim, and they may be at different levels of difficulty.

My objective for an oral presentation could be relatively simple: to actually stand up and talk for ten minutes. The objective need not say anything about how well I do it! Then again, I could choose a harder objective, which says I should give a presentation on a controversial topic at the end of which I will have persuaded more than 70 per cent of the group hearing it to vote in favour of my position on the subject. This would mean that in order to achieve it I have to be sufficiently good at persuasive speaking. Notice I have specified here how I am going to demonstrate success. Whenever you try to write objectives in this way, they should include within them the criteria for success.

The trick with objectives is to make them as clear and as concrete as possible, and at a level you can cope with but that stretches you and reflects your learning needs. Time and care spent on working out your objectives now will pay off later, when you get to assessment.

Stage 3a: identify your preferred means of achieving these objectives (learning tasks)

Stage 3 involves working on three linked areas: identifying your preferred means of achieving your objectives, the resources needed and the means of assessment. As far as possible plan these three in parallel rather than getting ahead with the means, say, and then realizing you can't get the resources to finish what you wanted to do.

Starting with Stage 3a, you can see that the kind of skill you want to work on will affect how you go about finding, or defining, a learning task or event. If it's numeracy, you could look for extra learning tasks in a textbook, but if it's something at the qualities end you may need to be more imaginative or simply be ready to seize an opportunity when it comes by. You can often find your chance within another, more formal, learning event. Self confidence, for example, can be worked on by choosing to take any opportunity to stand up and be counted. You could volunteer for that presentation, or to be a class representative. It is helpful at this stage to be very specific as to what your chosen learning task will involve. Describe it carefully in words, as concisely and accurately as you can, and try to visualize exactly what you will be doing. It may help to put times or dates against tasks, when they should occur or be finished by. Use the skills development form on p. 260 for this.

Stage 3b: identify resources needed

Consider whether your learning task will involve any resources; books, people, money and so on. If so, note it down and decide whether it is practicable, or it might be better to look for an alternative task. People resources include friends and family, who may be happy to give you feedback or help in some other way. You may want to involve your tutors (if, for example, you can't think of a suitable learning task) or some other sort of advice or assessment. Most tutors would be only too pleased to find you are taking responsibility for your own learning development.

Stage 3c: identify means of assessment

You also need to think about assessment. This may sound a bit formal and daunting; it doesn't need to be in practice, but it is a necessary part of the process.

Summative assessment tends to involve actual marking and is most often done to you or for you by tutors, although it can include self and peer assessment marks as well. *Formative assessment* may or may not involve actual marks or grades, but where it does they are there as indicators to help you see how you are doing. Marks are just one possible form of the feedback for learning which is the essential part of formative assessment. This feedback can come from tutors but also, very importantly, from your peers and yourself. Summative and formative assessment can occur together, as in an essay the marks for which will go forward, hence be summative, while the comments written on it will be formative – especially if you really use them to help you learn for next time.

It should be easy to see that we're into the formative version of assessment here. So you can forget about marks if you want to (although you could use marks, or grades, to help yourself see where you're at, particularly with things at the true skills end, like numeracy). You can also, if you want to, forget about tutor assessment, though you might still decide you would like some other input or advice from tutors.

Achieving objectives

In essence, assessment in the sense we're using it here means checking you have got to wherever you wanted to go for your own learning purposes, including whether you have achieved your objectives. It may include finding some evidence to show that you have successfully performed a task, as seen by other people. It should definitely include your own feedback to yourself, on reflection, about how you performed.

The most obvious and important check you can do is that you have achieved your objectives. Have you learned or changed? How are you going to check this? What evidence can you present? What are the criteria by which you will judge this? Depending on the objectives you wrote earlier you may need to formulate some criteria at this point (or perhaps re-write the objectives). To take our example of a presentation, the objective (that we should persuade 70 per cent of the audience to our viewpoint) wouldn't need any extra criteria. But if our objective had simply been to give as good a presentation as possible, we would now need to decide what exactly makes a good presentation. This could be a short list of the criteria or aspects involved (content, structure, voice, visual aids, etc.) or of the 'hallmarks' of a good presenter.

Peer feedback

An oral presentation is a good example of a skill where peer assessment and feedback can be very helpful to you. You could ask a friend to assess your presentation according to the criteria you have listed for your own use, using numbers or grades. Getting feedback in this way can sometimes be a risky business, but there's quite a lot you can do to make sure it's a positive experience. If you use a friend it's a good idea to have a reciprocal arrangement, so that you give them feedback too. Knowing that it's two-way tends to improve the quality!

Decide what you want feedback about: a general overview or how you did on one specific item? Brief your feedback person carefully to make sure you get constructive rather than destructive criticism. You could use the idea of saying one positive thing, that is done well, for everything that still needs working on (and express the latter in that way, rather than as something badly done).

Stage 4: undertake the relevant tasks and processes and/or adapt your behaviour as appropriate

Now, at last, you get to do the thing itself! Perhaps I should stress that although this stage seems to be the most obvious and active learning phase it's not just here that learning occurs. The whole process of skills self development involves learning.

Whatever skill you are working on, try to think and feel yourself into doing it with self confidence. This is much more important than it may seem at first sight. The degree of self confidence really does affect skills learning and performance.

Stage 5: self assessment of your performance and peer feedback

After the event itself you move into the assessment stage. This includes checking objectives have been reached, your self assessment procedures and getting and taking on board assessment and feedback from others. It's also important that you spend time on reflection. Are there any special observations you could make? These could include realizations or illuminations about your skills and performances or behaviour patterns. Writing them down helps make sure they won't be lost. And what are you going to do with the feedback you get and the illuminations you have? What does it tell you about how you might have performed, or could perform in the future?

Stage 6: review the process and repeat if necessary

When you feel you've got everything you can from the assessment stage, then step back and look at the whole process as if it were from a distance. Think back to your planning and decide how appropriate and effective it was in the light of what you know now, after the event. Do the same for the skills practice stage and the assessment stage. You now need to decide whether to go through the whole process again, for the same skill (in the same or in a new improved format) or whether to take a different skill and work on that.

Using the questionnaire

The questionnaire isn't something to use once and then not look at again. You could try asking a friend to score question B for you and discuss any discrepancies. It can also be helpful to go through the whole list of skills again at a later date and compare your scores with your previous form. Hopefully those skills you have chosen to work on will have improved! But what about those you have not been working on? If you are scoring them much later, then we would expect many of these to have got better too. You may find, though, if you check back, that your scores for importance have gone up, while your scores for skill level have gone down. This probably doesn't mean you have actually got worse! As you grow in awareness you are likely to become more conscious of the importance of these skills, and as you gain wider experience you are likely to become more discerning and hence rate yourself lower. Meanwhile, you are honing your skills in self assessment.

The learning cycle

Looking back through the self development process you can see you have gone through four main phases. This is known as the learning cycle:

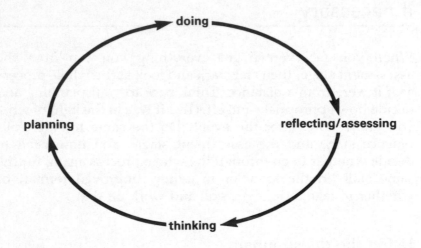

Learning occurs in each of these phases. You are now in the 'thinking' phase, reviewing what has gone before then deciding on the next planning stage. You can keep going round the cycle in a deliberate and structured way, each time building on what you have learnt the time before. This may seem to take extra, even unnecessary, effort. But if you only work on skills in the 'doing' (practice) phase you miss out on the possible learning that could occur in the other three phases. Each time you go round the full cycle you spiral upwards in learning, increasing your skills as you go.

Making use of your learning records

It's helpful to make sure that you record all the work you do on skills development. Fill in and date the questionnaire and the skills development form. An important use for your records is as part of your careers folder or portfolio. You could see the questionnaire as a primitive kind of profile (see chapter 16). You could add your self-development work to any other you do in this area, but make it clear that this part of it was done of your own volition. It certainly shows initiative to undertake learning in this way.

You can use your material to show prospective employers. At the very least it forms raw material for interview preparation or for constructing your application for work placements or jobs. It should help, especially if you can show evidence of having worked on your weaker areas.

Even more important, the skills development process forms part of your commitment to lifelong learning and personal skills growth. This process doesn't stop when you leave formal education: you need to develop an outlook that means you will want to keep on learning, and seizing learning opportunities, during the years to come.

We have gone through the skills self-development process step by step and you can see the whole. Now it is time to go back and make a start at engaging in the process yourself. You could make an informal learning contract with yourself to complete the sequence. Good luck!

Personal transferable skills: questionnaire

Complete this questionnaire by ticking the appropriate boxes, according to:

A How *important* you think it is that you should possess/acquire the following skills:

6 – very important
5 – important
4 – slightly important
3 – slightly unimportant
2 – unimportant
1 – very unimportant

B The extent to which you think you *already possess* the following skills (i.e. your *self assessment* of your present skill level):

6 – very good at this
5 – good at this
4 – slightly good at this
3 – slightly poor at this
2 – poor at this
1 – very poor at this

LIST OF SKILLS

	A (importance) high low	B (your present skills) high low
	6 5 4 3 2 1	6 5 4 3 2 1

Communication skills

1 ORAL – ability to communicate effectively and appropriately on a one-to-one basis

    ( ) ( ) ( ) ( ) ( ) ( ) ( ) ( ) ( ) ( ) ( ) ( )

2 ORAL PRESENTATIONS – ability to present ideas orally to an audience; to discuss and argue a case

    ( ) ( ) ( ) ( ) ( ) ( ) ( ) ( ) ( ) ( ) ( ) ( )

3 LISTENING – willing and able to hear and actively comprehend verbal messages without undue blocking through, for example, prejudice or assumptions

    ( ) ( ) ( ) ( ) ( ) ( ) ( ) ( ) ( ) ( ) ( ) ( )

	A (importance) high ⟶ low	B (your present skills) high ⟶ low
	6 5 4 3 2 1	6 5 4 3 2 1
4 WRITTEN – well constructed and grammatically accurate essays, reports; the right style for the right occasion	( ) ( ) ( ) ( ) ( ) ( )	( ) ( ) ( ) ( ) ( ) ( )
5 READING – ability to absorb written material sufficiently rapidly and at a level of accuracy and completeness appropriate to the need	( ) ( ) ( ) ( ) ( ) ( )	( ) ( ) ( ) ( ) ( ) ( )
6 VISUAL – represent in drawn or diagrammatic form, use of a range of visual aids	( ) ( ) ( ) ( ) ( ) ( )	( ) ( ) ( ) ( ) ( ) ( )
7 NUMERACY – sufficient ability to manipulate numbers in those contexts in which you might expect to participate	( ) ( ) ( ) ( ) ( ) ( )	( ) ( ) ( ) ( ) ( ) ( )
8 INFORMATION SKILLS – ability to seek, store, retrieve, synthesize, use and present information in a manner appropriate to the objectives you are pursuing	( ) ( ) ( ) ( ) ( ) ( )	( ) ( ) ( ) ( ) ( ) ( )
9 KEYBOARD SKILLS – ability to use a typewriter/ computer keyboard to a level sufficient for your own use	( ) ( ) ( ) ( ) ( ) ( )	( ) ( ) ( ) ( ) ( ) ( )
10 COMPUTER LITERACY – ability to use computer applications (e.g word-processing, databases, spreadsheets) appropriate to the vocational direction you are pursuing	( ) ( ) ( ) ( ) ( ) ( )	( ) ( ) ( ) ( ) ( ) ( )

	A (importance) high — low 6 5 4 3 2 1	**B** (your present skills) high — low 6 5 4 3 2 1
11 FOREIGN LANGUAGES – speak and understand a foreign language	( ) ( ) ( ) ( ) ( ) ( )	( ) ( ) ( ) ( ) ( ) ( )

Other similar skills
Specify _____

_____

Interpersonal skills

12 SOCIAL COMPETENCE – ability to relate to others; socially at ease with people from a variety of backgrounds	( ) ( ) ( ) ( ) ( ) ( )	( ) ( ) ( ) ( ) ( ) ( )
13 ASSERTIVENESS – know what you want and be able to negotiate for it in a way which is assertive rather than aggressive, manipulative or passive	( ) ( ) ( ) ( ) ( ) ( )	( ) ( ) ( ) ( ) ( ) ( )
14 GROUPWORK/ TEAMWORK – ability to co-operate with others and carry out a variety of roles (ideas, organization, task-performance) in a joint venture	( ) ( ) ( ) ( ) ( ) ( )	( ) ( ) ( ) ( ) ( ) ( )
15 LEADERSHIP – ability to manage, guide, facilitate a group or activity so as to maximize its success and the contribution of participants	( ) ( ) ( ) ( ) ( ) ( )	( ) ( ) ( ) ( ) ( ) ( )

Other similar skills

Specify _____

_____

| | A
(importance)
high   low
6 5 4 3 2 1 | B
(your present skills)
high   low
6 5 4 3 2 1 |

Intellectual skills

16   USE OF CREATIVITY – ability to use your imagination and creativity fully in order to innovate, develop ideas and carry out plans

    ( ) ( ) ( ) ( ) ( ) ( )   ( ) ( ) ( ) ( ) ( ) ( )

17   CRITICAL/ANALYTICAL THINKING – ability to consider issues from a range of perspectives, to understand them and draw upon appropriate concepts and values in arriving at a critical assessment of them

    ( ) ( ) ( ) ( ) ( ) ( )   ( ) ( ) ( ) ( ) ( ) ( )

18   PROBLEM SOLVING – ability to confront obstacles in pursuing an objective and arrive at positive ways of overcoming them

    ( ) ( ) ( ) ( ) ( ) ( )   ( ) ( ) ( ) ( ) ( ) ( )

Other similar skills

Specify _____

_____

Self-management skills

    ( ) ( ) ( ) ( ) ( ) ( )   ( ) ( ) ( ) ( ) ( ) ( )

19   SELF ASSESSMENT – ability to evaluate your own strengths, weaknesses, progress and future learning objectives

20   SELF CONFIDENCE – trust in your own worth and ability sufficient to enable you to make a full contribution

    ( ) ( ) ( ) ( ) ( ) ( )   ( ) ( ) ( ) ( ) ( ) ( )

	A (importance) high low 6 5 4 3 2 1	**B** (your present skills) high low 6 5 4 3 2 1
21 SELF PRESENTATION – ability to demonstrate in an appropriate manner, in oral, written and physical form, the qualities you possess	( ) ( ) ( ) ( ) ( ) ( )	( ) ( ) ( ) ( ) ( ) ( )
22 RESPONSIBILITY – ability to act or decide on your own without supervision	( ) ( ) ( ) ( ) ( ) ( )	( ) ( ) ( ) ( ) ( ) ( )
23 SELF DISCIPLINE – ability to manage yourself in reaching goals and carrying out tasks	( ) ( ) ( ) ( ) ( ) ( )	( ) ( ) ( ) ( ) ( ) ( )
24 PRO-ACTIVE APPROACH – ability to initiate activities without needing prompting from others	( ) ( ) ( ) ( ) ( ) ( )	( ) ( ) ( ) ( ) ( ) ( )
25 CHANGE – willing and able to manage change; comfortable with facing new situations	( ) ( ) ( ) ( ) ( ) ( )	( ) ( ) ( ) ( ) ( ) ( )
26 TIME MANAGEMENT – ability to make appropriate use of your own time in managing and achieving tasks	( ) ( ) ( ) ( ) ( ) ( )	( ) ( ) ( ) ( ) ( ) ( )

Other similar skills

Specify _____

_____

Learning skills

| 27 ACTIVE LEARNING – willingness to take an active role and take responsibility for your own learning | ( ) ( ) ( ) ( ) ( ) ( ) | ( ) ( ) ( ) ( ) ( ) ( ) |

	A (importance) high low	B (your present skills) high low
	6 5 4 3 2 1	6 5 4 3 2 1

28 LEARNING DIAGNOSIS – ability to diagnose what you know and what you don't know   ( ) ( ) ( ) ( ) ( ) ( )   ( ) ( ) ( ) ( ) ( ) ( )

29 LEARNING PLANNING – ability to plan learning and to set targets   ( ) ( ) ( ) ( ) ( ) ( )   ( ) ( ) ( ) ( ) ( ) ( )

30 LEARNING RESOURCES – ability to identify resources for learning (people, books, software, etc.)   ( ) ( ) ( ) ( ) ( ) ( )   ( ) ( ) ( ) ( ) ( ) ( )

31 LEARNING REFLECTION – ability to reflect on learning   ( ) ( ) ( ) ( ) ( ) ( )   ( ) ( ) ( ) ( ) ( ) ( )

Other similar skills

Specify _____

_____

Management and career development skills

32 CAREER/EMPLOYMENT AWARENESS – ability to identify a range of options open to you in work and in community life and have a realistic sense of what qualities they might require   ( ) ( ) ( ) ( ) ( ) ( )   ( ) ( ) ( ) ( ) ( ) ( )

33 DECISION MAKING – ability to weigh up alternative approaches and make a commitment to and carry through a selected option   ( ) ( ) ( ) ( ) ( ) ( )   ( ) ( ) ( ) ( ) ( ) ( )

		A (importance)							B (your present skills)					
		high					low		high					low
		6	5	4	3	2	1		6	5	4	3	2	1
34	MANAGEMENT OF PEOPLE – assessing contribution and utilizing potential of others, delegation	( )	( )	( )	( )	( )	( )		( )	( )	( )	( )	( )	( )
35	ORGANIZATIONAL SKILLS – ability to make and carry through an action plan with others to achieve a given objective	( )	( )	( )	( )	( )	( )		( )	( )	( )	( )	( )	( )
36	MANAGEMENT OF RESOURCES – ability to gauge resources (finance, materials, staff, etc.) required for specific operations and to work within those allocated	( )	( )	( )	( )	( )	( )		( )	( )	( )	( )	( )	( )
37	BREADTH OF VISION – recognition of opportunities; ability to perceive the possibility of future developments	( )	( )	( )	( )	( )	( )		( )	( )	( )	( )	( )	( )
38	IMPLICATIONS OF DECISIONS – appreciation of financial, design resource and other implications of decisions/activities	( )	( )	( )	( )	( )	( )		( )	( )	( )	( )	( )	( )
39	ENVIRONMENTAL AWARENESS – recognition of the importance of natural resources and of the implications of certain acts on the environment	( )	( )	( )	( )	( )	( )		( )	( )	( )	( )	( )	( )

	A (importance) high — low 6 5 4 3 2 1	B (your present skills) high — low 6 5 4 3 2 1
40 INTERNATIONAL/ COSMOPOLITAN OUTLOOK/ AWARENESS — recognition and sufficient knowledge of characteristics of other contemporary societies; ability to look at the broader pattern in economic and social terms	( ) ( ) ( ) ( ) ( ) ( )	( ) ( ) ( ) ( ) ( ) ( )

Other similar skills

Specify _____

_____

Action plan

- Ensure you are familiar with all of the definitions for the PTS items.
- Work through the 40 skill areas and rate how important you think they are (you may prefer to do this in chunks, having a rest between each section) – be honest!
- Now rate yourself for the 40 items as regards the extent to which you already possess the skill.
- Obtain feedback from others about their views on your abilities and your self assessment.
- Identify areas which you think are important, and where you need to develop further. Draw up a plan for such development, and if possible ask academic staff to introduce activities which will help you to do this.
- Return to the PTS questionnaire later on, and keep a record of development and progress.
- Draw up a profile when applying for jobs, as outlined in chapter 16.

Skills development form

Skill area

General learning aim:

Specific learning objective:

Learning task

Description:

Resources needed:

Assessment:

Date and event for learning task – to be completed by:

Observation, reflection and self assessment:

Assessment/feedback from others:

Review – decision as to future learning needs:

Crosslink chapters

Further reading

Bourner, T. and Race, P. (1990) *How to Win as a Part-Time Student*. London: Kogan Page. (NB. equally useful for full-time students)

Dainow, S. and Bailey, C. (1988) *Developing Skills with People*. Chichester: Wiley.

Francis, D. and Woodcock, M. (1982) *50 Activities for Self-Development*. Aldershot: Gower.

Guirdham, M. and Tyler, K. (1992) *Enterprise Skills for Students*. London: Butterworth–Heinemann.

Pedler, M. and Boydell, T. (1990) *Managing Yourself*. Aldershot: Gower.

Part III

Getting Out of College

16

Employment Profiles

Malcolm Pike

'Well, it boils down to ballet, or computers...'

A profile is a very brief summary of your achievements, background experience and skills. It is often based on consultations with academic staff and personal tutors who have watched and encouraged your development since coming to college. Profiles can include short written statements, graphical summaries and/or skills checklists which are scored in some way. In this chapter Malcolm Pike concentrates on what employers value, and on the use of his employment EmPro profile – in using checklists to feed into a final two-page statement written by students about themselves. This is then added to your job applications. It can also be included within such documents as the National Record of Achievement.

An analogy that I use to introduce employment profiles to my students uses H.G. Wells' *The War of the Worlds*. If you are a sci-fi fan you will know the story is about an attempted invasion of earth by martians. They came in huge cylinders and emerged to devastate humankind with vastly superior weapons. The fiends, it seems, had thought of everything, even anticipating our extra gravitational pull by moving around in sophisticated machines. Only one small factor had been overlooked: the microbial life of planet earth. The result, an untimely and unpleasant death for the inhabitants of planet Mars, was brought about by tiny life forms – 'germs'. I offer three conclusions:

1 The martians failed to recognize fully the difference between Earth and Mars.
2 They assumed the things that made them successful in one world would be equally effective in the other.

3 Their preparations had not been adequate, having been ignorant of, or having chosen to ignore, potentially harmful factors.

What has this to do with employment profiles? Replace 'martians' with 'students', 'Mars' with 'education', 'Earth' with 'employment' and I believe you have a set of statements that applies equally well to sophisticated, well qualified graduates and diploma holders who find it difficult to get a job. Though students realize there are differences between the world of education and employment, many fail to recognize the full extent of the differences. It is much more than 'being on time or you won't get paid'; there is a fundamental difference in philosophy. To the educational purist 'education for education's sake' is the maxim. Not so the employer, to whom 'relevance' and 'value for money' are the guiding principles.

What do employers want?

Your qualification entitles you to apply for a certain level of work in a particular area. An LL.B (Hons) would be unlikely to apply for a post that specified B.Eng.(Hons). A diploma or degree, however, is an indicator of intellectual ability not of suitability for any particular work, and employers know that. You may have come top of your class, be in-line for a 'first' even, but if you are totally unreliable, no good at working in a team, ignorant of world issues, you may not be the sort of person an employer is looking for. You may have been successful in targeting and developing the skills and qualities needed to attain educational objectives, but are they the ones required to achieve success in industry and commerce?

The problem with many vocational initiatives in education is that they give the potential employer masses of documentation about their students, much of which is irrelevant, but which purports to give the whole picture. Employers generally don't want the whole picture; they want the relevant 'bits', and the first problem is that the educator and employer may not agree as to what the relevant bits are. A second problem is simpler to understand. An employer does not have the time to deal with masses of paperwork – give him or her too much and you are already a problem before you go for the interview. So the golden rules of adequate preparation are to find out exactly everything that is required by asking employers and taking the necessary steps as suggested by their answers. Then you can, with confidence, take that 'giant step'.

Giving employers what they want

Having applied the conclusions in theory the important next step is to look at the practical applications. What can you actually do to make sure that you have more success 'invading' employment than the martians had when invading Earth? Is there some means by which you can prepare yourself in a way that is relevant to the needs of the employers, recognizing the factors that are giving you success now, and developing those that will help you to overcome the differences between your world and theirs? If the answer were no, there would be little point in continuing. Fortunately the answer is yes.

An obvious step is to use the Careers Guidance Service (see chapter 19). You will also find chapter 15 useful for identifying personal transferable skills. For the remainder of this chapter I want to concentrate on something else that you can do to help you 'get a job', namely to construct a profile. A profile is a *brief* summary of your achievements and personal qualities based on levels of performance that are supported by some kind of evidence.

An employment profile can be started as early in your course as you like: the earlier the better. It involves discussing, with your tutor, progress or lack of it, achievement and the possession or lack of skills and qualities that *employers* think important. The importance of working with your tutor is paramount, as his or her feedback on the profile gives it credibility. Most colleges, if not all, have a personal tutoring system where each student has a member of staff to talk to about anything. The personal tutor takes an interest in you and should be prepared to help you in the construction of your profile. As a result of your discussion you can write a fairly short statement about yourself making reference to things employers want to read about.

But will employers read it? Who is going to take notice of anything you write about yourself? These are the natural questions of a student reluctant to spend time on what might be considered, at first glance, a waste of time. Because over 150 employers (large, small, private, public, local, national) have been consulted and because a representative sample helped to design our own employment profile, we are very confident it will be read. Everything in our employment profile is relevant and the documentation is kept to a welcome minimum. We find that many educationalists are wary of EmPro (short for employment profile) but employers love it; they have told us so in no uncertain terms.

One of the surprising patterns to emerge from our consultations with employers was that though the type of employment varied enormously, the qualities, skills and other information required was remarkably uniform. You would think that the sorts of information required about a potential nursing officer would be totally different to that required for an embryo architect. There are, however, more similarities than differences. Nearly all employers want to know the following about candidates:

Personal qualities	(A)
Social or group activities	(A)
Leisure activities	(B)
General knowledge/awareness	(A)
Ability to communicate	(A)
Appearance	(A)
Health	(A)
Time keeping	(A)
Work qualities	(A)

Careers research	(A/B)
Work experience	(B)
Work skills	(B)
Work preferences	(B)
Educational attainments	(A/B)

and briefly about their present course; for example, how it was taught and assessed.

Many of these things are asked about in 'confidential' references. It seems rather unfair that your referee should be asked to write about you under headings you might not know exist. How can you perform well in an area if you don't even know what the area is? If you knew in advance that riding a bicycle was an important skill for the job you wanted, you would obviously make sure that you could ride a bike really well and insist that your referee saw you do it. Thus EmPro is not like any other reference. You know in advance what employers want to know and you can make sure that what is said under these headings is to your advantage. A critical point, when undertaking EmPro, is that you must discuss and negotiate with your tutor on a fairly regular basis. In that way you gain a realistic appraisal of how you are doing. Your tutor gets to know more about you and, eventually, when called upon to do so, can write a much more meaningful reference. The final report that you write about yourself will be a much more important influence on the employer because it is the result of a negotiated process, a process that has concentrated on things important to him or her.

Using EmPro

EmPro gives relevant information about yourself to an employer on two sides of A4 paper. It is called the 'final' or 'summative profile'. What you write on those two sides, however, will have been the subject of discussion with your tutor. This 'process' is also recorded in the document. In addition there is a side of A4 on which you can add any other information you may think necessary. Another page, which only requires you to tick boxes, tells the employer about your course (not the content, but how it was delivered, evaluated, assessed and so on).

However useful the final profile may be to employers, they also like to see the process by which it was delivered. If you refer back to the list of things employers want to know about, some areas (we call them targets) are marked with an A, B or A/B. The Bs are the easiest targets to deal with because all you have to do is to give preferences and/or examples. For example, what your sport, leisure activities are; any work experience you have done; any skills you have that are particular to the job for which you are applying, and any preferences for your conditions of work. Employers are interested in your leisure: what you do in your spare time is a good indicator of the 'sort' of person you are.

Having some work experience is also an advantage. Many students already have some through their schools with varying degrees of success (a frequent problem at school is that pupils are 'placed' and that in turn depends on what is available – meaning you might get stuck in some 'hell-hole' for a fortnight and, therefore, have a decidedly 'non-experience').

The holiday postman is one of the nation's most trusted workers and the occasional labourer shows not only blisters but 'gut' determination to get through the day. Don't undervalue any work experience you have had. Bar staff, waiters and waitresses and checkout operatives still have to display punctuality, reliability, honesty and an ability to deal with those awful customers. The very fact that you are prepared to work in various situations impresses employers.

Word-processing and information technology expertise is becoming essential in areas of work where there are more screens than faces. Even the driving licence – have you got one? – can mean that extra factor in getting a job. When I first applied for a teaching post the only one available was in a junior school. I got the job, not because I was the most experienced (I'd never taught before), not because I was the best qualified (I was a zoologist with no educational training), but because I, alone of the candidates, could play the piano, and they needed someone to play their piano for morning assemblies. How little did I think when struggling at the keyboard all those years ago that one day it would mean the difference between employment and unemployment. The advice is clear: develop skills you may have and look for opportunities to obtain more.

Dealing with the Bs therefore is straightforward. Simply put to your tutor what relevant experience you may think you have had and decide which is the most appropriate. Try and be selective but I would guess you could record quite a lot under each target heading.

The As are a little more involved. To give you an idea of how one actually tackles a target from this group it is best to look at one of them in detail. What you would see in EmPro under target heading 'Social/group qualities' would be the following:

```
Enjoy meeting people                      ( . . )
Enjoy working with people                 ( . . )
Enjoy serving people                      ( . . )
Enjoy helping people                      ( . . )
Sensitive to others' needs               ( . . )
Listen well to others                     ( . . )
Contribute readily to groups              ( . . )
Always co-operative                       ( . . )
A good team leader                        ( . . )
A leader in a group                       ( . . )
Argue without aggression                  ( . . )
Caring                                    ( . . )
Put others first                          ( . . )
Respect other values and beliefs          ( . . )
Fit in well with all ages                 ( . . )
Mix well with different people            ( . . )
```

Where did these words or phrases come from? When we were asking employers what areas they were interested in, many not only gave what became our targets, but also examples of words and phrases associated with them. EmPro lists the most commonly occurring and these have, therefore, become the descriptors. It is worth noting that all the descriptors given occurred in more than half of the replies we received, reinforcing our belief that no matter what the employment the qualities and skills looked for are largely the same.

Let us, however, deal with our chosen target. The idea is to indicate how well the descriptor applies to you. There is no need to consider all the descriptors in a particular group. For instance, there are 32 descriptors in the target 'Personal qualities' and you would have to be a 'very special person' for all to apply. You need to be selective, but having selected you need to indicate a level of appropriateness. Do it this way. Give yourself mental applause and pretend the applause is being measured by a 'clapometer'. Level 1 means the descriptor doesn't apply and 5 means it really does apply to you very well indeed. Now put your level in the first space in the bracket and ask your tutor's opinion. Imagine your level is recorded as this:

(I) Enjoy meeting people   (4, ,)

What would your tutor say?

I would ask you to give me some reasons why you are giving yourself a high level. You might say you share a flat, you belong to various societies, you work part-time behind a bar, you enjoy, and have travelled with, friends around France. I would agree and tick and date the record. If you had said you rarely go out, you prefer to stay in your room, you don't belong to any clubs, you like reading on your own, it does not mean that you are any 'less a person', but I certainly wouldn't think you enjoy meeting people. So we would negotiate an altered score that, hopefully, would reflect the real situation. Now, if 'meeting people' is a factor in your future career, yet is a problem with you, it is something that has to be tackled and, hopefully, between your tutor and yourself you will be able to do something that will help. If your tutor can't help then you should be put in touch with someone who can. Then, later, you can increase the level, for example:

(I) Enjoy meeting people	(2,3,4)

The employer, by quickly scanning these targets and descriptors, can actually see that you have discussed your strengths and weaknesses and done something to correct the weakness.

Fortunately most targets and their descriptors are not such minefields. Having dealt with the descriptors selected in the particular target and, where needed, been given time to show improvement, you may feel ready to tackle the final profile.

I recommend a minimum of two sides of A4 to cover a maximum of 14 targets. Being brief and to the point is, in itself, a most valuable skill and in the final profile you have a marvellous opportunity to show it because this is what the employers will definitely read. You must take care not to simply regurgitate the descriptors in a slightly altered form. Write in your own style, preferably (employers tell us) in your own handwriting.

There is nothing wrong in adding or deleting descriptors or indeed targets. EmPro is only the starting point for your preparation to enter that 'other world', and you are invited to develop and modify it for yourself according to the qualities relevant to your career choice. Thus a graphic designer needs to be creative, a programmer, logical, and a social worker, caring. Some qualities are inborn but you still have to develop them. Others like 'politeness' and 'firmness' can be acquired.

Any employer likes to feel that you have used the Career Service, indeed any agency that specializes in helping you select a career. It is important that you show them you have not stumbled into a career but have consciously taken steps to help you in your choice. Consulting the college careers officer sooner rather than later is a wise choice because, having decided on a possible career area, it is possible to match your EmPro more closely with the demands of your future job.

An example

This particular student is a male undergraduate studying for a mathematics degree, who wanted to go into the world of finance following work experience in a firm of accountants. The student had met his tutor fairly regularly since the middle of the first year and used EmPro as a basis for discussing his career. At first the discussion was general, but as the student became more certain about career plans they spent more time on the targets and descriptors most appropriate to finance and accountancy.

The list on pp. 276–7 shows you which descriptors, previously referred to as As, were thought to be most important. The student then wrote the summative or final profile based on the targets and descriptors. It is important to realize that the profile you are about to read is only an example and its style is not to be followed rigidly. You have your own style use it.

An example of a final profile

Leaving home and the structured life of a comprehensive school came as a great shock. It took time to learn how to organize myself and set my own targets. At first managing my time was a real problem. I am a conscientious person, however, and as I got to grips with my mathematics course I found I was using my time much more productively and achieving my targets, not least of which was handing in work to very demanding deadlines.

Having an enquiring mind I particularly enjoy problem solving. This is an ability that has been tested to the full during a very difficult 'honours' course. The practical applications of mathematics to real situations has always been my main interest, demanding speed, accuracy and attention to detail if there is to be a satisfactory outcome. It is this real application, where solutions depend as much on resources as on theory, which has attracted me to a career in finance.

I have been fortunate enough to obtain some summer employment. Working as a part-time barman certainly developed

Targets	Descriptors (Relevant examples)	Performance levels
Personal qualities	An enquiring mind	(5, ,)
	Enjoy solving problems	(5, ,)
	Logical	(4,5,)
	Think clearly	(3,4,5)
	Well motivated	(2,4,5)
	Self confident	(3,5,)
	Honest	(5, ,)
	Responsible	(3,5,)
	Reliable	(4,5,)
	Patient	(2,3,5)
	Firm	(2,3,5)
	Polite	(4,4,5)
	Pleasant	(4,5,)
	Adaptable	(2,4,5)
Social qualities	Enjoy working with people	(4,5,)
	Enjoy helping people	(4, ,)
	Contribute readily to a group	(3,4,5)
	A good team member	(5,4,)
	A leader in a group	(2,3,4)
	Argue without aggression	(1,2,4)
	Mix well with people from different backgrounds	(3,5,)
General knowledge	Good general knowledge	(4,5,)
	A knowledge of national/international issues	(2,3,4)
	Aware of basic economic issues	(2,4,)
	Aware of European society	(3,4,)
	Aware of impact of IT on work	(3,4,5)
Appearance	Well groomed	(4, ,)
	Dress appropriately	(4,5,)

Targets	Descriptors (Relevant examples)	Performance levels
Health	Stamina	(4,5,)
	Good general health	(5, ,)
	Good eyesight	(5, ,)
Work qualities	Quick	(3,5,)
	Methodical/accurate	(4,5,)
	Conscientious	(4,5,)
	Pay attention to detail	(3,5,)
	Enjoy providing a service	(2,4,5)
	Use my time productively	(1,3,4)
	Attain objective set	(2,4,)
	Produce work of high quality	(3,4,)
	Reliable	(5, ,)
	Good attitude to training	(3,4,)
	Review my own progress	(2,4,)
	Set targets for myself	(1,3,4)
Timekeeping/ absenteeism	Punctual	(3,5,)
	Good attendance record	(4,5,)
Career research	Sought/obtained relevant work experience	(2,5,)
	Visited places of employment	(5, ,)
Educational attainments	A high level of numeracy	(5, ,)
	Work as a team member to solve problems	(3,4,)
	A good level of general literacy	(4,4,)
	Recognize that solutions may depend on resources	(2,3,4)
	Speak another language	(3,4,)

my ability to deal with people and tested my patience. I was, however, often left to look after the premises, an experience that taught me a lot about responsibility and increased my self confidence. For two summers I worked for a fairly large firm of accountants. After a while I was considered reliable enough to do some work on actual accounts. I enjoyed the experience very much, especially working with, and for, different people. I certainly learned the value of 'local information', but because some of the clients had European connections, I also became very interested in the financial institutions of the European Community. I speak French fairly well so was able to help with some translations. Having realized the importance of a second language in business transactions, I have since enrolled on an Advanced Business Conversational French Course in college. As parts of my degree involved computerized systems I was able to use many of the accountancy software packages I encountered during my work experience.

During my time with the accountancy firm, I found I enjoyed providing a useful service. I appreciated the chance to meet new people and quickly learned the importance of appearance and punctuality when dealing with clients. I believe I am fairly adaptable so I welcome the varied challenges that accountancy, as a profession, has to offer. I would, eventually, like to specialize in some aspect of company finance and combine this with the possibility of some travel.

I have travelled in Europe since I was a child. Thus I am aware of the varied cultures and customs to be found. I know France very well having travelled with friends on youth hostelling holidays. Because of my ability with the language I tend to be placed in the role of group leader, something which I enjoy. As social secretary of my hall, and later as the 'organizer' in a house shared by a group of five students, I think I have demonstrated leadership qualities in the widest sense, often listening sensitively to others and putting their needs before mine.

Sport has always played a big part in my life. As a student I have enjoyed the demands of fitness training and the social life to the full. I am captain of the college IIIrd XV and was for two years its treasurer. I have, therefore, experience of leadership on the field and of public speaking off it. I also play golf to a middle handicap and this, perhaps more than rugby, has given me the chance to meet and mix with a variety of people from different backgrounds. Above all, sport has taught me to value my health and I can claim to be very fit.

The college careers service has been invaluable in helping me to choose a suitable career. After a great number of careers interviews, and having read a great deal of literature, I am now confident that I have the qualities and abilities that would suit me for a career in accountancy.

| Student | Signed: | J. Smith | Date: | 7/4/94 |
| Tutor | Signed: | A. Last | Date: | 9/4/94 |

Conclusion

This student was fortunate. He had, because of high quality work experience, discovered fairly early on what he wanted to do. Therefore, his EmPro could be focused without too much trouble and the process made to relate to a particular career.

Most of us are not that lucky. We are not sure, even after consulting the careers service, what we want to do. Sometimes, we do know when there are no jobs available in that particular field. But remember, the EmPro process is relevant to *all* employers and the final profile can be adapted to suit *any* employer.

Remember what EmPro is. It is a short, concise document that contains a brief statement about yourself that is relevant to employers. You can include a table of statements or you can go for the more textual presentation as included in this example. If you are brief you can do both.

It also shows that the final statement was arrived at after discussion and negotiation with your tutor. EmPro is such a slim document you may ask if you really need it – 'Can't I build up an employment profile of my own?' Yes, of course you can. However, you are turning your back on a lot of experience and research. Your attempt has to have credibility and you must have a document to send or take to an interview. It is no good claiming that you have gone through the process of producing a profile and then saying 'but you can't see it, it's all in my head'. A document of some description is essential if you are going to construct an employment profile. I hope you will, and I hope you think it's worth it.

You may be looking at your future career in much the same way as the martians looked at earth: excited, anxious, determined to succeed. However, don't assume success, you have to prepare and work for it. Above all, remember the world that you will enter is very different, but you can prepare for it now. Don't rely on the rocketeers who will blast you into space – they won't be making the journey, you will. How well you do when you land will depend on the preparations you, as an individual, will have made.

Action plan

- Identify likely employment targets based on liaison with your careers service.
- Draw up a provisional list of skills you consider to be relevant and important (see chapter 15 as well as EmPro).
- Contact a personal tutor or lecturer of your choice in order to obtain their ratings of you for the same skills, and negotiate an agreed rating.
- Identify those skills which need to be worked on, and plan activities which will support such development.
- Try to get further feedback about your progress in these selected areas at a later date, and negotiate new ratings.
- Decide on your preferred format for the final profile, be it a written statement or checklist or even a set of graphs and tables – but remember to keep it short.
- Show the draft to your tutor or lecturer, make modifications and draw up the final version.
- Obtain your tutor's signature on the final version, and add your own. Make copies and enclose one with each job application you make. If possible use official headed notepaper or obtain a college 'stamp' for the document.

Crosslink chapters

1 Time Management
5 Live Projects

Further reading

EMPRO. Record of Achievement Office, Resources Centre, Crosskeys College, Risca Road, Gwent.

Francis, D. and Woodcock, M. (1982) *50 Activities for Self Development*. Aldershot: Gower.

Guirdham, M. and Tyler, K. (1992) *Enterprise Skills for Students*. London: Butterworth-Heinemann.

17
Portfolios

Sally Brown and Paddy Maher

A portfolio used to be part of the domain of Art, Design or Architecture students. Over the last few years, however, portfolios have become popular with all kinds of subject areas and courses. The actual container for the contents can be anything from a box file or cardboard folder to a laminated wallet which contains your name, college title and logo. In this chapter, Sally Brown and Paddy Maher outline the very varied contents for a portfolio, and explain the clear advantages when you take a portfolio with you to a job interview. Additional benefits appear when you want to present a portfolio of evidence to lecturers or tutors showing that you already have enough experience to gain additional course credits without having to study further!

Assessment by portfolio?

Students on all kinds of courses in increasing numbers are being asked to present portfolios of their work for assessment. A portfolio is a portable collection of items which will allow you to use a wider range of media than is normally permitted for assessment. These may include:

- documents of all kinds;
- video and audio tapes;
- visual display/exhibition material such as charts, posters, plans, flow charts, drawings, diagrams;
- computer discs/programs including spreadsheets and databases.

You will need to show judgement and common sense in putting together a portfolio, so that it is in a form manageable for you and for the assessors. Some students will find that the format is stipulated; for example, a box file or portfolio case; others will be given a greater degree of flexibility. Do, however, ensure that it can be carried readily, is ordered systematically and can be handled by the assessors with relative ease.

Why use portfolios?

They are a valuable method because they:

- let you as students show more of yourselves and demonstrate your individuality;
- allow for assessment of experience gained in non-traditional learning environments; for example, before you became a student or in your life outside your studies;
- allow for a variety of means of self expression, letting you set the agenda to a greater extent than, for example, in examinations;
- give you greater control of the assessment media;
- enable you to demonstrate flexibility and coherence in a compact format, with you setting the limits rather than anyone else.

Outside the course, you can use a portfolio for the secondary purpose of selection and recruitment. In completing application forms and compiling a curriculum vitae (see chapter 20) your portfolio will be a valuable resource in helping you to give a brief account of your achievements and experience and to draw out the particular strengths you can offer an employer. A portfolio that demonstrates your skills, knowledge and abilities assembled over a period of time will be invaluable to you at interviews, because it will let you demonstrate the qualities that you know are your best, rather than leaving you in the passive role of most interviewees, who just respond to questions. Many employers are also keen to introduce port-folios as part of the appraisal scheme for their employees, who can use them as evidence for promotion and career progres-sion, or as a means of reflecting on their own development needs.

They are also very widely used in the *Accreditation of Prior Learning* (APL), that is to allow students to get credit for experience and knowledge gained outside formal study, and entry to higher education can often be claimed this way rather than through 'A' levels or BTEC qualifications.

Accreditation of prior learning

The way in which APL operates will depend on the particular institution or professional body which is prepared to give credit for prior learning. If you are considering the APL route, you should find out exactly what would be required of you and in particular the format of the portfolio, the forms of evidence that would be acceptable and whether any personal guidance is available. In general, the APL process requires you to:

- review in a systematic way, your past and present experiences which have led to learning relevant to your current requirements;
- identify what you have learned from your experiences and the evidence for this learning;
- match your relevant learning to the requirements of the institution or professional body;
- compile a portfolio which clearly states the learning you are claiming and provides appropriate evidence for it.

APL is not an easy route to credit but the learning you are claiming and self assessment inherent in the APL process can be very valuable in terms of your own personal development.

What should they contain?

Portfolios may contain a range of materials including, for example:

- Documents from the student's workbooks/learning contracts, including log books, self profiles, individual targets, action plans and evaluation sheets, records of achievement, statements of competence.
- Tutor comments and feedback.
- Comments from your industrial supervisor if appropriate.
- Peer assessment documents.
- A *selection* of coursework from the taught components of your course (if you include everything, this will be bulky and tedious for the assessors). Examples might be reports, essays, specifications, instructions, correspondence, press releases, minutes of meetings, notebooks and financial statements.
- Examples of the actual products you have created on work-placement or in employment which demonstrate what you have learned and how you have progressed during the course.

This is supposed to be a menu rather than a checklist! You could not possibly expect to include all or even most of these things. You will need to discuss what you put into the portfolio with your tutor so you can demonstrate *variety* of achievement, *excellence* of what you have achieved and *progression*. You will have to take into account who your audience is, and this will tend to determine the kind of language and style you use. Your aim will be to assemble a balanced portfolio which will contain materials that show you and your work to the best effect.

Presentation is an important feature of portfolios, and you may find it expensive to produce good quality documentation and visual material. This has been a problem for many years for Art and Design students, with the less well off feeling disadvantaged if they can't afford, for example, top quality materials and glossy photographs. Colleges and institutions of higher education are aware of this problem, and you may find that there is some financial support available for you. If there is not, the assessment process will need to be devised to take this into account. You will need to be resourceful and creative in your presentation of material to the best of your abilities.

Portfolios often have multiple uses; they are often used to enable your institution to find out how you are doing on placement if you are on a sandwich course, or in employment if you are a part-time student.

How can portfolios be used to demonstrate learning in the workplace?

Portfolios can achieve this by:

- providing evidence of what you can achieve away from your institution, particularly in the application of what you have learned in the classroom;
- showing you have done what you said you would do in a learning contract (see chapter 6);
- offering you an opportunity to show that you have developed and progressed throughout your course.

In this context, they are valuable to:

- you, so that you can provide evidence of your competences and achievements;
- your tutors, so they can assess you on what you are doing away from the normal study;
- your industrial supervisor (where relevant), so they can see how you have progressed and done useful work for the company.

How can portfolios be used?

You can develop your own abilities for self evaluation through portfolios; it is a valuable skill in the lifelong learning process to be able to assess accurately how well you are doing. This is also a quality much prized by employers.

A good starting point is to complete a self-profile with guidance from your tutor, showing your abilities and achievements early on in a programme of learning. It might also be valuable to get colleagues and friends to help you to arrive at a realistic view of what you know and can do.

Next you can produce an audit of your own abilities in a range of areas, listing your competences, alone or with guidance (see also chapter 15 on personal transferable skills). This is most useful if you are able to systematically *define* the knowledge and skill you have and to give a reasonable estimate of the *level* of your competence.

Following this, it is valuable to set yourself quite specific goals and action plans in negotiation with your tutor and, possibly, industrial supervisor; perhaps using some kind of learning contract which sets out what is expected of all parties to the agreement. Having done that, it will be possible for you to evaluate your achievements at key stages and then modify your targets accordingly and as appropriate.

The portfolio should also include a self-evaluative and critical preview of your own portfolio. This will be more than just a detailed contents list; it should give the assessors insights into the processes you have gone through over a period of time to assemble the portfolio and also about your own feelings and reactions.

You may be aware that all kinds of agencies, including schools, colleges, BTEC, NCVQ and City and Guilds and the Open University are keen for students to be able to produce personal competence statements, which may be free standing (with material in the portfolio to be used as evidence of competence) or externally moderated. Briefly stated, competence statements are simple but detailed statements about what you can *do* as opposed to vague references to 'knowing' or 'understanding' theories in methodology. Some institutions will help you develop these as part of your coursework, others will leave the initiative up to you. The Open University has developed an accredited Personal and Careers Development Portfolio pack, which will enable you to do this for yourself.

A distance-learning portfolio

The Open University is particularly aimed at adult learners in any subject area who want to improve their career prospects and enhance their personal development. The pack guides learners through the process of self assessment, action planning, skills development and reflection to:

- recognize and value past and present achievements;
- clarify personal and career goals;
- assess strengths and weaknesses;
- produce individual development plans;
- develop and demonstrate relevant transferable skills of communication, problem solving and personal effectiveness;
- reflect on performance.

The pack can be built into a personal portfolio for use and reuse in planning for personal and career development and as a resource for assessment. Assessment is optional and focuses on activities in the pack and on the learning and reflection demonstrated in work-based projects.

Conclusions

Portfolios are not a new method of assessment, but their wider application to all kinds of courses beyond Art and Design is novel. If you are given the chance to be assessed for all or part of your course by portfolio, you should make the most of the opportunity and use it to demonstrate the breadth and extent of your abilities. Remember that it is not a static end product of a one-off experience; rather it is a dynamic means by which you can demonstrate your competences, updating it and changing it for different purposes after the formal assessment procedure is finished.

Action plan

- Collect together a range of coursework from a variety of modules, levels or years of study. Include any posters, slides, video/audio tapes and software you may have helped to produce.
- Select what you consider to be the best 'pieces of evidence' – if possible, ask your tutor or lecturer to help you. Ensure your selection shows off a range of skills and achievements.
- Photocopy positive written feedback from people who have marked your work, and compile a condensed document entitled 'Feedback from lecturers/employers'.
- Draw up a profile – if you have done reasonably well in your studies, give a table or matrix of coursework and exam grades or percentages.
- Compile an index for the contents, and if possible get some lecturers or tutors to give an 'open reference', which is signed by them verifying the authenticity of the content.
- Select an appropriate container for the contents and make the cover as professional looking as possible; you can ask your college for help or sponsorship here, as your portfolio can be an excellent advertisement for them as well as you.

Crosslink chapters

Further reading

Maher, P. and Harrison, R. (1991) *The Personal and Career Development Portfolio Package*. Milton Keynes: The Open University.
Tallantyre, F. (1987) *The Assessment of Prior Learning from Experience*. University of Northumbria at Newcastle Enterprise Unit.

18

The Placement Experience

Jen Harvey and Fiona Campbell

When it comes to getting employment after leaving college, work placement can be a deciding factor. It can establish excellent contacts, provide a wealth of experience for inclusion in profiles, portfolios and references, and it helps you decide what kinds of things you are good at doing and – more importantly – what you enjoy doing. The problem is that courses and colleges vary greatly in what they expect of their placement students. Jen Harvey and Fiona Campbell provide close guidelines on finding your own placement to returning to college. Case studies illustrate a range of students' placement experiences.

Placements provide students with the opportunity to gain supervised work experience as part of their degree or diploma course. Work experience usually forms part of a designated sandwich course but can involve a short period (or several periods) within a standard course.

Initially, a placement might seem daunting, particularly if you have never worked before. However, there are many advantages to be gained by going on work experience. You can, for example:

- see how the theory from your course relates (and fails to relate?) to practice;
- experience industrial and professional situations;
- develop personal skills through working with others;
- obtain 'hands on' technical expertise not possible in college.

Perhaps more importantly, you can improve your future employment prospects. These benefits are not just one sided:

employers gain valuable training experience and your college gains by establishing links with Industry. This can then feed back into the development of courses, making them better equipped to prepare students for employment.

Placements are organized in a number of ways depending on your particular college or course. For example, you might be assessed on how you obtain and plan your placement with the drawing up of a learning contract included as part of the exercise. Alternatively, your college might do most of the organization for you and set up interviews and training schedules. Whatever role you take in these arrangements, ultimately it will be up to *you* to get what you want from the 'workplace experience'.

Before the placement: getting started

Dear Becky,

Remember last year, when you said that you would help me find a placement when I reached that part of the course?

Well, I need help now! I have to organize my placement before the end of term – the exams start in two weeks – and I have to get something good. Where do I start? Help !!!

Craig
(Sorry I've not written before)

When should I start looking?

Finding a placement need not be a traumatic event – however, it is easier if you leave plenty of time to look around! After all, you want one that suits your individual needs. Students sometimes complain that they started looking for a placement too late and as a result were left with very little choice of employer. It is best to start hunting as soon as your college advises you to, even though your placement seems months away.

Where do I start?

A good place to start is to think about the *kind* of job you might like when you graduate. At this stage, you need only a rough idea.

Make a list

A list of the type of jobs or further training you *could* apply for is helpful, and from there you can begin to eliminate what does and doesn't interest you (try your students careers office or library for this.) Remember, one of the reasons for going on placement is to improve your future employment prospects so it's a good idea to try and plan towards an area which you like.

What next!

Once you have a rough idea of the type of work, the next step is to try and find a suitable employer to take you on. Colleges will often offer potential placements on course notice boards and will sometimes organize 'milk round' interviews for particular courses.

Something different?

If you want to try something a bit different, perhaps in another town, then it will probably be up to you to do the groundwork.

Try Exercise 1 for some assistance in making up your mind about the kind of placement that would suit you.

EXERCISE 1

What kind of placement would suit me?

1 Which parts of your course do you **like** and which do you **dislike** e.g. subject areas, types of classes, study methods etc?

LIKE   DISLIKE

2 Go through a list of last year's placements (this should be available from your tutor) and pick out one which you think looks interesting, bearing in mind your profile above. Write down a brief description of the responsibilities you imagine the job involves.

3 Go through your job description ticking and crossing out the parts which you think you **would** and **would not** enjoy. This should make you think more about the kind of job which would suit you. How many other jobs would offer work of a similar nature?

Once you have a rough idea of the kind of placement you would like, it should be easier for the library and the careers service to help you find potential employers.

Before the placement: preparing yourself

Dear Becky,

I just thought I'd write to thank you for all your help – I'd <u>never</u> have thought about asking the library and careers officer about getting a placement. They were able to give me a list of employers and descriptions of their research interests.

There's one I really like the sound of and, as you also suggested, I spoke to some of the final year students and found somebody who had worked there before AND thought it was brilliant – so fingers crossed. I just have to get in touch with the employer now but I'm not sure what to write – I don't suppose you could give me some advice?

Craig
(How's <u>your</u> new job going?)

Approaching an employer

You will probably have to make some speculative approaches to prospective employers if you are looking for a specific placement. This first approach is very important and can determine whether or not you are taken on. Try to find out as much as you can about the employer before you start to write a letter. This will not only help plan your letter but demonstrate your interest in them, when you make contact.

Market yourself!

Once you have obtained a list of possible placements or even one you think looks interesting, then it is time to market yourself. Consider the placement from the employer's perspective and try to think about what they would be looking for from an employee.

Your strengths

Try to match your strengths with your potential employer's requirements – a brief job description would help. Remember, they don't want to know what you *can't* do or *don't* like – so always be positive!

Other aspects to consider

Although training is usually the most important aspect of the placement, some students are interested only in the personal development gained through the experience of working. If this is you, *think* – before you jump at the first job available, try to find out more about it. Factors such as isolation, poor wages, long travelling times and lack of transport can dramatically affect your situation once you are on placement, so check these out before formally applying.

For help with your speculative letter try Exercise 2.

Once you have organized a placement

It is always a good idea to check up on some other aspects of the job before you leave. For example, do you need to take any special clothing, how much money will you need to last until pay day, would you be better to organize your own accommodation, do you need to provide your own transport? You don't want to have to spend your first few days rushing around shopping and the rest of the time worrying about whether or not you will have enough money to last until pay day!

EXERCISE 2

What are you looking for from a placement?

1 Start by making a list of the objectives you hope to fulfil by
going on placement, e.g. type of training, experience, etc.
Prioritize these objectives by writing them in descending
order to demonstrate their importance to you.

2 What can you offer to a potential employer? Try to match this
with what you see as their requirements. Make a list of the
strengths which you have and prioritize their importance.

3 Using the results generated by (1) and (2), construct a letter
to an employer offering a student placement. The letter
should communicate what you seek in a placement and
emphasize the experience, skills and qualities which you
could bring to such a position.

During your placement

Dear Becky,

I've now started working on the placement thanks to your advice about preparing for the interview. When I got there I found that none of the other students had even bothered to find out anything about the company and one had turned up looking like a real scruff. That made all the difference – I felt really confident when I went into the interview room and I think it must have showed because they phoned me up later to offer me the placement. I wish they hadn't though – you have no idea how boring it is – I'm getting no training and if I have to make another cup of tea I'll scream!!!

Craig
(Sorry to hear about you losing your job)

Going to work!

If you have never worked before, you might find that the placement is not quite as you expected. Naturally, everyone is apprehensive before they start – an unfamiliar environment, strange people and even new accommodation can be intimidating. However, many students find that their placement is a successful and rewarding experience. Although you might feel personally challenged to cope within a working environment, remember that you will be developing many skills which will equip you for later employment – even if it doesn't quite seem like it at the time!

Training

Your training will probably be discussed during your interview and that is the time to either back out if you are unhappy or to try and compromise and obtain something more suitable. Don't let yourself be bulldozed into anything you don't want or you will probably regret it later.

A plan

If you did not formally agree on a learning contract with your employer it is a good idea to draft a brief training schedule. Try going back to your list of objectives (Exercise 2) if you are stuck. Arrange a meeting with your workplace supervisor, either before you start or on your first day and discuss your objectives. Although you might not like the idea of making an approach, be assured it will save any misunderstandings later.

Once you have agreed and drafted a rough training schedule it is a good idea to keep a record of what you *have achieved* and *hope to achieve* as your placement progresses. For some ideas as how to go about this try Exercise 3.

What happens if I have a problem?

Sometimes problems can arise during placement. These can vary from the work being boring and repetitive to you being asked to do unreasonable tasks or to personality clashes between you and your workmates. It will be up to you to decide what is appropriate action, if any, for the circumstances. *What are your options?*

Not do anything?

This will depend on the severity of the problem. Some students not receiving adequate training, for example, will just try to weather it out and work towards a good reference. However, you must do something if there is ever any risk to your personal safety – TAKE IMMEDIATE ACTION.

Wait for my placement officer?

This is an option if you can depend on an early visit or your problem is a minor one. Waiting, however, can make you feel

EXERCISE 3
What am I doing? Where am I going?

Training plan

Having discussed your schedule with your workplace supervisor make a list of the objectives or skills you would most like to advance.

My priorities are:

1
2
3
4
5

A diary is a useful method of recording your progress and development through your placement. Are you achieving your objectives? Is your progress to target? This record does not have to be very detailed but should contain sufficient information to act as a memory jog when writing your report or applying for a job.

An idea for a diary layout

WEEK 6   Planned work
Completed work Monday Tuesday Wednesday Thursday Friday
Uncompleted work
WEEK 7   Planned work

very isolated and powerless, particularly if you are facing a worsening problem of harassment or unreasonable working conditions. In addition, you might also find that in the end 'the visit' is only a quick phone call or a few minutes along with your workplace supervisor. If things *are* bad, phone to try to speed up a visit, explaining that you have an urgent problem.

Contact my placement officer?

This is the best idea if your problem is severe – don't do something drastic like walk out of the job. Remember, your placement officer is there to help you. Getting in touch with them might not prove so easy during the summer months as they are likely to be away on other visits or on a holiday, so try and arrange some means of contacting them before you leave on placement.

Approach my workplace supervisor?

If you agreed on a training schedule and discussed a job description before you started, it should be easier to make an approach if the working conditions are not fulfilled later on. You might find, however, that your supervisor becomes rather evasive when it comes to problems, so it will be up to you to persevere if you want to take action. After all, they won't realize there is a problem unless you tell them!

Personal problems You can't expect to get on well with everyone and like any working situation you will have to cope with this. If problems arise with your supervisor try and make an extra effort to sort things out – you want a good reference!

Health and safety Do not under any circumstances undertake anything which is dangerous or hazardous to your health. If you are in doubt check up first!

Overworked/underpaid! You are not there as slave labour, so don't be pushed into longer hours than other employees, particularly if you don't get paid extra. Negotiate your wages beforehand and find out about any extra costs like travelling expenses which you might have to pay in advance.

After the placement

Dear Becky,

Thanks for the advice, I did as you suggested and dropped a note to my workplace supervisor. We then met and discussed a more suitable training schedule which would tie in with what I was wanting to do when I graduate.

From then on, everything changed and the training worked really well and you'll never guess what! He called me into the office at the end of the placement and offered me a job when my course finishes.

Craig
(Well you can't say I haven't been writing to you now!)

Once you finish

After you complete your placement, you will probably be required to write a report or complete an assessment form. This might be added to your workplace supervisor's report. The format of these and the overall assessment varies considerably between courses and colleges depending on the emphasis put on the workplace experience. Some colleges might assess your placement on a pass or fail, while others will allocate marks for different components.

Quantity or quality?

Placements are notoriously difficult to assess because of differences in the quantity or quality of the work undertaken. Some students will seem to have an easier time: finding work with an established firm and going on to a formalized training or research programme. Others seem to have an endless struggle with all sorts of problems and, in the end, little to show for their time of employment.

Is that fair?

The only consolation for this discrepancy in challenge is that for what the seemingly more fortunate gains in the product of their work, the seemingly less fortunate can gain in personal development skills. If this still does not seem fair to you make sure you start looking for your placement early and you can decide what *you* want to get from your placement.

What next?

Once you have returned to college, it is always a good idea to reflect on what you have gained from working. You might have discovered, for example, what kind of work suited or didn't suit you, or how you could negotiate with management, or how you could successfully fend for yourself in a difficult situation. Whatever, in your 'workplace experience' you will have gained valuable skills which should prepare you for future employment and set you apart from those who haven't worked before.

To focus on the more positive aspects of your placement work through Exercise 4.

Case studies

How to use these case studies

Firstly, read through the case study and consider what action you would take under the given circumstances. The problems outlined might be experienced by any student going on placement. Now consider how you would react if you found

EXERCISE 4

What did I gain from my placement?

Reflecting on your placement and the skills you have gained
is an important part of your workplace experience. Work your
way through the following questions, thinking carefully about
the answers.

What was the most important thing that you learned while
on your placement?

What personal skills do you feel you have gained from the
workplace experience?

If you had to give a student advice on looking for
placements, what would it be?

yourself in such a situation. Is there any difference in the answers?

There are no right and wrong answers, but some general comments are included at the end of the section.

Case study 1: Faculty of Professional Studies
Mary is a business studies student and wants eventually to go into personnel management. She always works hard and spent a long time looking for her placement as she knows exactly what she wants out of her work experience.

Once on her placement she finds that there is a bad personality clash between her and her immediate supervisor from whom she would be expecting to get a reference. **What would you advise her to do?**

Case study 2: Faculty of Science
James is a computing student. He enjoys working with computers and hopes to go out into Industry and work as a computer programmer when he graduates.

The placement he is offered is based a long way from home. He has no accommodation organized and knows nobody there. Travelling to and from home would be difficult and expensive and his main concern is how he will cope with being in a strange place and being away from home for the first time. **What would you advise him to do?**

Case study 3: Faculty of Humanities
George is a catering student and hopes to go into Hotel Management when he graduates. He has always looked for hotel work during his holidays and has undertaken a wide range of general hotel duties. For his degree placement he has

arranged to work in one of the city's largest hotels and is hoping that he will get some junior management experience during this time.

However, when he starts his placement he finds, yet again, that he is only expected to do basic hotel duties. When he approaches his workplace supervisor he is told that he is only an unqualified student and is therefore not able to take any more responsibility and that, besides, there is nobody available at junior management level to supervise or train him. **What would you advise him to do?**

Case study 4: Faculty of Technology
Lucy is studying for a degree in Building and having completed the first two weeks of her course has arranged for her one year work experience to be with a well known building company in her town.

Once she starts working with the building company, Lucy finds that the range of jobs which she is given is rather restricted, with the emphasis on general office work rather than the more practical site experience for which she had hoped. In addition, she finds that she is able to finish her delegated work by lunchtime, which leaves her nothing to do in the afternoon.

When she approaches her workplace supervisor she is told that she should try and spread the work out over the day as there is no rush to complete it. He also says that she should be glad she is in the office with the other women and does not have to go out onto the site with all the 'rough' men. **What would you advise her to do?**

Case study 5: Faculty of Business
Peter is training for a degree in Commerce and had a very useful and enjoyable placement in the company secretary's office of a large brewery. At the end of his placement he was offered a permanent post in the company, but he has been asked to start immediately, which would not allow him to complete the remaining year of the course and obtain a degree. **What would you advise him to do?**

Case study 6: Faculty of Science
Michael is a biology student and has taken a placement which involves testing biological samples. However, he discovers that he is required, after some initial training, to travel about town doing these tests for clients of the company.

He expected to be based in a lab and is worried that he won't have enough money to cover his travelling expenses. In addition, he is expected to carry out far more tests than he feels he can manage because of his travelling time. When he approaches his supervisor he is told that it is not company practice to hand out expenses in advance, and that if he doesn't complete his allocated daily work he will be sacked and replaced by someone who will. **What would you advise him to do?**

Responses

These notes are only comments on the students' problems. There are no right or wrong answers.

Case 1

It is a good idea to know what you want from a placement and to plan accordingly. But future work in this line is likely to involve elements of personnel management, so it is important that the situation is resolved satisfactorily. If there is no luck, she could ask for a move if a good reference is a priority, but it is probably best to try and resolve the situation – is some of the fault on her side?

Case 2

He could try to find accommodation which would give him the opportunity to make friends (in a flat or hall, for example). He could advertise in the local paper to share with someone with similar interests and find out from the library if there are any local groups with similar interests. He could find out about travel allowances and arrangements for flexitime to allow him to travel back at a weekend, i.e. have Friday afternoon off. He should encourage his friends and family to visit him while he is there.

Case 3

He should have tried to confirm a training schedule before starting placement. He could speak to the workplace supervisor again, perhaps asking for a transfer to a more suitable area where someone could train him – is there another hotel in the chain which could offer more suitable training? He could also try the approach that he has up-to-date knowledge which would be of benefit to them.

Case 4

She should have checked what the training schedule was before starting. In larger established firms training can sometimes be restricted, whereas a smaller firm can offer a wider range of duties. If the attitude of the workplace supervisor is sexist (from the start she should try to make clear that she wants her training to include 'man's work') she could ask her placement officer to have a word. She could possibly try to offer to help the other office workers for extra work, suggest going 'on site' on a trial basis to see how it goes and she can still ask to see what others are doing and ask them about their work. If all else fails she should try to get another placement before it is too late.

Case 5

He should consider this situation very carefully – it could be a good opportunity or it could result in limited career potential. If he wants the post and to complete the course he should seek possible compromise situations, for example by delaying start date until the end of the course. Does he need to start immediately? Are there alternative methods of gaining the qualification e.g. day release, distance learning? Would his new employer support his attendance – could he obtain advance standing for the part of the course completed? Does he have the motivation to complete the course? He should try to weigh up the pros and cons of his individual circumstances.

Case 6

He should have tried to find out more about the placement before starting, making it easier to negotiate later – he would then have found out about travelling expenses and arranged to have enough money with him. He could find out about cost cutting methods of travelling; for example, bike, bus cards. Are all employees required to undertake similar workloads? If not, he could approach his supervisor, putting forward the case of what was physically possible. When threatened with the sack he should immediately get in touch with his placement officer emphasizing the urgency of the situation and asking for an immediate visit. He shouldn't have allowed the problem to reach this stage without contacting the officer before – if no resolution is possible then he should try to negotiate another placement and warn the college about future placements there.

Action plan

An *applied* course	An applied course containing a work experience element should improve your future job prospects.
What placement?	When you are looking for a placement try to select one which will relate to your future employment and contains the types of work which you enjoy.
Making an approach	Try to find out about a potential employer before making an approach. Make sure you show interest in the work during speculative approaches and at interview.
Before you go	Confirm your training schedule and any necessary equipment or arrangements you might have to make prior to leaving.
During your placement	It's up to you to get what you want from the placement – learn by keeping your eyes and ears open to everything going on.
Problems?!?	If a problem arises it will be up to you to decide whether to take action – speak to someone if a problem is getting worse.
Wot no problems?	Most people don't have problems when they go on placement, so don't worry! Just be aware of what your options are should a problem arise.
'An experience'	Most students find that after initial panic their placement gives them an opportunity to learn, not only about work, but about themselves, and that this can be a positive and rewarding experience.

Crosslink chapters

5 Live Projects
8 Working in Teams and Syndicates
15 Personal Transferable Skills
16 Employment Profiles
19 Investigating Careers
20 Applying for a Job

Further reading

Campbell, F. and Harvey, J. (1992) *The Workplace Experience*. (A user guide with video) Edinburgh: Available from Napier University.

19

Investigating Careers

Jim McNally

Here we emphasize the value of researching into various career paths and opportunities at an early stage in your studies: too often careers advisers and actual employers meet final-year students who show naivety and a lack of understanding when it comes to decisions which potentially affect the rest of their lives. Jim McNally reminds you that your chosen subject at college can be fed into a wide variety of jobs, and gives advice about what to do and who to contact when exploring possible career openings. Especially useful is the insider's guide to the 'milk round', along with six categories of experience and ability which employers often look for when looking through applications from students.

This chapter will address five main questions:

1 When should students start to *think* about careers?
2 Why should students investigate careers?
3 How should this investigation be done?
4 What help is available?
5 When should students actually do something about investigating careers?

When should you start to think about careers?

Now, if you are not already doing so.

Why should you investigate careers?

Put simply, you should investigate careers now to allow you to plan:

- your courses of study, with some vocational criteria in mind;
- modes of study; for example, sandwich courses;
- the pursuit of work-related options;
- significant extra-curricular activities.

Students' responses to vocational courses

If you do not think about careers until approaching the end of your studies you will not be able to plan *additional personal development* while you are a student. Many students think they have chosen their career by following an obviously vocational course such as medicine, dentistry or divinity. The statistics in tables 1, 2 and 3 will be enlightening.

Table 1 Graduate first destinations: known first destinations of 1988 graduates in full-time employment – type of work (%)

	Chemistry		Physics	
	University	Poly-technic*	University	Poly-technic*
Science and Technology	54.5	72.1	65.1	76.1
Finance**	24.3	6.0	17.9	3.6
Uncertain***	21.3	21.9	17.0	20.3

  * From 1991 polytechnics became universities.
 ** Includes accounting, banking, insurance, capital markets.
*** Includes *inter alia* sales, marketing, buying.

Source: Association of Graduate Careers Advisory Services (AGCAS), *What do graduates do?* 1990

Table 2 Graduate vacancies

Year	'Any discipline'	Total	% any discipline
1980	2,431	7,731	31.4
1990	6,568	12,324	53.3

Source: Central Services Unit, *Current Vacancies*

Table 3 Final year students on subject choice

Satisfied with subject studied	20%
Dissatisfied with subject studied	80%

Source: *Independent* 13 June 1991

What can you learn from the above? Perhaps that:

- ultimate choice of discipline is often regretted, and hence unlikely to be the basis of a connected career choice;
- the subject of your degree, diploma or certificate is of diminishing significance by the time you apply for a job and look for a possible career;
- increasingly, recruiters are looking for something other than discipline-specific expertise.

What exactly are recruiters seeking in graduates? (This might prompt ideas for a project or dissertation.) What should you *do* in response to the above points? Perhaps:

- be assured that if your discipline is of decreasing attraction to you it will still be possible to seek a career in the 'any discipline' category;
- seek to develop the *knowledge, skills* and *perspectives* which recruiters seek from those who pass the hurdle of gaining a degree;
- sample as many disciplines and career options as your *studies, extra-curricular activities* and *work experience* permit.

Personal development

Very few graduates of, say, history or engineering will be recruited only for their expertise in those disciplines. Tables 4, 5 and 6 indicate:

- what organizations seek when they advertise vacancies for graduates;
- what graduates see as less fully developed in higher education;
- what additional skills engineers use in the workplace.

In sum, you should investigate careers in order to gain insight into the personal development you can seek above and beyond your discipline-specific expertise, and plan and act accordingly.

Table 4 Characteristics significant to recruiters

1	Oral communication
2	Teamwork
3	Enthusiasm
4	Motivation
5	Initiative
6	Leadership
7	Commitment
8	Interpersonal
9	Organizing
10	Foreign language competence
11	Energetic
12	Innovative
13	Ambitious
14	Managing
15	Drive
16	Dynamic
17	Determination

Source: Personal Skills Unit, Sheffield University, 1991

Table 5   University development of skills/capabilities: chemistry students' perceptions

	Satisfied (%)	Dissatisfied (%)
Computer proficiency	51	49
Negotiating skills	21	79
Communication	56	43
Objectives setting	43	57
Teamwork/management	56	42
Problem solving	63	37
Generation of novel ideas/ ability to direct project	67	33
Literature searching	26	74
Assessing hazards at work	78	22

Source: Imrie, B. W., McNally, J., Webb, G., Baird, T., Brown, W. A. C. (1991) *Proceedings of 17th International Conference of Improving University Teaching*. University of Maryland.

Table 6   Engineers at study and at work

	Work	Education
Time spent on ICs	20%	80%+
Time spent on INGs	80%	0%

ICs = physics, mathematics, electronics, etc.
INGs = communicating, persuading, managing, proposing, etc.

Source: Harrisberger, L. in S. Goodlad (ed.) (1984) *Education for the Professions: Quis custodiet . . .* Guildford: SRHE and NFER-Nelson.

How should you investigate careers?

Important options which can help you investigate careers are work placements and work-based projects, now arranged on many courses (see chapters 5 and 13). You should plan to gain at least the following benefits from such options.

1 That experience, usually undefined, which is sought by recruiters and which you should seek to define for inclusion in, for example, your application form or curriculum vitae. You might gain experience of the organization's ethos and conventions which will be reflected in modes of recruitment, interview technique, management style.

More specifically, you should seek to acquire knowledge, skills and perspectives in your time in an organization. For example, what techniques/principles are staff expected to know and apply to ensure that customers are satisfied; what particular skills, intellectual and technical, are required for effective and efficient operation; and what perspectives must be considered when a decision is made.

2 If you are innovative and enterprising on a project you may gain acclaim from the organization. Projects can be devised to be of practical benefit to an organization which has a problem, a decision to make or a conflict to resolve. Use contacts in the organization and in education for support.

> The recommendations made by the students in their report have in part been implemented and others are being considered. (John Milligan of Scottish Power on the outcomes of a workplace project undertaken by Medieval History students at the University of Glasgow.)

Offers of jobs, testimonials and references follow on for students who make such an impact.

3 Anticipating the question of when to investigate careers, the sooner you gain access to a workplace the more experience you can gain. If your work is clearly beneficial you can easily use the evidence to gain repeat projects in the same or other organizations. A 'portfolio of achievement' (see chapter 17) is worth displaying as tangible evidence of your success.

4 Opportunities may exist to publish you work in, for example, in-house journals, student newspapers, your college's newsletter.

5   You should seek to gain knowledge of state-of-the-art technology along with additional features of software and equipment; and to take opportunities to extend your skills through the use of the technology. If open learning training packages are available, request access and use in any free time you have.

6   The contacts you make can begin a network which gives access to job market intelligence, introductions, references. Staff involved in recruitment take it as axiomatic that 75 per cent of jobs are filled without being formally advertised. Look for examples of alternative means of filling, and creating, jobs in any organization you work in.

What help can you get for this investigation?

1   Your careers service should be your first source of support. It may provide a register of holiday jobs for which you can apply.

2   Academic staff will have industrial and commercial contacts gained through research, consultancy or previous employment. If you have a subject-based research project to undertake it might be possible to give your approach a work-based perspective. For example, a case study of local individuals or organizations will allow you to compare and contrast your findings with national, or other regional, results.

3   Many central bodies have an educational interest. Understanding British Industry has a scheme which arranges placements. Enterprise initiatives (for example, Training and Enterprise Companies and Local Enterprise Companies) in many areas have a directory of local firms which can provide contact names.

4   Libraries have directories which give details of awards and grants available to students in higher education, for example, the Scottish Tourist Board (STB) and the

Committee for the Public Understanding of Science. Joyce Powers, a student at Glasgow University, gained one of the first STB research awards and states that she has 'gained immeasurably from the experience of taking a project from concept to completion.'

5 If your careers service does not offer any support to students seeking workplace experience (paid or unpaid) why not offer to undertake a feasibility study to consider its worth?

6 Other chapters of this book should be used to support your investigations. For example, make sure you heed the advice on presentations given in chapter 12 and on producing a curriculum vitae in chapter 20.

Information on course design

Another aspect of your education worth considering is the approach to teaching and learning offered in courses and modules. For example, an unremitting diet of lectures will require little more than passive absorption of off-the-peg wisdom. Assessment by terminal essay will require little beyond restatement of this wisdom; bespoke at best but often restatement will suffice.

Alternative teaching, learning and assessment methods which promote thinking and doing are on offer, for example:

- *Project-based learning.* You might be operating 'ventures' such as a student newspaper or undertaking work-based activities. These can yield tangible examples of your attainments for your portfolio.
- *Dissertations.* Here search and research is required and allows you to develop your information and communication skills.
- *Case studies.* Here roles are to be played, decisions made and problems solved giving you an introduction to those high-level skills which managers are expected to deploy.
- *Workshops and seminars.* Here skills in oral communication, teamwork and leadership can be developed.

- *Negotiated learning.* This approach offers students the chance to show imagination in deciding the perspectives to be adopted and the issues to be pursued.
- *Peer group learning and assessment.* These can accompany projects and devolve additional responsibilities on to the student group.
- *Computer supported learning.* Increasing opportunities are available for such learning which allows self-paced learning and assessment.

When should you do something about investigating careers?

Now.

PS: an insider's guide to the milk round

Possibly the most formal method of recruiting graduates is the so-called milk round. A recruitment consultant who previously recruited in this way for ICI recently visited Glasgow University to give an insider's view of the milk round. In particular she explained:

- how large companies like ICI approach recruitment of graduates and post graduates;
- what students should do to increase their chances of success.

She gave a very lucid and comprehensive explanation of ICI's methods of selecting for first interview. The application form is scored on a points system with a maximum of 36 points possible. There are six categories, each with a possible six points, and these are:

1   Academic achievements at school/college
2   Academic achievements in higher education
3   Work experience

4 Leisure pursuits
5 Style
6 Content

Academic achievements should list awards gained, year obtained, and include grades known and anticipated.

Within each further category crucial tests must be passed. For example, work experience is judged as to its relevance to study. A chemistry student who obtains unpaid work in an environmental health unit laboratory will score more than a student working in a pub. (If, however, you used your chemistry expertise to improve hygiene following an outbreak of dysentery this should be explained!)

The university student who lists enjoyment of reading as a leisure pursuit is advised that this is likely to annoy the recruiter: it is axiomatic that students enjoy reading. Representing the university in a sport or intellectual pursuit will score more highly, particularly if a position of leadership or responsibility was held.

Style is concerned with the legibility, readability, grammar and spelling in the application form. 'Whiting out' and spelling mistakes are common causes of low scores here. A crucial point is that the recruiters for first interview will probably not be specialists in the applicants' discipline. Thus the content must be written to be understood by, and make an impact on, a 'lay' recruiter. Success at first interview will lead to a second interview by a specialist panel where the advice is 'be yourself': the interviewers are experts at finding out what they want to know about applicants.

In order to get a first interview a score of about 28 is needed. Those students who have no workplace employment for project experience require to score 28 out of 30, which is thought very unlikely. The earlier you plan to obtain workplace experience the better!

A further benefit of undertaking a workplace project is that you can aim to secure tangible evidence of your efforts, in completed work, designs or reports, for example, and which are supported by employer testimonials and references. Stress is placed on the importance of giving evidence in support of an application, which can be displayed as part of your portfolio of achievement, which will also include your certificates and diplomas.

Action plan

- List the types of employment you might be interested in and, if possible, the skills you already have (especially useful if you are involved in a profiling exercise).
- Now go to your careers service and ask for a preliminary interview and aptitude test. You can also go to other careers advisers (for example, attached to local educational authorities, or your old school or college) or use/develop contacts with employers themselves.
- Obtain literature about specific careers/organizations and try to get some vocation or part-time employment in order to gain experience. If this isn't possible it's often possible to 'shadow' employees for a day or two, especially if you enlist the help of your college when making such requests to potentially helpful employers.
- Prepare yourself for each of the six categories associated with milk round recruitments.
- Do not put all your eggs in one basket! Make sure you investigate 'fall-back' positions.

Crosslink chapters

3   Active Reading
4   Creative Problem Solving
15   Personal Transferable Skills
18   The Placement Experience
20   Applying for a Job

Further reading

Cleaton, D. (1991) *Making a Choice from 21 Onwards*. Dalkeith: Charles Letts and Co.

20

Applying for a Job

Jim Macdonald

In this chapter, Jim Macdonald gives a down-to-earth guide for getting yourself an interview for a job. Many promising, talented and suitable candidates do not get an interview because their application forms fail to interest employers. Three crucial stages are outlined to ensure that you avoid some of the common pitfalls: filling in an application form, producing a curriculum vitae (CV) and writing a covering letter.

Filling in an application form

Application forms are a highly standardized method of communication. They take time and effort to prepare and fill in. It is important to ensure that you match the employer's viewpoint with your own so that you don't sell yourself short when applying for jobs. In this section you will be asked to:

- suggest your purposes in completing an application form;
- suggest the employer's purpose in reading your application form;
- describe yourself in terms of your aptitudes, your disposition and your achievements.

There is little to be gained from completing and submitting an application which is promptly rejected. It's worth taking the time and trouble to work through this process.

Can you quickly suggest what your purpose in completing an application form might be?

1

2

3

Now suggest what the employer's purpose is in reading your application:

1

2

3

Perhaps this all seems rather too simplistic. But without asking these types of questions as a starting point, you're liable to waste your own time and the prospective employer's. We have made suggestions on the next two pages to paint a picture of the two sides we are trying to bring together.

Why are you filling in the application form?

When you complete your application form you are in effect selling yourself to an employer and, like any salesperson, you will concentrate on your good points, for example:

- your achievements;
- your experiences;
- your perceived skills.

Although of course you shouldn't tell lies or make false claims, you are not expected to reveal your weak points. Everyone has their weaknesses: it is up to the employer to find these. Here are some basic rules for guidance; you can probably think of others.

1   Write or print legibly and neatly using black ink (because the form may be photocopied). Avoid corrections and deletions.
2   Be careful to avoid grammatical errors and spelling mistakes.
3   Do not type unless you are a good (professional standard) typist and even then only if your writing is not easy to read.
4   Keep the form clean. Blots, stains and creases create a bad initial impression which will act to your disadvantage.
5   Read questions carefully. Make sure you understand them before you answer them.
6   Do rough drafts of your answers on scrap paper first, to allow for correction of grammar, punctuation, spelling and chronology.
7   When supplying information on, for instance, your education or work experiences, provide it in chronological sequence.
8   Do not leave blanks. Reply to all questions even if it is only to state 'none' or 'not applicable'.
9   Employment forms usually allocate a certain amount of space for your answer to a particular question: the amount of space provided is an indication of its significance so try to fill the space meaningfully. Avoid padding out your reply just to fill the space.
10 Retain a copy or rough draft of your completed application and use it to refresh your memory if and when you are called for an interview. Differing replies to the same question on the application form and at an interview will create an unfavourable impression.

Why is the employer reading your application form?

Bearing in mind that employers of graduates often advertise nationally, there can be hundreds of applications to sift through for each vacancy. From these the employer has to find candidates who appear to have all the qualifications and qualities the post will demand. It would be too expensive to interview all the candidates.

Many national and most multinational employers devise their own application forms because they do not all seek the same qualities or attach equal significance to common qualities. Such application forms are referred to in careers literature as Employers' Application Forms (EAFs or EFs).

Smaller organizations frequently cannot afford the expense of developing, printing and distributing their own forms. They use a Standard Application Form (SAF) devised by the Association of Graduate Careers Advisory Services and the Association of Graduate Recruiters. SAFs are available at all careers services.

Recruiters often use a framework, known as a seven point plan, as a basis for selection. It is of value to bear this in mind when completing an application and when attending a first interview (see also chapter 21 on being interviewed).

Seven point plan

1 *Physical makeup* (This of course only applies to interviews) Covers manner, dress, appearance, health.
2 *Attainments*
   Covers education performance, training prizes.
3 *Intelligence*
   Covers general IQ, initiative.
4 *Aptitudes*
   For example, literacy, numeracy, keyboard skills.
5 *Sports and interests*
   Such as competitive sports, social activities, hobbies.
6 *Disposition*
   Is the candidate confident? Talkative? A good mixer? Cautious?
7 *Circumstances*
   For example, family, social, domestic.

Now turn to page 332.

Aptitudes	Strong	Average	Weak	Don't know, not tried
Design Creating attractive forms in different materials				
Manual dexterity Doing practical work using hands and tools				
Communication Understanding by means of listening or reading and explaining orally or on paper				
Presentation skills Speaking to and convincing an audience				
Numeracy Coping with figures/ numbers and mathematical concepts				
Methodical work Neatness, accuracy, attention to detail				
Originality Developing new solutions to problems or situations				

Aptitudes	Strong	Average	Weak	Don't know, not tried
Logic Suppressing preconceived ideas and/or personal prejudice in favour of the facts				
Decision making The ability to make and accept responsibility for decisions				
Relationships Getting on well with others; being an effective team member				
Reliability Regular time keeping; fulfilling promises; earning trust				
Ambition How strongly will you work for success and at what cost to your personal life or that of your colleagues?				

How you rate in the seven point plan: aptitudes and disposition

Two points from the plan which you can think about just now are aptitudes and disposition. How do you rate your aptitudes? For convenience, use the table on pp.330–1 and assess yourself as strong, average or weak (if you can).

Have you been totally honest in making these assessments? Too often we tend to *underrate* our abilities and aptitudes because we do not wish to appear too boastful. As a rough guide, if you can talk knowledgeably and at some length on any of the listed headings (for example, give a five minute presentation) you should class that aptitude as 'strong'. If you feel happy with your aptitude (doing a satisfactory job), grade yourself 'average'.

Now look again at your assessments. If they are all in the average or weak categories you are underselling yourself. Revise them. We all have above average aptitude in some areas. Write down an aptitude and remember to include it on your EAF/CV.

Consider your *disposition*: have you ever examined it honestly? Below there is a series of adjectives, some of which you might use to describe yourself. Let's call these 'appropriate'. Equally there must be some of which you believe do not apply. We shall call them 'inappropriate'. (Of course, appropriateness will sometimes depend on the occasion – but you're describing yourself in general terms.) Look at the adjectives below and extract those which you feel you can allocate to either the appropriate or inappropriate columns. List those you extract.

The list of adjectives is not exhaustive. You should think of others. Add them to your lists. Now consider whether these lists accurately reflect the sort of person you are, or whether they paint a word-picture of the sort of person you like others to see. Think about how truly the adjectives relate to your disposition and amend your lists if necessary. You will perhaps recognize aspects which require development or control.

Finally, try them on an honest friend and revise if necessary. When you are satisfied, you will have a number of adjectives

Disposition

quiet   cheerful   moody   talkative   taciturn   confident

shy   sociable   adventurous   competitive   impulsive

aggressive   methodical   careful   hesitant   anxious

resourceful   determined   inventive   co-operative

sensitive   artistic   easy-going   sympathetic   optimistic

humorous   even-tempered   patient   ambitious

energetic   dominant   restless   critical   popular

Appropriate (I am. . .)   Inappropriate (I am not. . .)

which can be used on your application form. But remember, you should be in a position to provide evidence to justify your assessments of your disposition.

What about your achievements?

Employers' forms often ask you to list your achievements. This can be perplexing, because many of us feel we have not achieved anything worthy of putting on a form, except passing various examinations. Here is a list of achievements which might be considered worthwhile:

- a successful holiday job;
- organizing a club or society;

- reporting for the college newspaper;
- completing work placement;
- award of Duke of Edinburgh medal;
- making a video;
- completing an Outward Bound course;
- helping to run a 'Niteline' or Samaritan service;
- becoming a Queen's scout/guide.

In the holiday job, for instance, you might have acquired the skills of organizing a day's work. An employer would be very interested in this.

Now try the following exercise. List your achievements and against them try listing skills you acquired as a result.

Other questions to think about

The advice given so far, even if you follow it as carefully as possible, will not guarantee success for any specific application you make. Employers will wish to have your answers to a range of further, vital questions such as:

- Why this career? What qualities do you have to offer?
- Why this organization? Why did you choose to apply?
- Have you applied to other organizations in our field?
- If you get more than one job offer, what criteria will you consider in making your decision?

To get answers, you need to research the prospective employer and the particular vacancy for which you intend to apply. An additional benefit will be an overall feeling for the company's 'ethos' with which you must conform if you are offered employment. If you find yourself unable to go along with the ethos you could well be advised to look for another employer where you would fit in.

Next, we think about what to do when a curriculum vitae is called for instead of – or as an accompaniment to – an application form.

Producing a curriculum vitae (CV)

Essentially, the CV is a concise, chronological history of your education, experience, achievements and interests; something like an application form where you answer questions about yourself before they are asked.

When should you use your CV?

You use a CV when:

- you are asked to supply a CV;
- the advertisement states 'send full details' or 'apply in writing';
- your application is speculative: that is, not directly in response to an advertisement.

What should it look like?

There is no definite layout. The aim is to convey essential information clearly and concisely. A skeletal CV is suggested on p. 336, which can be adapted to suit your requirements.

Your CV should be typed so that good photocopies can be made. Your aim is to capture the reader's interest, so the style must be easy to read. Use facts and figures whenever possible; this gives a more professional impression. You should ensure that all essential information is included on two sides of an A4 sheet. To that end you need not use complete sentences.

Unlike the application form, the CV does allow you to explain your skills, interests and motives fully. However, you should supply skeletal information which may 'lead' an interviewer to ask the questions which you can answer with confidence to substantiate your interests and motives. An alternative is to use the covering letter to get your message across, but there is a danger: the letter can expand into a potted biography. Your CV must always be up to date. Failing in this

Proposed layout for a sample curriculum vitae

CURRICULUM VITAE

Personal details

Name: (In full)	Date of birth:
Nationality:	Marital status:
Home address:	Term address:
(Include postcode and	(As for home address also give
telephone no.)	dates when contactable here)

Education and qualifications

Dates	School/college
Dates	Standard grades or GCSEs: subjects with pass grades; ONCs, BTECs.
Dates	Higher or 'A' levels: subjects with grades; HND, HNC, BTECs, GNVQs, etc. University, polytechnic, college Diploma/degree subject plus class (if already taken) Subjects studied Details of final year project/dissertation

Work experience

Dates	Description of work; for example, shelf-filling, bar work

Interests

At school	Clubs, societies, sports, hobbies, interests
At college	As for school. Detail positions of responsibility
Other skills	E.g. driving licence, computing experience, foreign language (and standard), travel (to which countries)

Referees

Include names and addresses of two referees, one of whom should be academic (make sure you have their approval before listing their names) area leads to suspicions of poor organization or carelessness, neither of which you wish to convey. Thus, do not include your age; give your date of birth.

Since laser printed CVs are expensive you obviously will not wish to create a new CV for each application. A cost effective method of bringing a CV up to date is to add a postscript with the new information. This will be on a separate sheet, also of good quality paper and reproduction. Remember: the object of the CV, like that of the application form, is to get you an interview.

Writing a covering letter

A covering letter is an essential accompaniment to your CV. It also may be used to advantage with an application form.

Why should you use a covering letter?

You use the covering letter to:

- Introduce yourself.
- Explain how you learned about the vacancy, why you are applying for it and why you consider yourself a suitable candidate.
- Emphasize aspects of your life, skills or experience which you believe will be of particular relevance to the employer. (You have, we hope, researched the employer and have a fair idea of the qualifications, experience and personal qualities sought).
- Provide details of when you will be available for interview or to start employment.

Proposed layout for covering letter

Your full postal address
to which any replies
will be sent.

Address of organization to which
you are applying. If you have a
name, use it.   Date

Dear Mr/Mrs (Surname)

(Opening paragraph identifies the job and your source of
information.) For example: I wish to apply for the post of
Trainee Manager as advertised in the latest issue of *Prospects
Today* and enclose my curriculum vitae for your attention. The
vacancy reference is PT4/1434.

Second paragraph draws attention to relevant training or
work experience and why you consider yourself ideally suited
for the post.

Third paragraph highlights any extra skills or experience
which may not be directly relevant but which add to the sum
of your achievement. For example, fluency in a foreign
language. You will already have included this information on
your CV. You are now highlighting it.

Fourth paragraph should suggest why this particular
company attracts you: perhaps because of its size, its type of
work, the people it recruits or the excellent training or
promotion prospects.

Final paragraph explains availability for the interview you
look forward to being invited to attend, and when you can
actually start work.

Yours sincerely (if no surname at top, use 'faithfully')

Signature

Name printed plus title (Mr, Ms, etc.)

Guidelines

- Keep it to one side of paper.
- Use good quality paper. Some notepaper torn from an exercise book creates an impression of haste, carelessness or lack of motivation.
- Write in your best longhand, using a black pen if possible.
- Do a draft first to eliminate errors, polish your English and establish the layout.
- Ask a friend to read through it and make suggestions.
- Remember the conventions. If writing to a named person (always to be preferred) end your letter 'Yours sincerely', otherwise use 'Yours faithfully'.
- Print your name below your signature (which may not be easily decipherable) and do not forget to date your letter.
- Keep a copy you can refer to when called for interview.

Action plan

- Complete the seven point plan covering aptitudes and dispositions.
- Prepare your CV and after typing run off good-quality photocopies which can be used for a variety of job applications.
- Do rough drafts of your answers to questions on the standard application form. Ensure that all questions are answered.
- When ready complete the final version and keep a photocopy for your own reference.
- Write your covering letter, trying to keep it to one side of A4. Keep a copy for use at interview.
- Enclose letter, application form and CV in a folder or binder, and insert in an A4 or larger sized envelope. Do not fold contents.
- If appropriate, enclose a stamped-addressed card for acknowledgement of receipt of your application.
- Post and wait!

Crosslink chapters

21

Being Interviewed

Phil Race

Most people's careers depend on interviews. To get the job you want, you normally need to give a successful interview. Then later, for promotion, there's usually another interview and so on – you'll have interviews of one sort or another throughout your career. With an interview, unlike an exam, if something goes wrong, you can't put the clock back and take it again. There's no second chance to make a good first impression. In this chapter Phil Race helps you prepare for interviews beforehand, and helps you put on a good show when you get there.

Paving your way to an interview

When you send in your application form and your curriculum vitae (CV), you may not realize it at the time, but you're determining quite a lot of the interview you may get. Interviewers, or interview panels, normally have in front of them the paperwork you sent in your application. As they prepare to ask you questions they see the information you supplied them with. Even with a large interviewing panel, it's usual for everyone to have in front of them a full copy of your application and also your CV if you sent one. As they prepare themselves to gain an impression of what you're really like, they have before them the words you used to set out the information you supplied – already starting to make an impression for you. As they decide what they want to find out about you, they have in front of them what you've already told them about yourself.

You should aim to make the paperwork you supply when

applying for any job serve as an ambassador for you. The main aim of the paperwork is to get your application to the top of the pile. You want your application to look impressive enough and interesting enough to make them want to find out more about you. You want to be shortlisted and there are three weapons in your campaign to be shortlisted:

- your completed application form;
- your CV;
- your letter of application.

What can these do for you? How can they help to get you on the shortlist? How can they help you when you are called for interview? Here are some ways.

Create a good first impression

If your paperwork looks good, this helps a lot. In other words, pay attention to neatness, structure and layout in all the paperwork you send with job applications.

Make the most of what you have

Let's assume there will be other people with the same qualifications and experience as you applying for the same job. Let's go one stage further, and assume that some people will have *better* qualifications and experience than you. This is why it's important that your paperwork makes *your* application look that bit more interesting than theirs.

Making yourself seem interesting

Let's face it, we're talking about the way human beings react to fellow human beings. Once the applications have been sorted in terms of qualifications and experience, the next stage of the sifting is often almost subconscious – it's based on whether they 'like' what they see about you. If you look 'interesting' the chances are they'll want to find out more about you – there's your chance of an interview.

Set *your* agenda

Interviewers or interview panels normally have their agendas already. By the time you get to an interview, they will have decided many of the questions they are going to ask all the candidates. There's not much you can do about the questions they are going to ask everyone. However, there is quite a lot you can do about the questions they're going to ask specifically of you. This is where your application form and CV can be really useful. You can use them to tempt interviewers to ask you questions you're really going to *enjoy* answering. When (for example) your leisure interests are so fascinating to interviewers that they ask you more about them, you get the chance to wax lyrical about something you *like* talking about.

Make your application seem 'special'

What happens when you're applying for a lot of different jobs? You send in lots of different application forms. Your CV may be much the same in each application, but the application forms are different, and so are the letters you send in support of each application. It's all too easy to arrive at an interview, having forgotten exactly what you said in the particular application that got you there. Suppose you're successful and get asked for interview. The last thing you want is for the interviewers to get the impression that this is just one of hundreds of applications you've got on the boil. So keep a copy of the paperwork you send with each application, so that when you're interviewed you remember exactly how you presented yourself.

Activity 1

Jot down reminders about things you intend to put into practice with your letters of application, application forms and CV. In particular, note down points which you want them to make for you, so that they will increase the chance your application will get you shortlisted.

-
-
-
-
-

Helping other people help you: cultivating referees

So far, we've looked at the paperwork *you* supply. However, that's not quite all the paperwork the interviewers will have about you – they'll also have references. You can't exercise direct control over the quality of what your referees write, but there's plenty you can do to try to influence them positively. Here are some suggestions.

Choose good referees in the first place

Obviously, you haven't got complete control here – one or more of your referees may be dictated by circumstances. For example, when you're already employed your present boss will be expected to be one of your referees. When you're at college, one of your referees will be expected to be a lecturer or tutor who's in a good position to comment about your abilities. That said, you may still be able to exercise some choice. Try, for example, to choose referees who are good at references. How can you tell? You may be able to find out whether they often give references – secretaries usually know this. You've got more control of your 'second' or 'third' referees. They need not be directly associated with your present job or your present course. These 'additional' referees are normally expected to furnish details about what a marvellous person you are in broad terms – so look out for people who think that you're something special, and who are credible as referees. By 'credible', we're thinking of people who themselves look 'distinguished' either in terms of their qualifications or their position in society – or both.

Ask your referees!

Seems obvious, doesn't it? Yet, so often, in the rush of sending applications here, there and everywhere, candidates forget to ask their referees whether they are willing to act in that capacity. Put yourself in their shoes. What would *you* do if you got an urgent request for a reference about someone of whom you had just a vague remembrance of saying 'yes' to? Compare this with what you might do for someone who regularly kept you informed about the applications that were in the pipeline, and regularly thanked you again for your willingness to act as referee.

Tell your referees what you're up to

It's worth dropping your referees a note every time you put their names on an application. Don't just ask their permission once, then continue to use their names on countless applications. Letting your referees keep up with the various applications you make gives them a chance to tailor their references to the particular firms or organizations you're applying to. Sometimes they'll already have contacts in particular firms or organizations. It's not unknown for a referee to telephone such a contact informally on your behalf, and help to pave the way for your application.

Update your referees

As you add new qualifications and experience to your CV, don't forget to make sure that your referees know your latest strengths and triumphs. Sending referees copies of your latest CV not only helps them keep up with your progress, it gives them the chance to give you some feedback about how your CV comes across to them. You can often get some valuable advice from referees, leading to improvements in the way you structure your CV.

Sometimes you may want to thank your referees. It takes time and skill to write good references, and most of them (however well intentioned) don't actually lead to the prize of the candidate being offered employment. A word or two of thanks can compensate for the effort that goes into trying to get you the job.

Activity 2

Imagine you're writing a reference for yourself! Make a few notes about the things you would like your referees to say about you:

-
-
-

Now jot down some things you hope your referees won't say about you:

-
-
-

Finally, think about how best you can make sure your referees are armed with the information they can use to your advantage – and that they don't have anything particularly negative to say about you (accidentally or deliberately).

On your way to the interview

As we've already seen, first impressions count a lot at interview. The first impression you create will depend to a considerable extent on how the previous few hours have gone for you, and on what mood you're in as you first walk into the interview room. Besides getting there in a good frame of mind, there are several valuable things you can do on your way to an interview, to prepare you for what may come. The following suggestions may help you put the journey to good use.

Plan to be early

If you're late, you'll not create a very good impression – that's obvious. It's less obvious if you're *almost* late. Some interviews may be carried out on your doorstep, but in general most interviews involve some travel. Suppose your train was delayed and you just arrived on time, but with no time to spare. It would show. You'd have spent quite a lot of your reserves of mental energy worrying about the possibility of being late. It's well worth planning a considerable safety margin into your journey time, especially for interviews which you regard as particularly important.

Plan how you'll look

Once, it used to be the norm that all males had grey interview suits and that females would be equally soberly dressed. Times have changed and so have cultures. How best to look for your interview is no longer a topic that it is possible to give definite advice about. You will have as good an idea as anyone. Anyway, you'll pick up clues on the interview trail, as you find out what most of your fellow candidates are choosing to wear. It's just as important for you to feel comfortable; you will come across more naturally and more confidently. If you have a long journey, there is one piece of general advice that may help: plan to change! There's nothing worse than travelling a long way in 'formal gear' for generating tension (and risking coffee spills on your clothes). With a bit of planning, you can normally work out some way to change into your 'finery' fairly close to your destination.

Use the pre-interview time wisely

Whether you're spending the few hours before an interview travelling, or whether the interview is 'at home', there are sensible ways of spending the time involved. One of the most useful things you can do is look afresh at your copy of the information you supplied with the application. Remind yourself of exactly what you entered in the various boxes on the application form. It's very likely that several of the questions you will be asked will arise directly from the words you wrote.

Do some research

It's useful to spend some time before an interview doing some fact-finding about the firm or organization you're applying to. Normally, by this stage, you'll have been sent a fair amount of documentation; skim through this before your interview, looking for sensible questions you can ask the interviewers, and become as knowledgeable as you reasonably can about how the firm or organization is structured. If you arrive early you may be surprised at the amount of useful information you can gain by just looking around and talking to anyone who's willing to talk to you. Your newly-gained information could become your 'leading edge' when it comes to interview; for example, you could be the only candidate to enquire 'What's the interesting-looking new building just to the north of the main entrance going to be?'

Avoid stressful situations

The hours leading up to an interview are not the most sensible time to have arguments with your nearest or dearest, or to make a vigorous complaint to the management, or to engage in other high-tension activities. If stressful situations arise during these hours 'put them on hold'. Remember that however stressful any situation is, how you react to stress is still up to you.

The waiting room

Waiting rooms are rarely one's favourite places. Think of airports, stations, surgeries, dentists, hospitals and so on! Waiting itself can be a stressful thing. Waiting in a competitive situation, alongside other people who are hoping to succeed in competition with you, is even more tension producing. That is, if you let it get to you. Some candidates have even been known to use the waiting-room situation to try and unnerve their competitors. It's far better to engage in non-threatening friendly conversation about neutral topics – or if that is not forthcoming, simply to keep your profile low; for example, by quietly reading something.

Activity 3

Jot down a few notes about your reactions to stressful situations and turn these into recommendations to yourself about the best way to get to your interviews in a relaxed, unruffled state of mind.

Making that first impression

As we've seen already, first impressions are important. What do you want the first impression to do for you? How do you want to come across in the first seconds?

- Confident or nervous?
- Likeable or arrogant?
- Friendly or withdrawn?
- Human or robotic?
- Polite or socially inept?

People make their first impressions on the basis of very primitive instincts and reactions. Some factors you can do little about (at least at short notice), including your size, shape and some aspects of your appearance. Others you can think about using to your advantage, such as your manner, your expression, your movement and the 'atmosphere' you create around you. Here are a few suggestions for the first seconds of any interview.

Smile with your eyes

Eye contact is a powerful instinctive process. Imagine what happens when eye contact is missing. If people start talking to you but without looking at you at all, you soon begin to feel uncomfortable with them. You somehow begin to distrust them. If, however, they look at you 'warmly', as though confirming through eye contact that they're pleased to meet you, it is the start of a much happier relationship.

When does the interview actually start?

The formal part of an interview is normally easy enough to tell. However, quite often before that there will be some sort of less formal interview. This may take the form of a preliminary chat, sometimes one-to-one, sometimes involving a whole group of candidates. Use any such times to gently build up rapport in any way you can.

Don't rush into the black chair!

Sooner or later you'll be in the 'hot seat'. However, if you come in through the door and make a beeline for the empty chair, and sit down as quickly as you can, it all seems too rushed. The first few seconds can seem to you like a very long time but not to your interviewers. It's better to take your time, and pick up the vibrations of what is expected of you. For example, the interviewer (or even the whole panel of interviewers) may want to shake hands with you before you sit down. Perhaps the first empty chair you see isn't the one they want you to sit in. Even though it seems to take ages, let yourself be guided by the signs and signals you receive. Let the interviewers feel that they are in control! Soon, someone will say something like 'Please have a seat' and motion you towards wherever you're intended to sit.

The 'interview-proper': putting on a good show

Most interviews last only minutes, rarely hours, yet they often determine how you will spend several years of your life. This is one reason for the tension that many people feel regarding interviews. However, interviews are a necessary part of job-application procedures for many reasons:

- They give employers the chance to see for themselves what sort of people candidates actually are – details on paper only tell part of the story.
- They give candidates the opportunity to find out whether they really want the posts or not – the jobs often turn out to be very different from what was imagined from job adverts and descriptions.
- They allow both employers and candidates to make a preliminary assessment of one very important aspect – whether it will be possible for them to 'get on together'. This is at least as important as candidates' abilities to do the job.

So, whether you like interviews or not, you're stuck with them, and it's therefore worthwhile developing your skills at handling them. It is true that you can do this just by trial and error. There's no substitute for lots of practice. Most things are best learned by doing – interviews are no exception. However, since interviews are so important, it's best not to leave it just to trial and error (or should we say 'error and trial', as there are many more interviews than there are jobs, statistically you should not expect every interview to lead to a job offer!).

Every interview is different. With a little thought, you can approach interviews (whether successful or not) as useful learning experiences. The following suggestions may help you pick up useful techniques a little faster than by trial and error.

Be pleased to be there

However nervous you feel, however intimidated by 'important people' or 'experts', try to feel pleased to have got this far. Moreover, try to feel pleased to meet your interviewers. If you manage to convey this feeling of being pleased to meet them, you're probably well on your way towards striking up some empathy with your interviewers – empathy that could well swing the eventual decision your way.

Never doubt yourself

Even if you already know that the other candidates have higher qualifications and better experience than you, don't resign yourself to losing the interview. After all, you would not have been asked in the first place if there was not a fair possibility that you may be just what they're looking for. Looking at it another way, if you do give in and resign yourself to failure it will show on your face. No one wants to offer a job to someone who looks 'down' and dispirited.

'Tell us about yourself'

Quite often, at the start of an interview, there will be an open-ended question such as this. From the interviewers' point of view, such a question serves several useful purposes, as it:

- gives them the chance to start to see what you're really like;
- gives you the chance to introduce yourself;
- gives them the chance to work out how to play the next part of the interview.

You can feel very 'alone' and embarrassed talking continuously for even just a minute or two about yourself. This is where practice comes in. Long before you go for interviews, start practising speaking aloud a short introduction about your education, your experience, your main aims in life and your interests. When you're ready, get some further practice in, using friends or colleagues as your audience (and helping them in the same way too).

Show due respect

We're not talking of going down on bended knee here! It's to do with simple etiquette. For example, suppose you're being seen by a medium sized interview panel, chaired by the Personnel Manager, who's introduced to you as Julie Bainbridge. Suppose later in the interview you wish to return to a point she made: it's best *not* to be so bold as to say 'Coming back to Julie's point. . .'. Nor may it be wise to say 'Coming back to Mrs Bainbridge's point. . .' (she could be Miss Bainbridge for all you know). It would be safest to say 'Coming back to the point the Personnel Manager made earlier (looking at her). . .'. While it's all right for the members of the panel to use first names when talking to each other, they may feel it strange if you join in this practice. Of course, don't reject direct invitations such as 'Please call me Bill'.

Silence is not golden!

At interviews, silence is generally a bad thing. It can feel very uncomfortable. Silence can be caused by you not knowing the answer to a question. Silence can be caused by you not having anything more to say about something you've already been talking about. Silence can be caused by something you've said momentarily taking the wind out of the sails of your inter- viewers. At the end of an interview, when the interviewers take stock in private, if they remember any awkward silences, they're unlikely to rate your interview performance very highly. But don't forget that when you're tense a few seconds can feel like an eternity. So don't jump in and break every *short* silence. Give your interviewers time to think of their next question, and to reflect on your answers to their last question.

What you know or what you don't know?

Remember that at an interview you can only give a fraction of what you know. There's little point trying to become a walking encyclopedia on the topics that may be involved. More important, at most interviews there will be some questions involving things you don't yet know. How you handle these is just as important as giving answers on things you already know. Therefore, it's useful to take the emphasis of your approach to interviews away from knowledge for its own sake, and direct your attention to the way you handle the interview situation itself.

Don't interrupt

At interviews you'll often be interrupted. When you're talking about something the interviewers don't want to know about they'll often stop you short. It can become tempting to do the same to them – but don't. No one likes being interrupted. Interrupting your interviewers is one of the fastest ways to alienate them. When they interrupt you, try not to let any irritation show. Accept that they want to move on to something different, and go with the flow.

Use eye contact

Even if you find it hard to look strangers straight in the eyes, it's a skill which you can develop much more easily than you may imagine. One way is to look firmly 'at them' but not into their eyes – the bridge of the nose does fine! Of course, if you're comfortable with genuine eye contact there's nothing better, especially when you're in the business of selling yourself to other people. However, make sure that eye contact is not overdone – there's a borderline beyond which it becomes uncomfortable for your interviewers. Think how you feel when someone stares at you in a penetrating way. You'll know you're overdoing the eye contact if you notice your listeners moving their own gaze away when you look directly at them. Avoid making your interviewers uncomfortable.

Don't waffle

Tempting as it is to make up something when you don't know the answer to a question, it's far too dangerous. Normally, at an interview, the people who ask you questions have very good ideas regarding what acceptable answers will be. If you then spin a yarn to them they will actually feel quite insulted, which will do your chances no good. Sometimes you can seek clarification of the question. If you still have no idea about the answer, it's usually best to admit it. You don't have to be as direct as to say 'I've got absolutely no idea'. There are milder ways of replying, along the lines of 'I'm sorry, but I haven't actually met this situation yet', or 'Would one way of dealing with this situation be to try the following approach. . .?'

Talk to everyone

Most important interviews involve a panel rather than just one or two interviewers. It's not uncommon to meet a panel of 20. For example, a Board of Directors or Board of Governors is sometimes assembled for particularly important interviews. As with any type of interview, the best preparation for 'big' interviews is practice, and you can make such practice with friends or colleagues. One particularly useful technique at big interviews is to make sure that you talk to the whole panel, and not just to the person who asked you the last question.

Remember, the person who asked the question probably already knows the answer, but the other members of the panel may well not know it. Talk to them too and give them the feeling that they're learning something useful from you. At the end of a big interview the panel normally 'takes stock', and if everyone feels that you've been talking to them they will feel positive about your performance.

'What are your ambitions?'

A question like this often comes up. Interviewers are normally looking for candidates who know where they are heading. However, don't make it too unreasonable. If you say 'I want to end up as Chief Executive of this company' the present Chief Executive may feel a little threatened! Better answers are along the lines of 'I'd like to gain experience of this, and try my hand at that, and gain some new skills in the other', (filling in the 'this', 'that' and 'the other' of course!).

'Why did you apply to this organization?

Quite often, interviewers want to know what attracted your attention to the particular firm or the specific post. 'It looked interesting' is too mild an answer. It's better to say something like 'Based on my existing training and experience, the post seems to offer a chance for me to use my present skills, and to progress from there'. There are all sorts of alternatives. You can say why you think you'll fit in to the organization. You can explain that you are already attracted to the location, or the reputation of the firm, or the kind of duties involved.

'Just relax'

Easier said than done. You've probably already noticed that when you're relaxed your brain works faster – and better – than when you're over-tense. However, it's not necessary to be completely relaxed to come across as being cool, calm and collected. Many famous television personalities admit privately that when they're 'on' (and especially when it's 'live') their pulse rate is up and their palms are moist. So simply relax as much as you can – and learn to live with a little tension when necessary.

Take your time

If you're feeling a bit tense and you're asked questions, it's tempting to speak as fast as your brain is thinking. This can come across as 'gabble'! This isn't the sort of impression you want to make. You will know people who seem to put their mouths into gear before they engage their brains. A short silence while you gather some thoughts is much better than saying the first few half-ideas that come into your mind. One way of manufacturing some breathing space is to lead in by repeating some key words from the question you're answering (watch politicians using this trick!).

Hobbies, interests, leisure activities. . .

Sooner or later at most interviews you're asked about these. There are many reasons why interviewers should ask you about your leisure activities and interests, including:

- to give you the chance to talk for a while on 'your own ground';
- to check that you're a 'normal, balanced person';
- to check that you get on well with other people.

When asked for such details, take full advantage of the opportunity you're given. Look at it this way: when talking about your own interests, there's every chance that you know more about what you're talking about than anyone else in the room. You are on your own territory. This gives you the chance to come across confidently and strongly. It gives you the chance to impress your interviewers with your enthusiasm.

Questions on your leisure activities will often be based on things you declared on the application form and in your CV. Make sure that you are able to give convincing answers when asked about any activity you've listed. In other words, don't pretend you're interested in weather forecasting if that interest only extends to the television forecast each morning! Someone genuinely interested in weather forecasting will be able to talk for some while about climatic trends, the features of anticyclones and the techniques used to gather data for computer predictions of the weather to come.

'Why should we offer *you* this post?'

This is an invitation to blow your own trumpet – but not *too* loudly. When asked this question, it's often a clear indication that they're thinking quite seriously about making you an offer. It would undo all the good work you'd already done if you were so bold as to say 'Because you won't find anyone as good as I am'. Yet this is the subconscious message you actually need to deliver – but with much greater subtlety. There are ways of doing it. For example, try something along the following lines: 'It would seem that my previous education and training are particularly relevant to what is required for the job, and I find the description very interesting and stimulating. I feel that this job would enable me to bring out the best I can do'.

Have *your* questions ready

At most interviews, the time will come when the interviewer (or Chair of the panel) will ask you whether you have any questions you would like to ask. If you haven't a couple of questions ready, there could be one of those long, negative silences. Of course, you could declare 'no thanks, you've made everything very clear to me already'. But that's not as good as having one or two useful questions of your own ready. It's easier to give advice about what *not* to ask at this stage than to suggest what to ask. For example, it's best that your 'top questions' aren't about holiday entitlements and salary details. (You should already have probed such things from the paperwork you were sent – or you can safely ask more about them when you're offered the job.) Asking something about opportunities for further training and development can be a much more positive question. Probably the best questions are those you can guess that your interviewers will be pleased to answer – on something you've already gathered they're particularly interested in, for example.

'If we offer you the post, will you accept it?'

This is sometimes asked. It's best to say 'Yes, thanks' even if you've not quite made up your mind. You can always back down later in one way or another if you have serious second-thoughts. If you were to say 'No, thanks' it would be almost like saying to the interviewers that you've been wasting their time (though if you've definitely decided against taking an offer it's best to be honest). When interviewers ask this question you can guess they're impressed, but don't assume that this in itself is the offer. They may ask the 'top three' candidates and then come to a decision about which one they call back for the final offer. So treat this question as a positive signal but don't get carried away in your delight.

Activity 4

Thinking back to interviews you've already had (and guessing at future interviews) try to add a couple of hints for your own use, in the same way as shown on the last few pages. Use this chance to think about any situations or questions which cause you particular concern at interviews.

●
●

After an interview

If you're offered the post, and you accept it, little needs to be said about what to do after an interview – though even then, it's worth doing your own analysis of how it went, what caused your success, and how you can build on that success at future interviews in your career. However, remember that statistically there are more 'losers' at interviews than there can be 'victors'. The main thing to say at once is *don't regard yourself as a loser* when you're not offered the post. Put it down to experience. Be more positive still – consciously decide that you're going to use the interview as a useful learning experience.

If you have the chance to talk to other candidates who, like you, were not offered the post, you can often pick up even more ideas to put into practice at future interviews. Here is a checklist of useful self-analysis questions to reflect on after each interview.

- What were the two best moments of the interview? Why? How can I make more such moments occur in future interviews?
- What were the two worst moments of the interview? Was this my fault, or was it quite unavoidable? What can I learn from these 'bad moments' that will help me combat similar circumstances in future interviews?
- If I could have done one extra thing to prepare for the interview, what would it have been? How can I ensure that this particular issue, at least, causes no problems in future interviews?
- Was there anything I could have added to the application form, or to my CV, which would have saved me some trouble at the interview?
- Was there anything on my application form or CV which actually led to problems at the interview? Can I delete or rephrase this information in future?
- How impressed or interested (or otherwise) did the interviewers seem with the information I had already supplied? Is there anything I can do in future to make my paperwork better serve its purpose?
- What did I learn about myself at the interview?
- What did I learn about other people, and how to respond to them, at the interview?

Action plan

- Ensure you know everything contained in your application form, covering letter and CV.
- Do some research on you chosen career, organization or company.
- Rehearse a range of possible answers to likely questions, especially the obvious ones such as:

  - Why do you want to go into this career?
  - Why have you applied to *us*, specifically?
  - Please tell us a few things about yourself.
  - What skills have you got?

- Prepare some key questions to ask at the end of the interview, based on any research you have done beforehand.
- Talk to your referees. Try to find out what, roughly, they have said about you. If you can, talk through your rehearsed answers to likely questions.
- If possible, experiment with mock interview techniques: your friends can help, as can a good careers service.
- Arrive early and, if you can, talk to employees already working there and generally find out more about the place. If you have a portfolio, take it with you.
- At the interview, show you are pleased to be there.

Crosslink chapters

Conclusion

Being a student is all about studying a subject or a discipline, and becoming something of an expert in your chosen specialism. Twenty authors have contributed to 21 chapters in order to help you do this. This book has been devoted to developing study skills and communication competences. Most of these transfer to later employment, but some remain as definitely 'studenty' – sitting exams and writing essays being the two bastions of college performance.

Many lecturers will support moves which help you learn and to show-off your skills to people outside college. I also have to say that some academic staff will be wary of our venture. I have listed four types of objection. First, some believe that college is about knowledge and understanding rather than skills *per se*: the curriculum is crowded enough and a skills orientation interferes with (especially) higher education. This kind of objection is well-founded in the sense of a distrust of methods and innovations which essentially 'train' rather than help people learn. It is true that early notions of training revolved around a set way of doing things with training courses producing cloned products – in the USA the signing-off phrase 'You're welcome, have a nice day' characterized people who had been trained to answer telephone calls.

In more modern times training is all about helping people to define their own needs and to agree ways of achieving objectives which will meet those needs. If these needs include the learning of new skills or the improvement of old ones, then so be it. The great irony is that whilst such skills are not always a part of your curriculum, they are often assessed by academic staff: back to essays and exams! This is why many initiatives in further and higher education are exploring ways of bringing skills in from the cold, but in a way that meets with student – and lecturer – agreement. As for the problem with the crowded curriculum: the skilled learner can handle more information, and so any move which helps the learner to do this effectively uncrowds it!

A second objection comes from what I would call the 'hard-line academics'. Here college can be viewed as a test and an institution of selection. It is up to *you* to prove that you are up to certain standards (which have probably never been openly specified – what do first, upper second, lower second and third-class classifications really mean?) It is not the responsibility of academic staff to help you along the way; their concern is with ensuring the maintenance of standards through the delivery of an accurate and contemporary curriculum.

You might argue that such a view is user unfriendly. I have to confess that it is an easy option for those lecturers who have so many students, that all they can do is give lectures and award final marks. The major objection, however, is that this sink-or-swim mentality drowns people who would have become excellent swimmers. Many talented and hard-working students simply lack exam technique or time management skills; a little help would ensure that their efforts are not wasted.

A third objection concerns a distrust and even dislike of employers. Many of the skills which we have covered in this book are geared towards 'transferability' and bridging the gaps between college and career employment. Some specialists are very keen on this kind of emphasis, especially when their courses are linked with accreditation by professional bodies. But other areas will be more cautious because they cannot confidently identify 'an employer' relevant to their students. In the Arts and Social Sciences, for example, there is a huge range of possible employment and career specialization. This is why we have included the most general work-based skills, in the hope that these are relevant to most later situations.

A final objection concerns the fact that there are so many skills to cover that a single book cannot hope to meet all interests and needs. In this volume, for example, we have not included skills associated with writing a dissertation (although we do cover the writing of essays and reports). This was a deliberate omission because there are so . many different expectations about what a dissertation should include. We therefore decided that with such diversity between subject areas and individual lecturers, we would only confuse readers by giving specific guidelines.

Contributors

Sally Brown, University of Northumbria at Newcastle
Fiona Campbell, Napier University, Edinburgh
Roger Coles, University of Glamorgan
Hannah Cowie, Gameston, Nottinghamshire
Peter Dove, University of Northumbria at Newcastle
Rod Gunn, University of Glamorgan
Jan Harvey, Napier University, Edinburgh
John Hughes, Imperial College, London
Alan Jenkins, Oxford Brooks University, Oxford
Richard Kemp, University of Glamorgan
Jim Macdonald, University of Glamorgan
Jim McNally, University of Glasgow
Paddy Maher, Open University in Scotland, Edinburgh
Roland Metcalfe, Nottingham Trent University, Nottingham
Malcolm Pike, Crosskeys College, Gwent
Robert Purvis, Queen Margaret College, Edinburgh
Phil Race, University of Glamorgan
Danny Saunders, University of Glamorgan
Christine Sinclair, University of Paisley
Lin Thorley, University of Hertfordshire

Index